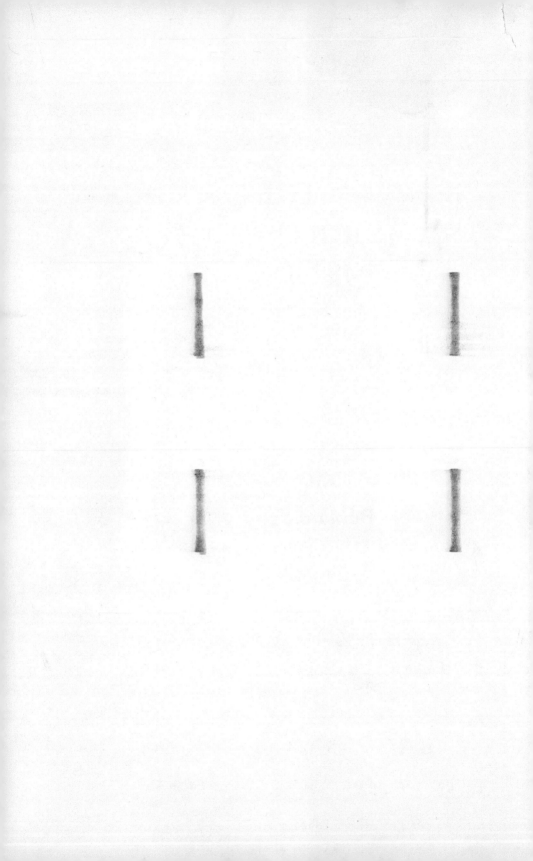

THE
FOURTEENTH
AMENDMENT

Centennial Volume

Edited by

Bernard Schwartz

New York New York University Press
London University of London Press Ltd
1970

Preface

This volume commemorates the centennial of the Fourteenth Amendment. It contains the papers delivered at a Centennial Conference held at the New York University School of Law on October 1, 3, and 4, 1968. The Conference was devoted to three themes: 1) The Fourteenth Amendment in historical perspective; 2) The Amendment and contemporary constitutional problems; 3) Constitutionalism in a changing world. The papers in this volume reflect this three-fold division.

The Fourteenth Amendment itself has become, in many ways, the most consequential part of the Federal Constitution. By nationalizing civil rights, it made the great guarantees for life, liberty, and property binding on governments throughout the land. It has served as the principal legal instrument for the Warren Court, particularly for the virtual equalitarian revolution which the Court's decisions have catalyzed. In many ways, indeed, present-day constitutional law is only a gloss on the Fourteenth Amendment's key provisions.

It was particularly gratifying that Chief Justice Warren was able to deliver the concluding address commemorating the organic fulcrum upon which the work of the Warren Court has turned. If the amendment is now construed as its framers intended, it is largely because of Earl Warren's leadership.

Public thanks must also be paid to the other contributors to this volume. Their papers mark a worthy commemoration of an event so important in constitutional history.

Bernard Schwartz

Contents

1

Landmarks of Legal Liberty

William J. Brennan, Jr.

We can start with the assumption that all of us would agree that the extent to which a document protects the individual from overreaching governmental regulation is the measure of its claim to the title of a Landmark of Legal Liberty. Under this test, the Fourteenth Amendment's credentials are impressive.

Surely the vindication of the legal right of Negroes to equality of opportunity was by itself one of the most remarkable achievements of law in our history. But the amendment has done much more. It has touched the life of every American by nationalizing the fundamental constitutional standards of freedom expressed in the federal Bill of Rights—thus meeting Madison's objection that although some states enacted notable bills of rights ". . . there are others whose bills of rights are not only defective, but absolutely improper; instead of securing some in the full extent which republican principles would require, they limit them too much to agree with the common ideas of liberty." [1] Were there a list of principles fundamental to the functioning of a free republic, it would, in addition to guaranteeing that no citizen would be denied an education, a house, or a job on account of the color of his skin, certainly include an assurance that each citizen's vote would count no more or no less than that of any other citizen, that his government would take no voice in or interfere with his religion, that he would enjoy freedom of speech and a free press, and that the administration of criminal laws would adhere to civilized standards of fairness and decency. The Fourteenth Amendment is assuring all of these things. In sum, it is the prime tool by which we as citizens are striving to shape a society which truly champions the dignity and worth of the individual as its supreme value.

The distinguished authorities who will follow during this Centennial

William J. Brennan, Jr., is an Associate Justice of the United States Supreme Court.

will trace the development of the enormous impact of the amendment upon specific areas of American life. We shall hear, too, something concerning the amendment's influence in other lands. These papers should convince us all that, in adopting the Fourteenth Amendment a century ago, America indeed created a great Landmark of Legal Liberty. It is true that, in the first half century of its existence, its function as a document of human freedom lay dormant; it was employed instead as a weapon by which to censor and strike down economic regulatory legislation of the States. This was in step with the compromise which settled the Hayes-Tilden Presidential election of 1876.[2] That compromise postponed the enforcement of the Fourteenth Amendment in behalf of the Negro, a result furthered by the decisions of the Supreme Court which invalidated the Civil Rights Act of 1875[3] and held that separate but equal facilities satisfied the demands of the equal protection clause.[4] In the last half century, however, the construction and application given the amendment by the federal judiciary has put it back on the track, and it has come into its own.

The importance of the role played by the federal courts in this development would not be surprising to the framers of the Fourteenth Amendment, nor should it be surprising to those who are acquainted with the earlier Landmarks of Legal Liberty in the common law system. For the investiture of independent tribunals with responsibility to define and guard personal liberties is a unique contribution of English speaking peoples to mankind's struggle for freedom. It was early recognized in England that high-sounding pronouncements of personal liberties are hollow when no enforcement role is given to an effective and independent court system. Indeed, it is not unfair to say that the impact of each great declaration of personal liberties in common law history can be measured by the degree to which reliance was placed upon independent judicial enforcement. It therefore seems appropriate that this paper should emphasize the role of the federal judiciary in the enforcement of the great guarantees of the Fourteenth Amendment.

The Founding Fathers of 1787 recognized that independent judicial enforcement was required if the limitations imposed by the new written Constitution were to be effective. The framers of the Fourteenth Amendment were heirs to this tradition. It is true that § 5 of the Fourteenth Amendment provides that "The Congress shall have power to enforce by appropriate legislation, the provisions of this Article" and that similar express authority is invested in the Congress under the Thirteenth and Fifteenth Amendments. But this does not indicate that the Thirteenth, Fourteenth, and Fifteenth Amendments were to be exceptions to the principle of judicial enforcement, or that enforcement was to be exclusively in the hands of Congress. Congress itself, contemporaneously with the proposal of the amendments, legislated an enormous expansion of the jurisdiction of the federal courts expressly to enlarge the federal judicial power to enforce the amendments' restraints and guarantees.

Until the time of the amendments, Congress had relied primarily on the state courts to vindicate essential rights under the Constitution and federal laws;[5] only the Supreme Court was invested with power to review the claimed denial by a state court of a federal right. Moreover, in 1833, the Supreme Court held in *Barron* v. *Baltimore* that the protections of the Bill of Rights comprised in the first eight amendments operated solely against federal power. However, as a complement to the adoption of the Reconstruction amendments, Congress completely altered the judicial structure of the country by legislation which "gave the federal courts the vast range of power which had lain dormant in the Constitution since 1789. These courts ceased to be restricted tribunals of fair dealing between citizens of different States and became the primary and powerful reliances for vindicating every right given by the Constitution, the laws, and the treaties of the United States."[6] The Act of March 3, 1875, was the principal ". . . measure of the broadening federal domain in the area of individual rights."[7] The 1875 statute granted the district courts "original cognizance, concurrent with the courts of the several States, of all suits of a civil nature at common law or in equity . . . arising under the Constitution or laws of the United States, or treaties made, or which shall be made, under their authority . . . ."[8] Indeed, in earlier statutes, the Civil Rights Acts of 1866 and 1871, Congress subjected to suit "every person who, under color of any statute . . . subjects, or causes to be subjected, any citizen of the United States or other person . . . to the deprivation of any rights . . . secured by the Constitution and laws . . . ,"[9] and it gave the district courts "original jurisdiction" over any action "to redress the deprivation, under color of any State law . . . of any right . . . secured by the Constitution . . . ."[10]

Congress thereby disclosed its intention to leave primarily to the federal judiciary the tasks of defining what constituted a denial of "due process of law" or "equal protection of the laws" and of applying the amendment's prohibitions as so defined where compliance counted, that is, against the excesses of state and local governments. Congress saw that to accord state and local governments immunity from effective federal court review would be to render the great guarantees nothing more than rhetoric. Congress did not use its § 5 powers to define the amendment's guarantees, but confined its role to the adoption of measures to enforce the guarantees as interpreted by the judiciary. And, of course, § 5 grants Congress no power to restrict, abrogate or dilute the guarantees as judicially construed.[11]

Congress' investiture of the federal judiciary with broad power to enforce the limits imposed by the amendment reflects acceptance of two fundamental propositions. First, it demonstrates a recognition that written guarantees of liberty are mere paper protections without a judiciary to define and enforce them. Second, it reflects acceptance of the lesson taught by the history of man's struggle for freedom that only a truly independent judiciary can properly play the role of definer and enforcer.

Consider, for example, the Universal Declaration of Human Rights in the Charter of the United Nations, which expresses in ringing words moral condemnation of the tragedy suffered by countless human beings over the face of the globe who are deprived of their liberty without accusation, without trial, upon nothing but the fiat of a sovereign government. The forthright prohibition of Article IX, solemnly joined by all the signatory powers, is that "No one shall be subject to arbitrary arrest, detention, or exile." But that has been no more than empty rhetoric, and must remain so, without an international tribunal and procedure to hold an offending signatory state to compliance with these great principles. As things stand, concepts of personal and territorial supremacy—national sovereignty—leave each member state free to grant its nationals only that measure of due process provided by its own laws, however far short that measure is of the standard of the Universal Declaration.

Contrast the way the declaration of similar substantive rights in the Fourteenth Amendment has been made meaningful by a system of judicial enforcement. Our concepts of due process in criminal proceedings are familiar to every American: a prompt and speedy trial, legal assistance (provided by government in the case of the indigent), prohibition of any kind of undue coercion or influence, freedom to conduct one's own defense, the right to a public trial and written proceedings, the presumption of innocence and the burden upon government to prove guilt beyond a reasonable doubt, and security against cruel and unusual punishments. Congress has ordained that the federal courts shall redress denial by any of the states of these standards of due process. In 1867, contemporaneously with its proposal of the Fourteenth Amendment to the states, Congress extended the ancient writ of *habeas corpus*—that most important writ to a free people, affording as it does a swift and imperative remedy in cases of illegal restraint or confinement—to any person claiming to be held in custody by a state in violation of the Constitution or laws or treaties of the United States.[12] The individual simply petitions a federal court to hear his claim that his detention by a state is a violation of federal guarantees. It avails the state nothing that the detention does no violence to state law or the state constitution. The guarantees of the federal Constitution are the higher law. It is true that the federal court will not hear a state prisoner who has not first exhausted any available state remedies for decision of his federal claims. For upon the state courts equally with the federal courts rests the obligation to guard, enforce and protect every right granted or secured by the Constitution of the United States. However, the state prisoner is not precluded from seeking federal relief by any determination of a state court that his federal claim has no merit. The prisoner may seek review of that holding in the federal courts, including the Supreme Court of the United States. Since he seeks his release on a claim of unconstitutional denial of a right secured to him by the federal Constitution, the last word as to its merits is for federal and not state tribunals.

In other words, Congress has provided a suprastate procedure for vindicating the guarantees which are the foundation of our free society. A most important corollary effect of the existence of this suprastate remedy is the incentive given to the judiciaries of the several states to secure every person against invasion of the rights guaranteed him by the basic law of the land.

When Congress decided to rely on the federal judiciary to define and enforce the guarantees of the Fourteenth Amendment, it was in effect acknowledging the peculiar competence of that branch of government to perform such tasks. For by that time it had long been clear that, because of its independence, the federal judiciary was an indispensable bulwark against disregard of constitutional limitations by those subject to them.

> Enforcement of these protections is entrusted by the Constitution to the "least dangerous branch" of government: a tribunal, insulated from direct political pressures, that has the power of neither purse, sword, nor administrative control; with authority only to decide disputes between contending parties; whose orders are dependent upon executive enforcement; whose size is subject to legislative variation; whose process of decision is reasoned analysis; and whose numbers are restrained by a long-standing professsional tradition.[13]

The Founding Fathers had taken particular care to create a federal judiciary of this nature precisely because their forefathers, first as Englishmen and then as colonists, had learned through bitter experience that an independent judiciary is the bedrock of a free society.

We know that in England today, despite an unwritten constitution and the doctrine of parliamentary supremacy, independent courts of justice enforcing the common law are the protectors of the fundamental liberties of the Englishman. E. C. S. Wade tells us, "It is only, where constitutional law is concerned, in that small but vital sphere where liberty of person and of speech are guarded that . . . [the rule of law] means the rule of common law. For here alone, has Parliament seen fit to leave the law substantially unaltered and to leave protection of the freedom of individuals to the operation of the common law." [14]

But this did not come about in England without centuries of struggle, and our Founding Fathers, as descendants of those who won the fight for an independent judiciary, were determined to leave their descendants that valuable heritage. Mackintosh said of Magna Carta, "To have produced it, to have preserved it, to have matured it, constitute the immortal claim of England upon the esteem of mankind." [15] The barons who wrung Magna Carta from King John in 1215 fought the first great battle for an independent judiciary. They were practical men of state and were not content that King John, representing the sovereignty of the nation, merely declare piously that "No free man shall be taken or imprisoned or disseised or outlawed or exiled or in any way ruined . . . ." [16] These lofty words were meaningless unless enforced, and King John had the habit of imprisoning or threatening to imprison opponents without formal prosecution, or, where formal prosecution was brought, of intervening with the judges and dictating the outcome. The barons therefore exacted provisions to assure that their fate would be determined by independent tribunals in accordance with the law of the land. King John was required to promise "nor will we go or send against him, except by the lawful judgment of his peers, or by the law of the land." [17] Furthermore, he was compelled to agree that the Court of Common Pleas would not be at his beck and call to follow him on his journeys in and out of England, but would sit at a fixed place, presumably Westminster.[18] He also was forced to agree not to appoint "justices, constables, sheriffs or bailiffs who do not know the law of the land and mean to observe it well." [19] He agreed that two of his justices would hold assizes four times a year in each county,[20] and that subjects would no longer be at the mercy of sheriffs, constables and other local officials.[21] Finally, he agreed that "to no one will we sell, to no one will we deny or delay right or justice" [22]—thus making access to the royal courts easier.

The next great battle was fought in the times of the Stuart Kings, whose claims to the sovereign prerogative and use of noncommon law courts were stoutly resisted by a coalition of Parliament and common lawyers led by Sir Edward Coke.

Under the Tudors the Star Chamber and other conciliar courts had been established as executive adjuncts to the Crown, in the belief that they were necessary because the traditional courts were inadequate to cope with the violence and disorder rampant throughout the country. Working outside and independently of the ordinary courts, the Star Chamber created new crimes and usually prosecuted accused persons without the safeguards provided in the traditional courts, often relying upon torture to assure convictions.[23] Seventeenth-century common lawyers began to see these executive courts as a serious threat to the independence of the judiciary, a threat heightened by the King's resumption of the practice of intervening in court proceedings to control their outcome.

Coke, as Chief Justice of the Court of Common Pleas, employed various means to curtail executive interference. Sometimes he employed writs of prohibition and *habeas corpus* to keep cases from the conciliar courts. But of greater significance for us in the light of the American concept of judicial review, was his development of the theory that the common law, including such fundamental documents of liberty as Magna Carta, was the supreme law of the land, and that the judges and not the King had responsibility for its interpretation and enforcement.[24] Coke was promoted in 1613 to Chief Justice of the King's Bench in the hope that the responsibility of that court to protect the Crown's rights would blunt his opposition. Coke promptly disappointed the King. In 1615, Coke held that the King violated the law when he sounded out the judges on their views as to whether conduct of certain dissenters might be regarded as high treason.[25] Coke compounded his defiance by refusing to acknowledge the King's power by royal writ to stop or delay proceedings in the Common Law Courts. Coke was instrumental in having a letter addressed to the King, concurred in by all the justices, defending the ruling that obedience to the royal writ was not required of the judges. The King thereupon summoned the judges in a body and upbraided them for their impertinence. Coke's colleagues capitulated under the King's assault, but Coke did not and was shortly thereafter dismissed as Chief Justice.[26] A few years later, he entered Parliament and inspired another great Landmark of Liberty, the Petition of Right, to the demands of which the King was compelled to accede in 1628.[27] That capitulation reaffirmed the principle that no man was to be deprived of his liberty except in accordance with the law of the land and, of equal significance, resulted in recognition of the right of subjects to have *habeas corpus* from the King's justices to challenge any detention as unlawful.

The Star Chamber and the Councils of the North and of Wales were finally abolished by the Long Parliament of 1641. The remedy of *habeas corpus* was perfected by the Act of 1679. And the Revolution of 1688 made these reforms permanent, together with those of the Petition of Right. Finally, in the Act of Settlement of 1701, Parliament legislated life tenure under fixed salaries for judges and provided that they could not be removed from office except on joint action of both Houses of Parliament.

Given this background of English experience, we can understand the colonists' outrage at King George III's refusal to grant the American Colonies an independent judiciary. They expressed their grievance, you will remember, in the protest in the Declaration of Independence that the King "has obstructed the administration of justice, by refusing his assent to laws for establishing judiciary powers." Specifically, they charged that "he has made judges dependent upon his will alone, for the tenure of their offices and the amount and payment of their salaries."

Thus, the Founding Fathers were determined to create a federal judiciary independent of the political branches of government. The Convention overwhelmingly rejected a proposal which would have provided that judges "may be removed by the Executive on the application by the Senate and House of Representatives." [28] The attitude of the Framers is apparent from the statements of some of the most respected and influential among them. James Wilson of Pennsylvania pointed out that "the Judges would be in a bad situation if made to depend on any gust of faction which might prevail in the two [political] branches of our government." [29] The result of life tenure for judges, he said, will be "that private property, so far as it comes before their courts, and personal liberty, so far as it is not forfeited by crimes, will be guarded with firmness and watchfulness." "I believe," he went on, "that public happiness, personal liberty and private property depend essentially upon the able and upright determinations of independent judges." [30]

In the Federalist papers, Alexander Hamilton wrote:

> The standard of good behavior for the continuance in office of the judicial magistracy, is certainly one of the most valuable of the modern improvements in the practice of government. In a monarchy it is an excellent barrier to the despotism of the prince; in a republic it is a no less excellent barrier to the encroachments and oppressions of the representative body. And it is the best expedient which can be devised in any government, to secure a steady, upright, and impartial administration of the laws. . . .[31]

Hamilton believed that independence of the judiciary was particularly necessary in this country because of the unique role assigned the judiciary in our then novel form of government:

> The complete independence of the courts of justice is particularly essential in a limited Constitution . . . one which contains certain specified exceptions to the legislative authority; such, for instance, as that it shall pass no bills of attainder, no *ex-post-facto* laws, and the like. Limitations of this kind can be preserved in practice no other way than through the medium of courts of justice, whose duty it must be to declare all acts contrary to the manifest tenor of the Constitution void. Without this, all the reservations of particular rights or privileges would amount to nothing.[32]

Madison expressed the thought more succinctly when, with particular reference to the Bill of Rights, he said, "independent tribunals of justice will consider themselves in a peculiar manner the guardian of those rights. . . ." [33]

We must therefore take it that the post-Civil War Congress, in enormously expanding federal judicial power to enable the federal courts effectively to enforce the new constitutional limits on state authority, fully expected that an independent federal judiciary would regard it a solemn duty to interpret and apply the new constitutional restraints in the spirit and sense intended by their framers, however unpopular with local authority or majority sentiment. Such expectation is, after all, the heart of our constitutional plan of judicially enforceable restraints.

The judicial task in defining and enforcing the Fourteenth Amendment was made particularly formidable by the patent ambiguity of the terms "due process of law" and "equal protection of the laws." By design, the great clauses of the Constitution had been broadly phrased to keep their noble principles adaptable to changing conditions and changing concepts of social justice, but "due process of law" and "equal protection of the laws" were particularly empty vessels.

It is true that the term "due process of law" derives from Magna Carta. It is the equivalent of the term, the "law of the land." But the Supreme Court from the beginning rejected the notion that "due process of law," as used in either the Fifth or Fourteenth Amendments, embraced nothing except what constituted the "law of the land," as sanctioned by settled usage in England or in this country. In a case decided in 1884, when the amendment was but 16 years old, the Court said:

> . . . to hold that such a characteristic is essential to due process of law, would be to deny every quality of the law but its age, and to render it incapable of progress or improvement. It would be to stamp upon our jurisprudence the unchangeableness attributed to the laws of the Medes and Persians.
> . . . it is better not to go too far back into antiquity for the best securities for our "ancient liberties." It is more consonant to the true philosophy of our historical legal institutions to say that the spirit of personal liberty and individual right, which they embodied, was preserved and developed by a progressive growth and wise adaptation to new circumstances and situations of the forms and processes found fit to give, from time to time, new expression and greater effect to modern ideas of self-government.[34]

Congress has not yet chosen to exercise its power under § 5 of the amendment fully to enlighten us as to the constitutional goals that should be furthered in applying the amendment's restraints; nor is the judiciary confined to discovering how the framers would have construed and applied those restraints. In the words of Chief Justice Hughes,

> if by the statement that what the Constitution meant at the time of its adoption it means to-day, it is intended to say that the great clauses of the Constitution must be confined to the interpretation which the framers, with the conditions and outlook of their time, would have placed upon them, the statement carries its own refutation. It was to guard against such a narrow conception that Chief Justice Marshall uttered the memorable warning—"We must never forget that it is a

constitution we are expounding" (*McCulloch* v. *Maryland* . . .)—"a constitution intended to endure for ages to come, and consequently, to be adapted to the various *crises* of human affairs." . . . When we are dealing with the words of the Constitution, said this Court in *Missouri* v. *Holland* . . . "we must realize that they have called into life a being the development of which could not have been forseen completely by the most gifted of its begetters . . . . The case before us must be considered in the light of our whole experience and not merely in that of what was said a hundred years ago." [35]

In giving meaning to the terms "due process of law" and "equal protection of the laws" the federal judges have therefore been aware, as Judge Learned Hand admonished,

> that there are before them more than verbal problems; more than final solutions cast in generalizations of universal applicability. They must be aware of the changing social tensions in every society which makes [*sic*] it an organism; which demand new schemata of adaptation; which will disrupt it, if rigidly confined. [36]

This approach of the federal judiciary has made the Fourteenth Amendment a potent tool in the attack upon the central problem of the twentieth century in our country. Society's overriding concern today is with providing freedom and equality, in a realistic and not merely formal sense, to all the people of this nation. We know that social realities do not yet fully correspond to the law of the Fourteenth Amendment. We do not yet have justice, equal and practical, for the poor, for the members of minority groups, for the criminally accused, for the displaced persons of the technological revolution, for alienated youth, for the urban masses, for the unrepresented consumer—for all, in short, who do not partake of the abundance of American life. Congress and the federal judiciary have done much in recent years to close the gap between promise and fulfillment, but who will deny that despite this great progress the goal of universal equality, freedom and prosperity is far from won and that ugly inequities continue to mar the face of our nation? We are surely nearer the beginning than the end of the struggle.

I do not know whether a 1964 American Bar Association report had Fourteenth Amendment jurisprudence in mind in observing that jurisprudence has shifted away from finespun technicalities and abstract rules to practical justice—to:

> a recognition of human beings, as the most distinctive and important feature of the universe which confronts our senses, and of the function of law as the historic means of guaranteeing that preeminence . . . . The new jurisprudence asks, in effect, what is the nature of man, and

what is the nature of the universe with which he is confronted. . . . Why is a human being important; what gives him dignity; what limits his freedom to do whatever he likes; what are his essential needs; whence comes his sense of injustice? [37]

I do know, however, that the content poured into the terms "due process of law" and "equal protection of the laws" surely has made more fruitful mankind's pursuit of the age-old dream for recognition of the inherent dignity and the equal and inalienable rights of all members of the human family. In its service of that dream, the Fourteenth Amendment, though 100 years old, can never be old. Like the poor old woman in Yeats' play, "Did you see an old woman going down the path?" asked Bridget. "I did not," replied Patrick, who had come into the house after the old woman left it, "But I saw a young girl and she had the walk of a queen." [38]

Notes

1. 1 Annals of Cong. 439 (1834 ed.).
2. For the history of the compromise, see C. Vann Woodward, *Reunion and Reaction* 266 (Anchor ed. 1956).
3. *Civil Rights Cases,* 109 U.S. 3 (1883).
4. *Plessy* v. *Ferguson,* 163 U.S. 537 (1896).
5. In the Judiciary Act of 1801, Congress had granted the federal courts extensive federal question jurisdiction, but this Act was repealed a year later. See Turner, *Federalist Policy and the Judiciary Act of 1801,* 22 William and Mary Q.3 (1965).
6. Frankfurter and Landis, *The Business of the Supreme Court: A Study of the Federal Judicial System* 65 (1927).
7. *McNeese* v. *Board of Education,* 373 U.S. 668, 673 (1963).
8. 18 Stat. 335 (1875).
9. 17 Stat. 13 (1871).
10. 14 Stat. 27 (1866).
11. See *Katzenbach* v. *Morgan,* 384 U.S. 643, 651, n. 10 (1966).
12. 14 Stat. 385 (1867). See the discussion in *Fay* v. *Noia,* 372 U.S. 391 (1963).
13. Ratner, *The Function of the Due Process Clause,* 116 U. Pa. L. Rev. 1048, 1061–1062 (1968). See also *The Federalist* No. 78 (Hamilton).
14. Introduction to A. V. Dicey, *The Law and the Constitution* lxxii (9th ed., 1939).
15. L. J. Mackintosh, *History of England* 188 (1830).
16. Magna Carta, ch. 39. The translations of Magna Carta quoted in the text are from Holt, *Magna Carta* Appendix IV (1965). For general discussions of the Charter see Holt, *supra;* McKechnie, *Magna Carta* (2d ed., 1958).
17. Magna Carta, ch. 39.
18. *Id.,* ch. 17.
19. *Id.,* ch. 45.
20. *Id.,* ch. 18.
21. *Id.,* ch. 24.
22. *Id.,* ch. 40.
23. See generally 5 Holdsworth, *History of English Law,* ch. IV (1927).
24. *Id.* at 428–436. See also Gough, *Fundamental Law in English History,* ch. 111 (1955).
25. See 5 Holdsworth, *supra,* note 23, at 438.
26. See 5 Holdsworth, *supra,* note 23, at 439–441.
27. *Id.* at 445–454.
28. U.S. Library of Congress, *The Creation of the Federal Judiciary* 31 (1938).
29. *Id.*
30. *Id.* at 46.
31. *The Federalist* No. 78 (Hamilton).
32. *Id.*
33. 1 Annals of Cong. 439 (1834 ed.).
34. *Hurtado* v. *California,* 110 U.S. 516, 529, 530 (1884).
35. *Home Building and Loan Assn.* v. *Blaisdell,* 290 U.S. 398, 442–443 (1934).

36. Hand, *Sources of Tolerance,* 79 U. Pa. L. Rev. 1, 13 (1930).
37. ABA Section of International and Comparative Law, *Report of the Committee on New Trends in Comparative Jurisprudence and Legal Philosophy* (M. Rooney, Chairman) 5–6, Aug. 10, 1954.
38. W. B. Yeats, *Cathleen Ni Hoolihan, The Hour-Glass and Other Plays* 80 (1912).

2

Historical Background of the Fourteenth Amendment

Henry Steele Commager

As an historian, the writer cannot, in all decency, launch this inquiry into the historical background of the Fourteenth Amendment without a preliminary glance at the question (or a glance at the preliminary question) of the relation of history to the law.

We stumble, at the very threshold, over two awkward problems. The first casts doubt upon the credentials of the whole enterprise, the second upon its usefulness.

Is it in fact possible to discover, with any reasonable certainty, the historical antecedents of so complex and miscellaneous a document as the Fourteenth Amendment? The evidence seems to be contrary. For almost a century now, jurists and historians have engaged in this challenging enterprise, and have come up with the most varied and conflicting answers to the most various and conflicting questions. Even the scope of the inquiry is, and has long been, a matter for dispute. After all what constitutes a proper historical background? Because we deal with due process, are we to go back to Magna Carta? Because we are concerned with a guarantee of a republican form of government, do we begin with Plato and trace (as John Adams did in a memorable but universally unread three-volume history) the history of republics? Because we must interpret the term liberty in the Fifth and Fourteenth Amendments, do we go back to Roman law and follow the explication of that term down the centuries?

How, after all, do we ascertain what statesmen and propagandists meant by the terms they used? It is a mistake to which historians and jurisprudents are peculiarly susceptible to assume that earlier generations used words with a precision foreign to most of us; that as individuals, or collectively as law makers, they knew precisely what they wanted in the way of legis-

Henry Steele Commager is Professor of History at Amherst College.

lation or policy, and that they chose precisely the right words and phrases to carry these ideas and policies to reality. It is this untested assumption which gives something of an air of unreality to much of the *explication du texte* of a Fairman, for example, or even a Boudin or a Crosskey: the careful analysis of every word and term. The majority of statesmen, past as present, use words with shocking carelessness, and even legislative drafting committees have been known to draw laws so loosely that the wisest judges differ about the meaning that is to be read into them. It is in part the ambiguity of words and phrases that largely justifies the existence of a judiciary: if every legal and constitutional term were clear beyond any doubt, there would be little work for lawyers or judges.

It is no use going back 100 years and demanding that busy men, in the heat of political campaigns or committee wrangles and eager, not only for the triumph of their own point of view but to persuade every one that their point of view is the majority one, always use words with precision and consistency, and with an awareness of the meaning that future generations of commentators will read into them.

This is equally unrealistic for students of law and of history. Not only do we not know what Jefferson meant when he wrote that all men are created equal, or what members of the Continental Congress thought the term meant when they endorsed it, but it is most improbable that Jefferson himself had any very clear idea what the phrase meant. So with many of the great phrases that have influenced history: "entangling alliances with none," "government of the people, by the people, for the people," "the world must be made safe for democracy" among them. This does not mean that these phrases were mere "glittering generalities" void of meaning; what it means is, rather, that there was a pretty common understanding or assumption about the implications of the phrases, and that it was this general understanding that a Jefferson, a Lincoln, a Wilson was able to lean back on.

There is no better illustration of this than the history of the debate over the Fourteenth Amendment. That debate has now been raging, in and out of the courtroom, since *Slaughterhouse,*[1] in 1873. Many of those who discuss most learnedly the meaning of the amendment—a Fairman, a Graham, a Crosskey, a Bickel—are, notwithstanding their sophistication, bemused by the potentialities of *explication du texte*. One might suppose that the amendment was unique in its use of controversial and imprecise words and phrases. But it is the character of our United States Constitution that it is full of these imprecisions; in fact, Thomas Reed Powell, beloved by many of us, used to warn his classes in constitutional law not to read the constitution as it tended to confuse the mind. Why should we expect to wrest precision out of the intransigent words of the Fourteenth Amendment when we have long been reconciled to our inability to know what the framers meant by words like "Commerce" or "the Executive Power"?

Nor can we assume that even familiar words mean the same thing, or radiate the same ideas from one generation to another. Consider, for example, the phrase "an establishment of religion." Whether interpreted broadly as in *Everson,*[2] or more narrowly as in *McCullom,*[3] it is generally supposed to imply, in Thomas Jefferson's felicitous phrase, "a wall of separation between church and state." But to Justice Story, who was appointed to the Court by the author of the First Amendment, James Madison, it meant no such thing. "There will probably be found few persons in this, or any other Christian country," wrote the great Commentator,

> who would deliberately contend, that it was unreasonable, or unjust to foster and encourage the Christian religion generally, as a matter of sound policy. [This policy, indeed] has continued to be the case . . . down to the present period without the slightest suspicion, that it was against the principles of public law, or republican liberty, [for] in a republic, there would seem to be a peculiar propriety in viewing the Christian religion, as the great basis, on which it must rest for its support and permanence.[4]

Or consider a phrase whose potentialities are only now, after a long lapse, beginning to be rediscovered: the guarantee of a republican form of government. Who can suppose that it carried the same connotations to those who drafted it—and who were animated by a lively fear of the establishment of monarchical government—or to those who applied it in the 1860's to exclude from representation states that had not yet conferred the suffrage on Negroes, and to President Taft who in 1911 vetoed the Arizona Enabling Act because its provision for the recall of judges violated the spirit of republican government?

A further, and familiar, difficulty in ascertaining meaning in the light of history is that we have different criteria for ordinary laws and for constitutional provisions. A law is not "designed to endure for ages to come" or to "adapt itself to the various crises of human affairs." If there are new crises, we can pass new laws. A law can, therefore, with somewhat better grace, be interpreted in terms of its immediate intention as declared or implied by its sponsors and critics. However, a constitutional provision is designed for a larger function and a longer life. It is therefore legitimate to insist that we go back to Congressional debates to discover, if we can, just what the Congress meant by the Sherman Anti-Trust Act or the Wagner Act. But recourse to Congressional, or to state legislative debates over a provision of the constitution, is allowed less authoritative credentials. Those who frame a constitutional provision must be assumed to know that it may be read one hundred years hence by men who listen to different semantic vibrations—or to none. Whatever we may think of the validity of the most famous footnote in constitutional law—footnote four of *Carolene Products* [5]—as a valid test for different parts of the United States Constitution, most of us would readily concede that the principle of *Carolene Products*—preferential treatment for one rather than another category of law—is valid as between the interpretation of ordinary legislation and of a constitutional amendment.

The second problem that confronts the historian is more awkward. It concerns the usefulness, rather than the theoretical validity of historical antecedents. For suppose that, by some miracle of research, we could ascertain precisely what the framers of the constitution or of amendments meant by the words they used. Would our problem then be at an end? Would we then consider ourselves bound by our findings, irretrievably condemned to repeat not only the words but the meanings of the past?

This, the conflict between the mechanical and the organic reading of the United States Constitution, is the oldest and most persistent in our constitutional law—from the dispute over "necessary and proper," in Washington's administration, to the dispute over "equal protection" today. *Dred Scott* provides the most nearly authoritative statement of the mechanical theory: the Constitution said Chief Justice Taney, "must be construed now as it was construed at the time of its adoption. It is not only the same in words, but the same in meaning." [6] Many judges have echoed his sentiment: Brewer, for example, who announced that the meaning of the constitution never alters—"that which it meant when adopted it means now," [7] or McReynolds in the *Gold Clause* cases, or Sutherland in *West Coast Hotel* v. *Parrish*. [8] On the whole, these views have been relegated to the realm of legal antiquarianism, but their ghosts still haunt the corridors of court rooms and law schools. However, most jurisprudents now endorse the principle laid down with classical simplicity by John Marshall in *McCulloch* [9]—one that deserves to be quoted in full because it commonly is not:

> This provision is made in a constitution, intended to endure for ages to come, and consequently, to be adapted to the various crises of human affairs. To have prescribed the means by which government should, in all future time, execute its powers, would have been to change, entirely, the character of the instrument. . . . It would have been an unwise attempt to provide, by immutable rules, for exigencies which, if foreseen at all, must have been seen dimly, and which can best be provided for as they occur. [To have limited the means, he added,] would have been to deprive the legislature of the capacity to avail itself of experience, to exercise its reason, and to accommodate its legislation to circumstances.

It is a principle crowned by the present Supreme Court in a series of epoch-making decisions from *Brown* v. *Board of Education* [10] to *Baker* v. *Carr* [11] and more recent cases.

The dynamic interpretation of constitutional concepts accentuates doubts as to the relevance of history. "I look forward to a time," said Justice Holmes, "when the part played by history in the explanation of dogma shall be very small, and instead of ingenious research we shall spend our energy on a study of the ends sought to be attained." Holmes's disciple, Judge Learned Hand, reminded historians that "the broad admonitory clauses of the Fourteenth Amendment are cast in such sweeping terms that their history does not elucidate their contents."

All this suggests that the search for really authoritative history is doomed to disappointment, not because historical antecedents cannot be found but because when found, they prove not to be authoritative. Yet it does not at all follow that exploration of the historical background of important constitutional doctrines is futile. Here we can take consolation from Justice Holmes who, though he disparaged "ingenious research," remarked later in life that "historical continuity with the past is not a duty, it is only a necessity."

If the meaning of our Constitution is not to be found in "ingenious research," neither is it to be found in an historical void, for our constitutional history is not catastrophic but evolutionary. We address ourselves, therefore, in this exploration of historical background, not to particular words, phrases, arguments, votes in the Congress or the States in 1866, 1867 and 1868, or to an eloquent phrase struck off in a Presidential campaign, or even to a stray word recollected in a courtroom in connection with a hotly contested piece of legislation, but to the larger purposes as they seem to emerge out of two generations of discussion.

This is, after all, what Blackstone himself said: that "when the words are dubious," you discover the meaning of the law "by considering the reason and spirit of it." It is what the Supreme Court admonished us in *Maxwell* v. *Dow:* [12] that the safe way to construe the Fourteenth Amendment is "to read its language in connection with the known condition of affairs out of which the occasion for its adoption may have arisen, and then construe it . . . so far as is reasonably possible, to forward the known purpose or object for which the Amendment was adopted."

It is the "reason" of the Fourteenth Amendment, and the "spirit" that infuses it—or infuses the historical background—to which we turn.

I

In the interpretation of the Fourteenth Amendment, as in the interpretation of the constitution, we can discern a broad and a narrow construction. Because the amendment worked a revolution in our constitutional system, we should not be surprised that under revolutionary pressure traditional broad and narrow constructions reversed themselves. Whereas, at the beginning of our national history, it was, on the whole, the libertarians like Jefferson and Madison who called for a narrow construction, and the conservative nationalists like Hamilton and Marshall who argued for a broad construction, it was, a century later, conservative business interests that took refuge in a narrow interpretation of the amendment, and libertarians who espoused a broad one. The division persists, though more commonly on philosophical than on economic grounds, in the court, as in public opinion. Over the years, Justices Bradley, Field and the first John Marshall Harlan, Black, Stewart, and Brennan, have championed the broad construction; Miller, Brewer, and Peckham, Frankfurter, Clark, and the second John Marshall Harlan, the narrow one.

If we consider first the anti-slavery origins of section 1 of the amendment, we do well to begin with Justice Miller's famous dicta in the *Slaughterhouse Cases:* [13]

> In the light of this recapitulation of events, almost too recent to be called history . . . and on the most casual examination of the language of these amendments [the 13th, 14th, and 15th], no one can fail to be impressed with the one pervading purpose found in them all, lying at the foundation of each, and without which none of them would have been even suggested; we mean the freedom of the slave race, the security and firm establishment of that freedom, and the protection of the newly made freeman and citizen from . . . oppression.

And, further:

> In any fair and just construction of any section or phrase of these amendments, it is necessary to look to the *purpose* which was . . . the pervading spirit of them all, the evil which they were designed to remedy.

We may take for granted familiarity with the immediate origins of the amendment: the *Dred Scott* decision; the Lincoln-Douglas debates; the climax of the Kansas struggle; secession; the formation of the Confederate States; war; emancipation in the District of Columbia and in the Territories; the Emancipation Proclamation; the struggle over control of Reconstruction culminating in the Wade-Davis bill and Lincoln's pocket-veto of that bill; Appomattox and the refusal of the South to accept the constitutional implications of defeat for race relations; the Black Codes and the Ku Klux Klan; the renewal of the struggle between Congress and the President, culminating in impeachment proceedings; Congressional response to Southern intransigence and to the constitutional attack upon the Freedmen's Bureau and the Civil Rights Acts.

All this is a thrice-told tale, and we are concerned with it here only in so far as it grew out of a deeper background, one whose roots go to the beginnings of national history.

Justice Miller's famous phrase, "one pervading purpose" is judicial short-hand for a long and crowded historical background sustaining a broad interpretation. That background would embrace, and absorb, not only legal and constitutional arguments, but the emotions, passions, arguments and policies of anti-slavery from the 1830's to the 1860's, inspired by fugitive slave rescues, the *Prudence Crandall* case, the argument of John Quincy Adams in the *Armistad* case, the sermons of Theodore Parker, the revivalism of Charles Grandison Finney and Theodore Weld, the organization of the Liberty, and the Free Soil parties, the Anthony Burns rescue crisis, "Bleeding Kansas," the publication of *Uncle Tom's Cabin,* and scores of similar episodes and issues charged with emotion and productive of political and constitutional argument.

Anti-slavery, or abolition as it speedily became, did not flourish in a vacuum; it was part of a much larger reform movement and drew from that movement much of its philosophy and its leadership. The philosophy was transcendental, the leadership was predominantly religious.

Nothing is more striking than the comprehensiveness of the reform movement. The reforms were universal, and radical; they embraced all mankind, white and black, men and women—and children too, the dangerous and the perishing classes of society (it is Theodore Parker's phrase) —and all institutions, religious and secular. Bronson Alcott proposed a club for "the study and diffusion of ideas and tendencies proper to the nineteenth century." Robert Owen—father of the Robert Dale Owen who helped draft the Fourteenth Amendment—called a "world convention to emancipate the human race from ignorance, poverty, division and misery." William Lloyd Garrison proclaimed that the world was his country and his countrymen all mankind, and meant it. The greatest of the clerical reformers, Theodore Parker, whose influence over Lincoln was significant, convened a council to discuss "the general principles of reform, and the means of promoting them," and when the Council met it devoted the first six hours to discussing "all the holy principles of reform."

Nothing was alien to the reformers: religious freedom, penal reform, temperance, child labor, education for Negroes and for whites, for girls as for boys, the emancipation of women, land reform, money reform, the welfare of workingmen, the elimination of slums, the end of war, the destruction of every form of privilege and inequality. "We are to revise the whole of our social structure," said Emerson, who was the cow from which they all drew their milk, "the State, the Church, Property."

Emerson himself was a minister who had left the pulpit but not the Church, and so were Channing and Parker and Ripley and so many of the others, for everywhere, East and West alike, it was the clergy who took the lead in this attempt to "revise" the whole of society. That meant emphasis on morality, and a habit of reading great moral lessons into law. The leadership was New England, too—a geographical concept, and a state of mind. Emerson and Parker, Garrison and Whittier, Margaret Fuller and Lydia Maria Child, Horace Mann and Samuel G. Howe, Charles Sumner and George Boutwell and Justin Morrill, Thomas Wentworth Higginson and Richard Henry Dana were New Englanders who stayed and worked in their country. The New York group—Horace Greeley and the Tappan brothers and the Rev. Samuel May—all had their roots in New England, while out in the Ohio country, the evangelists and Yankees joined hands to make the Western Reserve a moral extension of New England. Of the political leaders of anti-slavery in the West, Senator Chase was born in New England and so, too, were Zachariah Chandler and Jacob Howard of Michigan, Benjamin Wade, John Bingham, James Ashley, Joshua Giddings, William Lawrence of Ohio, Lyman Trumbull of Illinois and James Grimes of Iowa.

Slavery was originally but one of the many evils to be overcome before mankind could be regenerated, but it speedily emerged as the greatest of them. Convinced that they could make no progress as long as slavery blocked the road, reformers of all camps directed against that institution the whole weight of their moral, political, and constitutional arguments. Slavery as a general institution—like sin or infidelity—might have evoked only vague moral protest, but the manifestations of slavery in daily life required that the abolitionists formulate practical arguments and develop practical techniques. From the mid-1830's one crisis after another nudged the abolitionists onto a political course, and encouraged them to develop arguments and weapons that would be effective—which meant arguments that might win cases in the courtroom or send abolitionists to state or national legislatures.

It was in the furnace of these episodes and crises that the anti-slavery spokesmen forged their constitutional weapons. Thus, in the *Prudence Crandall* case in Connecticut, Ellsworth and Goddard formulated the principles of national citizenship and of the relevance of the comity clause as a guarantee of equal rights to education. Thus, in the *Matilda* and *Van Zandt* fugitive slave cases in Ohio, Samuel Portland Chase submitted arguments drawn from Higher Law to prove the unconstitutionality of the Fugitive Slave acts. Thus, in his memorable reply to the indictment for violation of the Fugitive Slave law, Theodore Parker ransacked history to prove the unconstitutionality as well as the immorality of slavery itself. Thus, in the *Armistad* case John Quincy Adams developed arguments which imposed international law upon American courts, and this even in the face of opposition from the President and the Attorney-General of the United States. The fight against the gag rule enabled antislavery forces to join with those deeply committed to protecting the right of petition, and to use the Congress as a forum for their propaganda. Bleeding Kansas raised once again the problem of the power of Congress in the Territories, a problem dramatized by *Dred Scott* in a fashion that won thousands of converts to the antislavery cause. The fight on the Oregon Constitution of 1859, which excluded free Negroes from the state, permitted Representative Bingham of Ohio to develop the argument of privileges and immunities in a fashion useful for the great debates of 1866. The indefatigable S. P. Chase and Joshua Giddings—likewise from Ohio—practiced their pens and their wits on the Liberty, the Free Soil-Democratic and the Republican party platforms from 1843 to 1860; all invoked as constitutional arguments the Declaration of Independence and the Bill of Rights. Thus—to cite only the first example—the platform of the Liberty Party in 1843 asserted that "the fundamental truth . . . of the Declaration of Independence was made the fundamental law of our national government by that Amendment which declares that no person shall be deprived of life, liberty or property without due process of law."

It would be tedious to trace each of the broad constitutional arguments to some particular document, platform, pamphlet, or debate, especially as Howard Graham and Jacobus ten Broek have already done this for us. Besides, there was no logical pattern in the selection of arguments that were used, but rather an indiscriminate blending of all that seemed relevant. Here is an example—William Goddell's call in 1847 for a national antislavery convention:

> Slavery in the United States is illegal, unconstitutional, and antirepublican. The federal judiciary is bound thus to decide in the case of any slave claiming his freedom. It is the business of the federal government . . . to provide such a judiciary, and Congress is bound to guarantee to every state . . . a republican form of government, which is incompatible with . . . slavery.

Or here is Charles Sumner asserting (for the first time, it is believed, in the *Roberts* case) that to exclude children from the schools of Boston was to deprive them of the equal protection of the laws . . . a concept which required "precise equality." Here is Theodore Weld insisting, in his dense monograph on *The Powers of Congress over Slavery* that allegiance and protection are two sides of the same coin, and that if slaves owe allegiance to the United States, then the United States is bound to provide protection for them. Here is Lysander Spooner, author of the formidable pamphlet, *The Unconstitutionality of Slavery,* asserting that "no law inconsistent with Natural Rights, can arise out of any compact of Government." Here is Charles Olcott, author of *Lectures on the Abolition of Slavery* (1838), insisting that the entire Bill of Rights applied to slaves as well as to freemen, because all were embraced in the term "people."

Representative Bingham, certainly one of the leading architects of the Fourteenth Amendment, had argued apropos the Kansas crisis, the admission of Oregon, and the Civil War legislation, that there was a national citizenship; that all citizens, black as well as white, were entitled to privileges and immunities, that the Fifth Amendment bound the states, and that the constitution, as it was, protected all of the Rights of Man but that government had heretofore lacked power to enforce its guarantees. James Wilson of Iowa asserted that slavery violated the Preamble of the Constitution and denied the privileges and immunities of citizens which were, quite simply, those contained in the Bill of Rights.

The line from the antislavery crusaders of the 1830's, 1840's and 1850's, to the Fourteenth Amendment, is clear and direct. The arguments that were advanced in the early agitation were refurbished and stiffened, and submitted as authoritative constitutional dogma in the debates over the Thirteenth Amendment, the Freedmen's Bureau and Civil Rights bills, and the Fourteenth Amendment. Even the men who inspired and who made the arguments were the same. A few, like Joshua Giddings, had passed from the scene, but most of those who contributed to the writing and the enactment of the Civil War amendments had served their apprenticeship in the earlier years of the abolitionist crusade.

Now this abolitionist background of the amendment sustains, as you will readily note, a broad construction of section one of that amendment. If we impose some order on what is essentially a disorderly body of arguments we can discern in them a group of plausible principles which most of the antislavery agitators espoused, and which they attempted to write into the Civil War amendments. If we may be guided, then, not by the words of the amendments, or the precise intentions of any of their authors —in so far as we can ascertain these—but by the purposes of the multiple authors, we must recognize the following arguments. It is not feasible here to determine whether these are sound (a matter on which opinion will always differ) but it is proper to say that they were persuasive in their day, and that they have not lost their persuasiveness, or their relevance, in our day.

1. That the rights to be protected by the Fourteenth Amendment were the rights of all persons, not just of freedmen.
2. That such terms as "persons," "citizens," "inhabitants," "people," "all men," and the like were used loosely, rhetorically and almost interchangeably in the propaganda of anti-slavery and in the debates on

the amendments, and that it is a mistake to read too much significance into the way particular words were used at any one moment.

3. That rights deserved to be protected not only when denied or abridged by a state or under cover of a state law, but whenever denied or abridged by individuals, groups, and organizations as well, because

4. Equal protection required *protection* in order to be equal, and failure to protect was itself a denial of equal protection, particularly flagrant when the failure was discriminatory, and that such failure required and authorized the federal government to make good the missing protection.

5. That the rights, privileges and immunities to be protected were not merely those attached, in some precise and narrow fashion, to national citizenship—as later set forth with limitless ingenuity by a long series of Court decisions culminating in *Screws* v. *United States*,[14] but that they were the whole spectrum of rights embraced in such phrases as "natural rights," "fundamental rights," "the rights of man," "God-given rights" and so forth, and in such documents as the Declaration of Independence, the Preamble to the Constitution, and the Bill of Rights. In throwing together this miscellany of philosophical and historical antecedents, the interpreters of the amendments followed the example of the abolitionists of an earlier generation.

6. That, in so far as we can penetrate the rhetoric of the time, the rights to be protected were substantially those embraced in the Federal Bill of Rights, in so far as these were applicable; and that some of the Congressmen who addressed themselves to this problem assumed that the amendment reversed *Barron* v. *Baltimore*.[15] The writer puts aside the question, raised by William Crosskey, whether *Barron* v. *Baltimore* was good law, but confesses his essential agreement with the arguments of Mr. Justice Black in *Adamson* v. *California*[16] and of Louis Boudin and Professor Crosskey on the larger issue of the relevance of the Fourteenth Amendment to the Bill of Rights.

7. That privileges and immunities, like rights in general, were not merely those supposed to be attached to United States citizenship, but embraced the natural rights of man, and that the term privileges and immunities must be given a positive, not a negative, interpretation. It was not to be invoked to cut down such rights as citizens might already enjoy in their own states, for if it were thus invoked to diminish existing rights the resulting condition could not logically be either a privilege or an immunity, but a limitation on the first and a restriction on the second; and thus the guarantee of privileges and immunities would be defeated.

8. That due process, as used in the Fourteenth Amendment, probably contained a mixture of ingredients, procedural and substantive; that

there were numerous precedents for a substantive reading of the term long before the *Wynehamer* [17] and *Dred Scott* cases, but that both interpretations, procedural and substantive, were directed primarily to the protection of the rights of men to life and liberty (whatever those words might have meant), and were pretty clearly not directed to the rights of corporations—rights which were never seriously discussed or contemplated in the debates of the time.

9. That the guarantee clause, which had long slumbered in innocuous desuetude, experienced during Reconstruction an interesting reinterpretation that opened up large possibilities for the future. As this consideration belongs rather to the prospective than the retrospective history of the amendment, we shall not pursue it here.

10. That section five of the amendment was designed to be an integral part of it, and that it was not mere rhetoric but meant what it said: namely, that Congress should have the "power *to enforce, by appropriate legislation,*" its provisions.

II

Turn, then, to the second large purpose which we can read into the Fourteenth Amendment: that of working a revolution in our federal system. The setting here is the long debate over the nature of the Union, a debate which had its origins in the Constitutional Convention and persisted through many vicissitudes down to what Andrew C. McLaughlin has called the greatest constitutional decision in American history, Grant's at Appomattox. With the bold judicial decision of the 1820's, the turning back of the dire threat to the supremacy of the federal judiciary from Virginia, Webster's reply to Hayne, Jackson's defiance of Calhoun, and the publication of Story's *Commentaries,* the broad construction of the Constitution reached one of its great climacterics. The next quarter-century saw a pronounced reaction towards particularism and a narrower interpretation of national powers. Slavery was growing and expanding and, during the Jacksonian era, it cemented a somewhat uneasy alliance with the Democratic party in the North as well as in the South. Defenders of slavery exalted States Rights for both legal and practical reasons: legal, because slavery existed only in the eyes of municipal law; practical because, notwithstanding its strength, only the states could be counted on to protect it, and the more rapid growth of free than of slave territory posed a most alarming threat to slavery in the national arena.

Events from the 1830's to Fort Sumter saw a corresponding weakening of the national authority. Marshall and Story gave way to Taney and Baldwin, Adams and Jackson to Pierce and Buchanan, the ardent nationalist principles of Webster to the doctrinaire, states rights theories of

Calhoun. And in the realm of fact, rather than principle, the effect of the acquisition of vast new territory seized from Mexico was to strengthen slavery more than freedom.

Yet all the time, nationalism itself was growing, not so much in dramatic decisions from the Supreme Court or through bold gestures from the Executive, but through the quiet workings of technology, transportation, immigration, language, literature, education, and law. It is customary to interpret abolition as a disrupting force, and in some ways it was that. However, the anti-slavery argument—expressed in a thousand speeches, resolutions, pamphlets and sermons, nationalist as a means rather than as an end—poured a continuous stream of rhetoric, logic, and sentiment into the great ocean of nationalism. Because much of this argument was inconsistent, disorganized, and vehement, we tend to neglect it; because much of its rhetoric despaired of a union with slaveholders, we tend to misconceive it. Nevertheless, *Uncle Tom's Cabin* (to take merely the most notable of all pieces of antislavery literature) did not create divisions, it merely advertised them; what it did create was something like a national sentiment.

The anti-slavery argument did not confine itself to the realm of morality; in the hands of shrewd leaders like Birney and Weld, Sumner and Parker, Giddings and Chase, it developed a substantial and even a respectable legal content as well. It argued the paramountcy of national power: that under the Constitution, as it then stood, Congress had the authority to abolish slavery not only in the District of Columbia and the Territories, but anywhere in the United States. It asserted that the comity clause of the Constitution meant what it seemed to say, and that the privileges and immunities which it protected were those which might be read out of the Federal Bill of Rights. It early developed the notion of equal protection and anticipated something of the use the Court would later develop out of it. It insisted, long before Bingham added the opening phrase to the Fourteenth Amendment, that citizenship was indeed national, and that national citizenship was paramount over state, and it also maintained that if the United States could protect an American citizen in France or Algiers, it could do so in Alabama and Mississippi—an argument that still has some interest. It anticipated, in the words of Charles Sumner, the potentialities of the guarantee clause as "a sleeping giant with a giant's power."

Because in *Barron* v. *Baltimore* and in *Dred Scott,* the Court rejected important ingredients of these claims, and because eventually it was to reject the broad interpretation of the Thirteenth and Fourteenth Amendments, we take for granted that the constitutional doctrines of the abolitionists were wrong-headed and misguided. It is not certain that they were. Perhaps we can say of them that they were ahead of their times. Perhaps we can say that if they were technically wrong (which we need not concede), they were historically right in their belief that American federalism should be nation-centered rather than state-centered. That is the kind of federalism we have now, if we can keep it—one whose center is in Washington, rather than in Montgomery or Jackson or Little Rock.

III

It is not a misreading of the judicial record to conclude that the last 15 or 20 years have witnessed an acceptance, perhaps even a vindication, of much of the antislavery argument that went into the making of the Fourteenth Amendment, and a return to the original intentions of those chiefly responsible for it. The so-called sociological arguments of *Brown* v. *Board of Education* are not very different from the philosophical arguments about equality from men like Birney and Weld, Bingham and Howard, and the decision of the Court in *Jones* v. *Mayer* [18] not only accepts the continuing validity of the Civil Rights Act of 1866, but goes out of its way to endorse the reading of that bill to forbid not only infringement of rights by state or local law, but by "custom or prejudice." Nor is this the only vindication of what we have called the broad construction. In relying on the equal protection clause to justify far-reaching reapportionment, the Court has ventured into areas that the most ardent of antislavery constitutionalists had seen but dimly, but never explored.

This volume commemorates the centennial of the Fourteenth Amendment at a time when we are in process of recovering, refurbishing and reinvigorating its original principles—original not in the literal sense that those finally responsible for it all subscribed to them, but in the deeper sense that the generation which fought the war and ended slavery meant them— thanks to the Negroes themselves, so long denied that protection the amendment was designed to secure them; thanks to the independence, the wisdom, and the courage of our highest court.

But we observe this centenary, too, at a time when some of its deepest purposes are called into question, and when that constitutional system of which it is an essential part is threatened by ignorance, and selfishness, and fear. Let us trust that our people may once again be animated by that devotion to the Union, that respect for the law and for the courts as the indispensable bulwark of the law, that passion for justice, that vision of liberty and equality, which animated the generation of the 1860's.

Notes

1. *Slaughterhouse Cases,* 16 Wall. 36 (U.S. 1873).
2. *Everson* v. *Board of Education,* 330 U.S. 1 (1947).
3. *McCollum* v. *Board of Education,* 333 U.S. 203 (1948).
4. Story, *Commentaries on the Constitution of the United States* § 1867 (1833).
5. *United States* v. *Carolene Products Co.,* 304 U.S. 144, 152, n. 4 (1938).
6. *Dred Scott* v. *Sandford,* 19 How. 393, 426 (U.S. 1857).
7. *Norman* v. *Baltimore & O.R. Co.,* 294 U.S. 240, 362, 381 (1935).
8. *West Coast Hotel Co.* v. *Parrish,* 300 U.S. 379, 402 (1937).
9. *McCulloch* v. *Maryland,* 4 Wheat. 316, 415 (U.S. 1819).
10. 347 U.S. 483 (1954).
11. 369 U.S. 186 (1962).
12. 176 U.S. 581, 602 (1900).
13. 16 Wall. at 71–72 (Emphasis added).
14. 325 U.S. 91 (1945).
15. 7 Pet. 243 (U.S. 1833).
16. 332 U.S. 46 (1947).
17. *Wynehamer* v. *People,* 13 N.Y. 378 (1856).
18. 392 U.S. 409 (1968).

3

The Amendment in Operation:
A Historical Overview

Bernard Schwartz

The Fourteenth Amendment in operation has been a virtual magic mirror wherein we see reflected every important development in American history during the past century.[1] Nor is it surprising that this should be so, when we bear in mind both the crucial part which constitutional issues play in this country and the cardinal significance of the amendment itself in the organic scheme.

The vital role played by constitutional issues in the American system has been stressed by observers at least since de Tocqueville. The perceptive Frenchman noted over a century ago the primordial place of the American Constitution and the judge who interprets it in our society. Scarcely any question arises in the United States, he wrote, that is not resolved, sooner or later, into a constitutional question.[2]

A more recent outside observer has made the point even more strikingly: "At the first sound of a new argument over the United States Constitution and its interpretation the hearts of Americans leap with a fearful joy. The blood stirs powerfully in their veins and a new lustre brightens their eyes. Like King Harry's men before Harfleur, they stand like greyhounds in the slips, straining upon the start."[3]

When we add to what has been said the crucial place of the Fourteenth Amendment in the organic framework, we can see that the assertion with which we began was more than mere hyperbole. In the century since it became a part of the fundamental law, the amendment has become, practically speaking, perhaps our most important constitutional provision—not even second in significance to the original basic document itself. That is true because the vast majority of cases now being brought to vindicate

Bernard Schwartz is Edwin D. Webb Professor of Law at New York University School of Law.

individual rights are, strictly speaking, brought under the Fourteenth Amendment rather than the original Bill of Rights. Thus it is the amendment that has served as the legal instrument of the egalitarian revolution which has so transformed the contemporary American society.

The Fourteenth Amendment itself was the most important of the post-bellum additions to the constitution, themselves the first changes in the organic text in over sixty years. The Thirteenth Amendment abolished slavery; the Fifteenth gave the emancipated race the right of suffrage. However, these were hardly enough to vest the Negro with anything like the civil status of others in the community, or to deal with the gross discriminations against the freedmen so graphically described in newspapers of the period. What was needed was an amendment designed specifically to protect the civil rights of the emancipated race against state infringements.

The need was met by adoption of the Fourteenth Amendment. It was intended by its draftsmen to have two principal effects. The first was to sweep away the 1857 *Dred Scott* decision [4] barring citizenship for the Negro. Hence the amendment's first sentence providing citizenship for all persons born or naturalized in this country. In addition, the intent was to make it illegal for the states to deny equal civil rights to those thus made citizens by providing that no state was to "deprive any person of life, liberty, or property without due process of law" or to "deny to any person within its jurisdiction the equal protection of the laws."

These two clauses—the Due-Process Clause and the Equal-Protection Clause—of the Fourteenth Amendment were completely to transform the constitutional system. Much of the stuff of our constitutional law in the century that has followed has, in truth, been in the nature of mere gloss upon those two seminal provisions.

The South has consistently attacked the Fourteenth Amendment as a force bill, steam-rollered through the Southern states as part of the Reconstruction program. Nevertheless, imposed by coercion or not, the Fourteenth Amendment must now clearly be considered a part of the constitution, for it was duly ratified in accordance with the established amending procedure. As the Supreme Court put it, with regard to the resolution and proclamation of ratification by Congress and the Secretary of State: "This decision by the political departments of the Government as to the validity of the adoption of the Fourteenth Amendment has been accepted." [5]

One may go further and say that, regardless of the manner of its adoption, the Fourteenth Amendment has been accepted without question as part of the supreme law of the land by most Americans. More than that, its provisions have accorded with the felt need for equal justice among all men; the Declaration of Independence did not, as Lincoln once expressed it, say that "all men are created equal, except Negroes." [6] The Fourteenth Amendment has by now been built into the conscience of the nation. In Senator Charles Sumner's phrase, "It has already taken its place in the immortal covenants of history. . . . As well attempt to undo the Declaration of Independence or suspend the law of gravitation." [7]

The adoption of the Fourteenth Amendment plainly marked a constitutional epoch in our history. Like the victory of the North itself, it constituted the culmination of the nationalistic theory that had first taken root 80 years earlier in Philadelphia.

From the founding of the Republic to the end of the Civil War, it was the states that were the primary guardians of their citizens' rights and liberties and they alone could determine the character and extent of such rights. That was true because the Bill of Rights was binding upon the federal government alone—not the states.[8] With the Fourteenth Amendment, all this was altered. That amendment called upon the national government to protect the citizens of a state against the state itself. Thenceforth, the safeguarding of civil rights was to become primarily a federal function.

Before Sumter, the great theme in our constitutional history was the nation-state problem. Nation and states appeared to confront each other as equals and all was overshadowed by the danger that centrifugal forces would rend the nation asunder.[9]

Appomattox put an end to this danger. Thenceforth, the Union was, as the Supreme Court put it in 1869, "indestructible" [10] and the supremacy of federal power was ensured. The focus of constitutional concern could be transferred from the protection of federal power to the safeguarding of individual rights.

Yet, even when the Fourteenth Amendment began to be given effect as a restraint upon state authority, its impact was almost entirely confined to the economic sphere. The decisions of the Supreme Court until our own day all but limited the amendment's impact to the area of property rights. Such limitation may have been understandable in an era of explosive industrial expansion, which so drastically modified the whole economic fabric. In such an era, it was not unnatural for the dominant emphasis to be placed upon the proper relationship between government and business. To the law (as to the society which it mirrored) the danger that state sovereignty would impair the power of the nation was replaced by the danger that government would unduly impede industry in its destined economic conquest of a continent.

The result was that the Fourteenth Amendment was converted into a Magna Carta for business, in place of the Great Charter for individual rights which its framers had intended. It is, indeed, one of the ironies of American constitutional history that, for the better part of a century, the

Fourteenth Amendment was of little practical help to the very race for whose benefit it was enacted, at the very time that it was serving to shield the excesses of expanding capital from governmental restraints.

The present-day observer must, however, note a sharp change of emphasis in the recent interpretation of the Fourteenth Amendment. As late as 1922, a federal judge could assert "that of the three fundamental principles which underlie government, and for which government exists, the protection of life, liberty, and property, the chief of these is property." [11]

If such judicial comment was not at variance with reality in 1922, the same is no longer true. The constitutional emphasis in our own day has shifted to one of ever-growing concern for "life and liberty" as the really basic rights which the constitution was meant to safeguard. The earlier stress upon the protection of *property* rights against governmental violations of due process has given way to one which has increasingly focused upon *personal* rights. Under the newer approach, the Fourteenth Amendment has at last become (as its framers intended) the shield of individual liberties throughout the nation.

To one familiar with the primary purpose of those who wrote the Fourteenth Amendment into our organic law, it is particularly satisfying to see equal protection become more than a mere slogan for the Negro. In 1896, the Supreme Court had held the guaranty of equal protection not violated by racial segregation.[12] The decision gave the lie to the American ideal, so eloquently stated in dissent by the first Justice Harlan: "Our Constitution is color-blind." [13] Upon the "separate but equal" doctrine approved by the court was built the whole structure of segregation that has been the very core of the Southern system of racial discrimination.

In the landmark 1954 case of *Brown* v. *Board of Education*,[14] the "separate but equal" doctrine was overruled, and segregation ruled violative of the equal-protection guaranty. The *Brown* decision itself, as is well known, has been subjected to severe criticism, ranging from extreme vituperation to more reasoned censure based upon an alleged lack of legal craftsmanship in the court's opinion. A decade and a half later, however, such criticisms have all but lost their relevancy. Perhaps the court did not articulate as clearly as it should have the juristic bases of the decision. But the *Brown* opinion is so plainly right in its conclusion that segregation denies equality, that one wonders whether additional labor in spelling out the obvious was really necessary.

What is clear is that the *Brown* decision has taken its place in the very forefront of the pantheon of historic high-bench decisions. For, make no mistake about it, it is having an impact upon a whole society's way of life comparable to that caused by political revolution or military conflict.

Most important, the *Brown* decision signals the present expansive attitude of the Supreme Court toward the Fourteenth Amendment which has already so transformed the entire constitutional system. From the field of racial equality involved in *Brown,* the high tribunal has more recently spread the Amendment's protective mantle over that of political rights and the rights of criminal defendants.

In the field of political rights, the key decision was *Baker* v. *Carr* (1962),[15] in which the federal courts were ruled competent to entertain an action challenging legislative apportionments as contrary to the equal protection clause. It has become all but constitutional cliché that *Baker* v. *Carr* has worked a virtual revolution in legislative representation throughout the land. For it has brought about a dramatic change in the manner in which legislative districts must be apportioned.

That has been true because, in 1964, the Supreme Court held that the Equal Protection Clause lays down an "equal population" principle for legislative apportionment.[16] The Fourteenth Amendment, under this principle, demands substantially equal legislative representation for all citizens. The result has already been a substantial shift in the political structure, with reduction of the disproportionate influence that rural areas have had and a transfer of the legislative balance to those urban concentrations in which the bulk of Americans now live.

In addition to racial and political equality, the Supreme Court has moved to ensure equality in criminal justice. Here, too, the constitutional instrument has been the Fourteenth Amendment. The basic theme of the Amendment in this area, the court declared in a noted case, is that "all people charged with crime must, so far as the law is concerned, 'stand on an equality before the bar of justice in every American court.' "[17]

To achieve this goal, the court during the past decade has used the guarantees of equal protection and due process both to ensure equality as between rich and poor defendants, and to eliminate the inherent inequality that exists between the prosecution and the defendant—dwarfed as he inevitably is when he finds himself in the dock, opposed by the state with all the wealth and power available to it.

In many ways, the landmark criminal case has been *Gideon* v. *Wainwright* (1963),[18] which ruled that the Fourteenth Amendment requires indigent defendants, upon their request, to be furnished counsel by the state—a holding which later cases have extended to virtually every stage of criminal process, from arrest to appeal. Under *Gideon* and its progeny, no man may be condemned because of poverty to run the gantlet of the criminal law without counsel at his side.

In other cases, the Fourteenth Amendment's requirement of due process has been held to demand adherence by the states to most of the rights guaranteed in the Bill of Rights. These have included the right to a jury trial,[19] confrontation of witnesses,[20] speedy trial,[21] and that against self-incrimination.[22] Ultimately, it may not be doubted, the Fourteenth Amendment will be deemed to include well-nigh all the specific rights safeguarded by the Bill of Rights.

If there is one great unifying theme in the recent decisions expansively interpreting the Fourteenth Amendment, it is that of equality: equality as between races, between citizens, between rich and poor, between prosecutor and defendant.

Equality itself has been the underlying concept of the American system since it was proclaimed as self-evident truth in the Declaration of Independence—in what Lincoln called "the electric cord in that Declaration that links the hearts of patriotic and liberty-loving men together." [23] More than the men who made the Revolution and wrote the constitution could possibly have foreseen, the twin levers of Liberty and Equality have accomplished in the field of political science virtually what Archimedes posited in that of mechanics: "Had we a place to stand upon, we might raise the world." [24]

The effort to give effect to the Declaration of Independence's great concept of the equality of man has been a constant driving force in our history. Though, at the beginning, the political and economic systems were permeated with inequalities, only a century later Bryce could declare, "The United States are deemed all the world over to be preeminently the land of equality." [25] In truth the paramount theme in any democratic polity must be the movement to provide equality, as well as liberty, for *all*. Democratic communities, concluded de Tocqueville, may "have a natural taste for freedom. . . . But for equality their passion is ardent, insatiable, incessant, invincible." [26]

Nevertheless, if the thrust for equality has always been a dominant force in our political history, it was not until after the Civil War that an express constitutional guaranty became appropriate. Before then, the notion of equality itself was most restricted; it did not include Negroes or women and was basically governed by the Aristotelian notion of the inherent inequality of persons outside the select circle of full citizenship.

With the express guaranty of equality in the Fourteenth Amendment, the picture was wholly changed. Yet, as already emphasized, only in our own day has the Equal Protection Clause really begun to be given practical reality—and that largely because of the expansive manner in which the Supreme Court under Chief Justice Warren has interpreted the clause.

The result has been what Justice Fortas calls "the most profound and pervasive revolution ever achieved by substantially peaceful means." More than that, it has been that rarest of all political animals: a judicially inspired and led revolution. Without the Supreme Court decisions giving ever-wider effect to the right to equal protection, it may be doubted that most of the movements for equality that permeate the society would even have gotten started.

Why, it may be asked, has the Fourteenth Amendment, which had, for so long, been a mere paper guaranty outside the field of economic rights, now been given effect as the great charter of personal rights?

In its recent decisions protecting individual liberties, the Supreme Court has been responding to the felt necessities of the mid-twentieth century. The society today suffers from ever-growing malaise, linked directly to recurring doubts about the survival of individual personality in a community dominated by the twin facts of accelerating urbanization and explosive scientific revolution. Can the individual exist, as an end in himself, in an age in which the machine tends more and more to despoil human personality?

The current concern of the Supreme Court for personal rights represents a direct judicial reaction to the vast concentrations of power confronting the individual in the urbanized industrial society. In such a society, the justices place a countervailing emphasis upon preserving an area of personal right consistent with the maintenance of individual development. Such emphasis, they feel, is vital if man is to continue to possess the essential attributes of humanity "lacking which," as William Faulkner puts it, "he cannot be an individual and lacking which individuality he is not worth the having or keeping." [27]

In this respect, the history of the Fourteenth Amendment confirms the crucial role played by the Supreme Court in the resolution of the nation's problems. From the beginning, the court has, in the main, functioned as an institution that has served the needs of the nation, its essential role being to maintain the balance which other institutions had failed to retain. At the outset, the primary needs of establishing national power on a firm basis and vindicating property rights against the excesses of state power were met in the now classic decisions of the Marshall Court. In the latter part of the last century, the need was to swing the balance the other way. If the high court was to elevate the rights of property to the plane of constitutional immunity, its decisions thus interpreting the Fourteenth Amendment were the necessary legal accompaniment of the post-Civil War economic expansion.

In our own day, the situation has become completely different. We have come to recognize that property rights must be restricted to an extent never before permitted in our law. Unless personal rights are correlatively expanded, the individual will virtually be shorn of constitutional protection —hence the recent shift in Supreme Court decisions to the protection of personal rights.

The justices, like the rest of us, are disturbed by the growth of authority and are seeking to preserve a sphere for individuality even in a society in which the individual stands dwarfed, if not overwhelmed, in the face of the power concentrations that confront him in the contemporary community. Only thus, they feel, can man be expected to retain a modicum of liberty in the face of Leviathan come to life.

There are, however, those who, more and more stridently, express the view that the law is merely a facade which can have no more than a surface impact upon the inequities in the society. Of what use, they ask, are concepts such as equal protection and due process in a system which, they claim, is so blatantly irrational that it can be ameliorated only by action which rejects the very tenets of the existing order, such as direct confrontation, violent disobedience of law, or even revolutionary tactics?

In a more restrained way, it may be asked whether the concept of constitutionalism embodied in the guarantees of the Fourteenth Amendment is relevant in the face of the injustice which inevitably exists in the contemporary community. All too many answers to such question are only one dimensional,[28] ignoring both the basic presuppositions of constitutional legality and the lessons of history.

The problem of the unjust law is, to be sure, most difficult both for society and the individual. The duty of the individual to obey such law, in the face of what he may deem the higher duty not to lend his obedience to public power exerted for unjust ends, may pose a crisis of conscience not readily resolved.

The community must, however, look beyond the alleged evil of the particular law. The rule of law itself becomes meaningless if we recognize in each individual a right, derived from what Martin Luther King called a "moral law of the universe," [29] not to comply with any law he deems unjust. "If one man," says Justice Frankfurter, "can be allowed to determine for himself what is law, every man can. That means first chaos, then tyranny." [30]

A prison may, under Thoreau's striking contention, be "the only house in a slave State in which a free man can abide with honor." [31] The same is scarcely true in a system such as ours, where every act of government can be challenged by an appeal to law. Such a system can work only while the notion of appeal to law, rather than to individual conscience, remains fundamental. "Americans are free . . . ," said John F. Kennedy in 1962, "to disagree with the law, but not to disobey it. For in a government of laws and not of men, no man, however powerful or prominent is entitled to defy a court of law." [32]

The history of the Fourteenth Amendment itself is striking proof of the extent to which our constitutional system can correct basic injustices. We forget how far we have come since Lord Acton, apostle of liberty though he was later to become, could write, "It is as impossible to sympathise on religious grounds with the categorical prohibition of slavery as, on political grounds, with the opinions of the abolitionists." [33] In those days, even a bitter opponent of slavery, like John Quincy Adams, could casually refer to slaves as "live stock." [34]

Since that time, the notion that a human being could be relegated to the status of mere property has been utterly repudiated. More than that, the Fourteenth Amendment has given full civil rights and legal equality to all persons, and, as it is being interpreted, regardless of race, creed, status, wealth, or sex. More and more, these factors are being treated as what they are: mere accidents of birth or condition which fade into insignificance in the face of our common humanity.

From this point of view, the Fourteenth Amendment has made the constitution not only color-blind, but also creed-blind, wealth-blind, status-blind, and sex-blind. The law regards man as man and takes no regard of those traits which are constitutional irrelevancies.

Of course, in what Justice Goldberg called "a world whose populations are everywhere fired by the notion of equality," [35] the movement to vindicate the right of equality has ramifications far beyond the legal order. Yet the gains made by such movement must, if they are to prove more than transitory, ultimately be translated into legal terms, in the form of enforceable precepts.

"All history," says Pere Teilhard, "bears witness to the fact that nothing has ever been able to prevent an idea from growing and spreading and finally becoming universal." [36] Such is manifestly the case in our own day with the idea of equality. In the legal field, such an idea, though elevated to the constitutional plane a century ago, has only recently become a substantial part of the living law. The centennial of the Fourteenth Amendment takes place in the midst of a tremendous evolutionary development, destined still to produce changes in the law fully as profound as those it will bring about in the society itself.

Notes

1. Compare Lerner, *The Mind and Faith of Justice Holmes* 29 (1954).
2. Quoted in *American Communications Association* v. *Douds,* 339 U.S. 382, 415 (1950).
3. *The Economist,* May 10, 1952, 370.
4. *Dred Scott* v. *Sandford,* 19 How. 393 (U.S. 1857).
5. Quoted in Schwartz, *The Reins of Power* 117 (1963).
6. 2 *The Collected Works of Abraham Lincoln* 323 (Basler ed., 1953).
7. 12 *The Works of Charles Sumner* 531 (1877).
8. *Barron* v. *Baltimore,* 7 Pet. 243 (U.S. 1833).
9. Compare McCloskey, *The American Supreme Court* 102 (1960).
10. *Texas* v. *White,* 7 Wall. 700, 725 (U.S. 1869).
11. *Children's Hospital* v. *Adkins,* 284 Fed. 613, 622 (D.C. Cir. 1922).
12. *Plessy* v. *Ferguson,* 163 U.S. 537 (1896).
13. *Id.* at 559.
14. 347 U.S. 483 (1954).
15. 369 U.S. 186 (1962).
16. *Reynolds* v. *Sims,* 377 U.S. 533 (1964).
17. *Griffin* v. *Illinois,* 351 U.S. 12, 17 (1956).
18. 372 U.S. 335 (1963).
19. *Duncan* v. *Louisiana,* 391 U.S. 145 (1968).
20. *Pointer* v. *Texas,* 380 U.S. 400 (1965).
21. *Klopfer* v. *North Carolina,* 383 U.S. 213 (1967).
22. *Malloy* v. *Hogan,* 378 U.S. 1 (1964).
23. Op. cit. *supra,* note 6, at 500.
24. Compare Paine, *Rights of Man* 155 (Heritage Press, 1961).
25. 2 Bryce, *The American Commonwealth* 810 (1916 ed.).
26. 2 Tocqueville, *Democracy in America* 102 (Bradley ed., 1954).
27. W. Faulkner, "Privacy—the American Dream: what happened to it," *Harper's* (July 1955, 33, 36).
28. The phrase is, of course, taken from a leading questioner of the relevancy of constitutionalism. Marcuse, *One Dimensional Man* (1968).
29. King, "The Civil Rights Struggle in the United States Today," 20 *The Record* (Assoc. of Bar of City of N.Y.), Supplement No. 5, 15 (1965).
30. Frankfurter, J., concurring, in *United States* v. *United Mine Workers,* 330 U.S. 258, 312 (1947).
31. Thoreau, "Unjust Laws," in *Voices in Court* 490 (Davenport ed., 1958).
32. Quoted in Correctional Ass'n of N.Y., Newsletter 3 (June, 1968).
33. Acton, *Essays on Freedom and Power* 246 (1948).
34. John Quincy Adams to Gerrit Smith, July 31, 1839 (unpublished).
35. Goldberg, *Equality and Governmental Action,* 39 N.Y.U.L. Rev. 205, 227.
36. Chardin, *The Future of Man* 283 (1964).

4

Sanctity of the Person

Walter V. Schaefer

One who is not acquainted with our institutions and our problems, and above all not acquainted with the common law process, might assume that a discussion of sanctity of the person in the context of the 100th anniversary of the adoption of the Fourteenth Amendment would be no more than an historical narrative—a description of the way in which each of the significant problems had been finally settled, many years ago. This is emphatically not the case. Not only do many important areas remain unsettled; there is fundamental disagreement as to the method to be used in interpreting and applying the words of the Amendment.

Let me attempt to state, in summary fashion, some of the reasons why an assumption of early, tidy and final interpretation of the Fourteenth Amendment is unwarranted. Uncertainty is inherent in any written text, for few words have a single meaning, and the content of the words used by any author is largely supplied by the reader. General terms, which are used so frequently in the great religious texts that have governed the moral conduct of mankind, are inevitably imprecise. There have been differing interpretations of the Talmud; the Koran has produced at least two major Islamic sects, and the forms of Buddhism are numberless, as are the Christian sects that have found their origins in the New Testament. And descending to a somewhat less exalted level, may I point out that the hazard of conflicting interpretations is not confined to great moral leaders; every judge who has been on a reviewing court for more than a few months has had to face it.

When a written constitution, designed to endure, moves from specification of the details of the structure of government into the area of relationships between the government and the people, it must speak in general terms. And those general terms will be read, over the years, by successive

Walter V. Schaefer is a Justice of the Supreme Court of Illinois.

generations in the light of their own interests and concerns, which will surely not be identical with those of the authors of the document.

Our judges who interpret the Constitution of the United States are lawyers trained in the common law process, and the common law process means a never ending quest for moral and logical consistency throughout the entire body of the law. No legal doctrine stands in isolation; each is part of the mainland, and the erosion of one has its effect on others. Law is never static, nor do we want it to be.

The interrelation of common law rules is neatly illustrated by a decision of the English Court of Appeal early in 1968.[1] Stated in general terms, the issue concerned the liability of an officer who, in executing a search warrant, seized property which was not named in the warrant, but which he reasonably believed to be stolen property. Again it might be thought that the English courts would have settled that issue many generations ago. The Master of the Rolls summarized the cases that bore upon the issue and then observed: "Such are the cases. They contain no broad statement of principle; but proceed, in our English fashion, from case to case until the principle emerges. Now the time has come when we must endeavor to settle it."[2]

Lord Justice Diplock (as he then was) introduced his more precise statement of the issue in this way: "The question in this appeal, therefore, is whether at common law *today* a police officer, . . ." He continued: "What answer does the common law today give to the question I have posed? No direct answer is to be found in any decision of the English courts, ancient or modern. From general observations, to be found in various judgments ranging over two centuries to which we have been referred, it is possible to discern where, upon this matter, various judges would have thought the balance lay between the inviolability of private property and the pursuit of public weal in a society of the kind in which they lived. But it is worth while remembering that until *Sommersett's Case* in 1771 the balance lay in favour of private property in slaves. This was six years later than *Entick* v. *Carrington,* a case to which we have been referred, whose reasoning we have been urged to follow. The society in which we live is not static, nor is the common law, since it comprises those rules which govern men's conduct in contemporary society on matters not expressly regulated by legislation. That is why in the question we have to answer I have stressed the word 'today.' "[3]

While it is thus a part of the duty of a common law court to make changes in the law, such a court lacks the power to initiate changes of its own volition. It can decide only as to the issues that are presented to it, and the scope of those issues is primarily determined not by the court, but by the litigants. Contrary to what some people think, and others wish, most courts are not eager to reach out for problems to decide. Judicial tenure is important not just because it ensures independence and freedom from the control of the demagogue, but also because it ensures a link with the past, and so guards against a too ready surrender to the claim of the present.

The late Professor Jacobus ten Broek has given us this capsule description of the shifting emphasis in the kinds of issues brought to and decided by the Supreme Court over the past century. His discussion is directed specifically at the equal protection clause, but it also serves to explain the course of decision with respect to other clauses of the Fourteenth Amendment:

> American political and constitutional assumptions and goals—liberty, the dignity of the human person, the right of private property, equality—intermingle and overlap. They are also fluid and variable in content. To the extent that they are living reality in a developing democracy, they are constantly growing, maturing, and changing. Every generation, every decade is a formative period in the constitutional life of the nation. Moreover, emphasis on the various elements has shifted at different periods in our history, in the documents that have embodied and expressed the different movements, forces, and times and among the prominent political writers and speakers. Equality was the dominant note in the Declaration of Independence. Property assumed a relatively stronger position in the Constitution. During the nineteenth century, when fortune and geography ensured the nation's military safety, and free land and the open frontier gave individuals a sense of economic safety, security was taken for granted, and liberty was elevated to a primary position. "When the traditional foundations of culture crumble," wrote Ralph Henry Gabriel concerning the impact of the world depression of the 1930's and the hot and cold wars of the 1940's, "when government by law gives way to government by irresponsible force, the preoccupation with liberty as an end in itself is replaced by a new search for security, mental, social, economic, and even physical." Tension can be endured, indeed can be felt, only so long. Eventually, although men live on the threshold of international doom, less spectacular but nevertheless urgent and pressing social, economic, and humanitarian problems force their way back into the nation's attention. And considerations of equality move again to the forefront. In some measure, this is the constitutional story of the 1950's and early 1960's in the United States.[4]

When we speak of "sanctity of the person," we are speaking of the right of each of us to be secure against unauthorized intrusions, our "right to be let alone." Unauthorized intrusions include, of course, burglary, robbery, rape, and the other crimes of violence which are the most serious assaults upon the sanctity of the person. But these intrusions are not relevant to our discussion, for protection against them must be found in the provisions of the criminal law. The prohibitions of the Fourteenth Amendment, and the other constitutional commands and prohibitions that are either absorbed or incorporated in that amendment, are addressed to State governments, and when they concern the conduct of individuals, they do so only indirectly, as is the case when First Amendment claims of freedom of the press compete with an individual's right of privacy.

I should like to begin by stating my reasons for excluding the Fifth Amendment's privilege against self-incrimination from a discussion of sanctity of the person under the Fourteenth Amendment. In my opinion, that privilege does not relate to the protection of the privacy of the individual, and I should like to reiterate my reasons for that opinion. Although the Supreme Court of the United States has vigorously applied the Fifth Amendment's privilege against self-incrimination and has even expanded the constitutional guarantee to prohibit comment upon the failure of a defendant to testify in his own defense, the court has not as yet settled upon a determination of the value that the privilege is intended to protect.

In 1957, in *Gruenwald* v. *United States*,[5] the court relied upon Dean Erwin N. Griswold for its assertion that "one of the basic functions of the privilege is to protect *innocent* men." Dean Griswold had indeed taken that position,[6] but he later stated that in his opinion it was a mistake to defend the privilege on that ground.[7] In *Griffin* v. *California*,[8] decided in 1965, the court expanded the privilege by prohibiting comment upon the failure of the accused to testify—an expansion based upon the ground that it was the purpose of the privilege to protect the innocent. Ten months after *Griffin* was decided, the court repudiated the ground on which expansion of the privilege had been based, saying: "[T]he basic purposes that lie behind the privilege against self-incrimination do not relate to protecting the innocent from conviction. . . ."[9] Instead, the Supreme Court expressed the view that the privilege reflects "the concern of our society for the right of each individual to be let alone,"[10] and that the privilege shows "our respect for the inviolability of the human personality and of the right of each individual 'to a private enclave where he may lead a private life.' "[11]

"That the protection of privacy is not a purpose of the privilege is demonstrated by the fact that a witness may constitutionally be granted immunity from prosecution and then be required to testify, under penalty of imprisonment for contempt, if he refused to do so. All concern for personal dignity disappears when the prospect of prosecution is removed. If privacy were our guide, moreover, we would be hard put to explain why a grocery list, or an automobile repair bill, is protected from disclosure if it incriminates, while disclosure of the most personal entries in a diary may be compelled if they do not incriminate. In a civil case the refusal of a party to come forward with evidence at his command, however intimate or personal it may be, routinely gives rise to an adverse inference, and it is hard to see why privacy, or the 'private enclave,' should be given greater protection in a criminal setting." [12]

In 1966, in *Johnson* v. *New Jersey*,[13] the court implied a new justification for the privilege, saying: ". . . we denied retroactive application to *Griffin* v. *California, supra,* despite the fact that comment on the failure to testify may sometimes mislead the jury concerning the reasons why the defendant has refused to take the witness stand." In a concurring opinion in a case decided in 1968, Justice Brennan said that it is clear that "the scope of the privilege does not coincide with the complex of values it helps to protect." [14] The court has still not definitively stated the values that the privilege was intended to protect. Indeed, it may be that the privilege rests primarily on the fact observed by Rupert Cross, Vinerian Professor of Law at Oxford, that there is in this country and in England, "an objection verging perhaps on the pathological to a man's incriminating himself out of his own mouth." [15]

The provision of the constitution that bears most directly upon the sanctity of the person is the Fourth Amendment with its statement of "the right of the people to be secure in their persons, houses, papers and effects, against unreasonable searches and seizures," and its further provision that no warrants shall issue without probable cause. In June, 1968, the Supreme Court handed down a landmark opinion dealing with the right to search, without a warrant, upon reasonable cause.[16] I propose to center my remarks upon this case, with only such deviations and departures as are required to accommodate by my own predilections and aberrations.

There were three cases decided in June, 1968, which had come to be known as the "stop and frisk" cases. Broadly stated, the problem they presented was this: What may a police officer do when he sees conduct which excites his suspicion, but which does not meet the traditional test that has justified an arrest—probable cause to believe that a felony has been or is being committed. As it turned out, the Supreme Court reached this problem in only one of the three cases. On the facts of one of them, the court held that the officer had no authority at all to interfere with the suspect,[17] and on the facts of another, the court held that the officer had probable cause to arrest in the traditional sense.[18]

Our interest centers on the remaining case, *Terry* v. *Ohio*.[19] There a police officer had observed two men take turns walking down the street and peering into a particular store. After each trip, the two men would confer, and after one of their expeditions they were joined by a third man. The officer followed, suspecting a daylight robbery, and when the three men met again in front of a store window, he asked them to identify themselves. In response they "mumbled something." Terry was one of the suspects. The officer spun him around so that he stood facing his companions, between them and the officer. The officer then patted his clothing, felt a pistol in his overcoat pocket, removed the coat and took the pistol out of the pocket. A frisk of another of the men uncovered another pistol; the third man was not armed. The defendant Terry was charged with carrying a concealed weapon. His motion to suppress the pistol which had been taken from him was denied. It was admitted in evidence, he was found guilty, and the Supreme Court of the United States affirmed his conviction in an opinion by the Chief Justice.

The case bristled with problems. The evils of promiscuous police use of the "stop and frisk" technique and the ease with which that technique may be abused are acknowledged in the opinion of the Chief Justice.[20] On the other hand, the opinion recognized that the authority of police officers to interfere with citizens cannot sensibly be restricted to those situations in which the officer has probable cause to believe that a felony has been or is being committed.[21] If that formulation ever operated satisfactorily in the past, it is not adequate today when resources of anonymity and mobility, to a degree heretofore unknown, are available to potential and actual criminals.

The opinion of the court stated the issue in narrow terms: "whether it is always unreasonable for a policeman to seize a person and subject him to a limited search for weapons unless there is probable cause for an arrest." [22] The court responded by holding that the validity of a search in circumstances like these, which cannot as a practical matter be subjected to "the Warrant Clause of the Fourth Amendment," with its requirement of probable cause, must be measured by determining whether the facts that confronted the officer, considered with the rational inferences to be drawn from those facts, reasonably warranted the action that he took. Subjective good faith on the part of the officer is not enough; his conduct must satisfy the objective standard of reasonableness that the Fourth Amendment requires.[23]

The approach of the Supreme Court in the *Terry* case differs sharply from the approach that it took in 1966 in *Miranda* v. *Arizona* [24] with respect to custodial interrogation, and in 1967 in *United States* v. *Wade* [25] with respect to identification lineups. And that difference prompts some reflections which may be incompetent, but which I hope are neither immaterial, irrelevant, or too impertinent.

When the court confronted the *Miranda* case in 1966, it had been dealing with contested claims of involuntary confessions on a wholesale basis for many years. Those claims had ranged from assertions of physical brutality to assertions of psychological compulsion. There are not very many cases in which it has been definitely established that improper police conduct has induced a confession. When there is incommunicado interrogation, improper conduct can only be brought to light by a combination of the utmost diligence on the part of counsel, plus a substantial ingredient of luck. Nevertheless, there have been enough cases in which coercion or other improper conduct had been established to justify a strong suspicion that there might be more.

The reaction of the Supreme Court to the *Miranda* cases must be measured against the background of the host of claims of improper police conduct that had been brought to its attention. Where there has been incommunicado interrogation, a reviewing court feels a sense of frustration, because the testimony of the police officers is usually consistent and it outweighs the testimony of the defendant. In almost all cases it is probably true. But the nagging possibility of that exceptional case, however rare, troubles a conscientious court, and repeated exposure to the problem enhances frustration.

The judges of a top State court have an advantage, in this respect, over the justices of the Supreme Court of the United States. A hearing upon a motion to suppress a confession takes place before the judge without a jury. Even in a state as large as Illinois, the reviewing court judges come to have a "feel" for the attitude of the trial judges on such an issue. Speaking for myself alone, my reaction to the record upon such a hearing is affected by my knowledge of the judge who made the ruling. In a close case, I suspect that I could not, even if I wished to do so, exclude from consideration my knowledge of the judge who has made the ruling, and my experience with his rulings over the years. And by way of indicating that my reaction is more than a personal idiosyncrasy, may I vouch to warranty the opinion of Justice Roberts in *Betts* v. *Brady,*[26] which referred to Chief Judge Bond of the Maryland Court of Appeals by name at least 14 times.

This is an advantage that the Supreme Court of the United States cannot often have, and its frustrations in the coerced confession cases were to that degree, which is in any event small, enhanced beyond those of the judges of the State courts. The outcome of the court's frustrations appears in *Miranda* v. *Arizona.* It was clear before those cases were decided that the Supreme Court would "be searching for some automatic device by which the potential evils of incommunicado detention can be controlled," and that "[a]ny technique by which its responsibility to guard against improper police conduct can be effectively delegated, with the assurance that the exercise of the delegated authority can be readily supervised, is bound to be attractive to the Court." [27]

In *Miranda,* the court announced the following procedural safeguards to govern the interrogation of suspects: "He must be warned prior to any questioning that he has the right to remain silent, that anything he says can be used against him in a court of law, that he has the right to the presence of an attorney, and that if he cannot afford an attorney one will be appointed for him prior to any questioning if he so desires. Opportunity to exercise these rights must be afforded to him throughout the interrogation. After such warnings have been given, and such opportunity afforded him, the individual may knowingly and intelligently waive these rights and agree to answer questions or make a statement. But unless and until such warnings and waiver are demonstrated by the prosecution at trial, no evidence obtained as a result of interrogation can be used against him." [28]

The *Miranda* warnings are designed to make it easy for the suspect to exercise his right to remain silent. I have lingering doubts, however, as to their essential fairness to the suspect. Nowhere do they tell him that his failure to answer, to explain or justify suspicious circumstances will inevitably weigh heavily against him in the event that he is charged with a crime and brought to trial. The Supreme Court of the United States may adhere to its holding in *Griffin* v. *California* that the Fifth Amendment prohibits comment upon a defendant's failure to testify in his own defense. But I would suggest that not even the Supreme Court can prevent the judge or the jurors who are trying the case from drawing adverse inferences from the silence of a defendant, whether at the trial or before it. The *Miranda* warnings stop just short of inviting the suspect not to explain, but they are silent as to the possible consequences that may flow from his failure to do so. To that extent, they do not, in my opinion, fairly advise the suspect of all of the relevant considerations that bear upon his choice.

One year after the *Miranda* decision, the Supreme Court adopted the same solution to deal with the problem it was sometimes called upon to face when a defendant had been identified at a lineup conducted by the police.[29] Some unfair identification procedures had unquestionably been used from time to time, and a valuable analysis of identification techniques, published in 1965, had spotlighted many improper practices.[30] The response of the court followed the *Miranda* pattern and laid down the requirement that a lawyer representing the defendant be present if the testimony as to the identification was to be admissible at the trial.

From the point of view of the court, the rules that it prescribed in *Miranda* and the lineup cases provided admirable solutions to the problems that confronted it. Enforcement of those rules throughout the entire judicial system should sharply reduce the number of hard cases involving lineups or involuntary confessions that the court will be called upon to determine. I leave it to others to fit these decisions into the late Edmond Cahn's classifications of "law in the consumer perspective" or "law in the official perspective." [31]

The Supreme Court will be criticized for its opinion in the *Terry* case but the ground of that criticism will, I anticipate, be the exact antithesis of the grounds upon which the opinions in the *Miranda* and in the lineup cases have been criticized. In *Terry,* the court made no attempt to formulate legislative standards to implement the Constitution. Instead, it based its opinion on the narrowest possible ground. The court rejected the notion that the search and seizure provisions of the Fourth Amendment are subject to verbal manipulation, and held that the constitutionality of a seizure of the person, and a search of the person seized, do not depend upon whether the seizure is labeled a "stop," and the search a "frisk."

The basic approach of the court is a straightforward determination that regardless of labels, the reasonableness of what an officer does is to be measured by the information available to him. The Supreme Court has thus moved in the direction of what has seemed to me to be a helpful way of looking at these cases. "If you would fire the police officer for not doing what he did, then what he did was reasonable." [32] Something of that approach is suggested, I think, when the court, after describing the conduct of *Terry* and his associates, makes this comment: "It would have been poor police work indeed for an officer of 30 years' experience in the detection of thievery from stores in this same neighborhood to have failed to investigate this behavior further." [33]

The opinion also minimizes the importance of another verbalism—the term "arrest"—which for generations has tended to dominate legal thinking in this area. Exaggerated emphasis upon the word "arrest" has had unfortunate consequences. It has often been assumed that whenever there is a right to arrest, there is also a right to search the person arrested. So, if my wife is arrested for parking too far from the curb, or for running through a red light, or driving too fast, the "arrest" talisman has meant that the police officer may search her person. This notion has been hard to kill in the state courts. But the Supreme Court has now emphasized that "The scope of the search must be 'strictly tied to and justified by' the circumstance which rendered its initiation permissible." [34]

It has often been assumed, on the other hand, that unless there is a right to arrest, there is no right to search. The fallacy of this assumption is apparent in the numerous cases in which police officers are confronted with ambiguous situations which may involve serious crimes, but may not involve criminal conduct at all. It is also apparent in those cases in which police officers must respond to anonymous phone calls, or take immediate action upon information furnished by persons whose reliability is unknown to the officer.

Moreover, the accepted justification for an arrest without a warrant "that the arresting officer has reasonable grounds to believe that the arrested person *has committed,* or *is committing,* an offense" has been inadequate. It has precluded the possibility of an arrest when the officer has reasonable grounds to believe that the person arrested *is about to commit* a crime. In his dissenting opinion in *Terry* v. *Ohio,* Justice Douglas explained the earlier statement of the right to arrest without a warrant on the ground that it was devised to fit the issues raised in the cases that had happened to come before the court, and so apparently was not meant to have a general restrictive effect. And, in that opinion, he added to the previous formulation of the rule the third situation, "probable cause to believe that a crime was about to be committed." [35]

I think that the majority reached the same result by squeezing the magic out of the term "arrest," with these words: "It does not follow that because an officer may lawfully arrest a person only when he is apprised of facts sufficient to warrant a belief that the person has committed or is committing a crime, the officer is equally unjustified, absent that kind of evidence, in making any intrusions short of an arrest . . . Petitioner's reliance on cases which have worked out standards of reasonableness with regard to 'seizures' constituting arrests and searches incident thereto is thus misplaced." [36]

Terry v. *Ohio* does not attempt to solve all of the problems concerning the sanctity of the person that will arise under the Fourth and Fourteenth Amendments. One unanswered question stems from the court's opinion in *Miranda* v. *Arizona*. *Terry* sustains the conduct of the police officer who, acting upon reasonable suspicion, searches the suspect to the extent necessary for his own protection. The product of the search is admissible in evidence. The officer can confront the suspect, and order him to halt, but beyond that there is little to suggest the kind of interrogation that is permitted. Obviously there will be some, if only "What are you doing here?" But as soon as there is some interrogation, after there has been a seizure of the person of the suspect, the *Miranda* safeguards are encountered.

Literally, the suspect is in police custody, and any interrogation is, in *Miranda* terms, custodial interrogation. Some passages in *Miranda* suggest that interrogation is prohibited, for in *Miranda* the court pointed out: "By custodial interrogation, we mean questioning initiated by law enforcement officers after a person has been taken into custody or otherwise deprived of his freedom of action in any significant way." [37]

But there are other indications in *Miranda* that are adequate to satisfy me, at least, that the kind of interrogation that would normally take place during an on-the-street encounter does not require compliance with the *Miranda* standards. Each interrogation in the *Miranda* cases took place in a police station. And the *Miranda* opinions heavily emphasized the environment in which those interrogations took place. The court spoke of "An individual swept from familiar surroundings into police custody, surrounded by antagonistic forces, and subject to" [38] techniques of persuasion, and of "the compulsion to speak in the isolated setting of the police station." [39] Again, the Supreme Court justfied the imposition of the burden of proving a waiver of the privilege against self-incrimination upon the State on the ground that "the State is responsible for establishing the isolated circumstances under which the interrogation takes place and has the only means of making available corroborated evidence of warnings given during the incommunicado interrogation. . . ." [40] Moreover, the court stated that "General on-the-street questioning as to facts surrounding a crime or other general questioning of citizens in the fact-finding process is not affected by our holding." [41] This statement appears to be deliberately ambiguous in its repetition of the undefined term "general questioning" and its reference to "questioning as to the facts surrounding the crime." It may be that the police officer who hears a shot as he is passing the saloon, enters and sees a body lying on the floor, violates the *Miranda* safeguards if he asks, without the required warnings, "Who shot him?" But I do not think so.

The question naturally arises as to what scope remains for "stop and frisk" legislation after the court's decision in *Terry*. In my opinion, it would be unwise to attempt to draft statutes that specify the circumstances under which an officer may confront and search a suspect. The danger is that such a statute might curtail the authority of the officer within limits narrower than those that would govern in the absence of any statute. And to the extent that a statute should attempt to broaden his authority beyond that permitted by the constitution, *Terry* makes it plain that the statute would be invalid.

But this does not mean that there is no room for constructive legislation in the "stop and frisk" area. The exclusionary rule, by which the Fourth Amendment is implemented, is not a satisfactory tool, and one of its deficiencies is that it is available only to those who are formally charged with criminal offenses. It does not bear at all upon the overzealous officer whose victims never appear in court. Thus, it does little to curb the obvious potential for evil in the promiscuous use of "stop and frisk" as a technique of harassment. This evil can be attacked directly through legislation. A requirement, for example, that an officer who stops a citizen and frisks him must report the circumstances in writing and in full detail, would tend to reduce abuses and to insure that police officers are always conscious of the necessity that every such detention be justified. And since the victim of the unwarranted "stop and frisk" which does not lead to arrest is unlikely to complain because of inertia, lack of time, fear of retribution or a host of other reasons, it might be desirable also to authorize the institution of disciplinary proceedings based upon such reports, by persons outside of the law enforcement agency. The court's decision in *Terry* invites legislative creativity, and other and better proposals, designed to insure that a citizen need not become a defendant in a criminal case to receive the protection of the Fourth Amendment, will undoubtedly be forthcoming.

Any discussion of "sanctity of the person" assumes that the permissible bounds of both individual and police conduct have been sufficiently defined to permit the formulation of law enforcement policies which reflect proper deference to personal liberties. Yet, in the course of the Supreme Court's rapid absorption or incorporation of specific provisions of the first eight amendments into the Fourteenth Amendment, it has necessarily over-turned many of its earlier decisions. The unsettling effect of this process upon the body of law that defines the boundaries of acceptable police conduct has been tempered somewhat by the court's adoption of the technique of prospective overruling. However, until a recent important change in the attitude of the court to the retroactivity of its overruling decisions, the significance of the fact that an officer had conducted himself in accordance with the law as it was when he acted, was disregarded. This change of attitude—which, so far as I am aware, has not been the subject of written comment—deserves attention because it should go far toward insuring that current precedent is a reliable guide for current action.

The justification for restricting the retroactive effect of an overruling decision is that persons who were entitled to do so have acted in reliance upon the former decision which the court now overrules. In its first ventures in prospective overruling, the Supreme Court was either not advised of the critical importance of the essential element of reliance, or overlooked that element. In 1949, the court decided that the federal exclusionary rule, which requires that the products of an illegal search be barred from admission in evidence, did not apply to the states.[42] In 1961, in *Mapp* v. *Ohio*,[43] the Supreme Court overruled its 1949 decision, but it did not at that time give any indication as to whether its overruling decision was to operate retroactively or prospectively. That issue was not considered until 1965, in *Linkletter* v. *Walker*.[44] There the court said: "Once the premise is accepted that we are neither required to nor prohibited from applying a decision retrospectively, we must then weigh the merits and demerits in each case by looking to the prior history of the rule in question, its purpose and effect, and whether retrospective operation will further retard its operation." [45] The court then held that its decision in *Mapp* applied only to cases in which the judgment of conviction had not yet become final—in the sense that direct appeal and certiorari were no longer available—when *Mapp* v. *Ohio* was decided in 1961.

"Two peculiarities stand out in this opinion. The first is that except as it may be subsumed in the 'prior history of the rule in question,' reliance upon the earlier decision, which is the fundamental justification for a prospective overruling, is not mentioned. But 'the prior history of the rule in question' emphasizes the history of a legal abstraction, developed through a series of judicial decisions, and ignores the earthly bearing of the legal doctrine upon the conduct of those affected by it. The second is that the Court makes retroactivity turn upon whether a particular judgment is being reviewed on direct appeal or on collateral attack, a matter that is totally unrelated to reliance upon the former legal doctrine. The only relevant reliance so far as the prospectivity of *Mapp* is concerned, occurred when the search was made. If the officers who made the search then acted in reliance upon existing constitutional standards, it is that reliance which is relevant in determining the retroactivity of a decision which alters those constitutional standards." [46]

In *Griffin* v. *California* [47] the Supreme Court held that the Fifth Amendment prohibits comment by the prosecutor upon the failure of the accused to testify at his trial. Ten months later, in *Tehan* v. *United States* ex rel. *Shott*,[48] the Supreme Court held that its decision in the *Griffin* case applied only to cases that were still pending in the line of direct appeal when *Griffin* was decided. Again, the factor of reliance was overlooked, because reliance took place when the comment was made, which is totally unrelated to the stage that the case had reached upon appeal. In *Johnson* v. *New Jersey*,[49] the Supreme Court held that the standards governing custodial interrogation which it had announced a week earlier in *Miranda* v. *Arizona* [50] were to apply only to those cases in which trials were commenced after the decision in *Miranda* was announced. Again, however, in its determination of the cutoff date for the application of the new constitutional doctrines, the court overlooked the factor of reliance. A police officer conducting an interrogation prior to *Miranda* could have complied fully with the then applicable constitutional standards, but still have failed to comply with the newly added requirements. The earlier constitutional standards were relied upon, not at the moment that the trial commenced, but at the moment that the interrogation took place. There have been cases, and there will be more, in which this distinction is critical.

Finally, in its decisions in the lineup cases the Supreme Court came to recognize the full significance of reliance in determining the extent of the retroactivity of new judgemade law. In *Stovall* v. *Denno*,[51] the court held that the new standards it announced to govern identification lineup procedures would apply only to lineups conducted after the date of those decisions.

As I read the *Stovall* opinion, the Supreme Court there acknowledges that its earlier determinations of retroactivity were erroneous. The court said: "We also conclude that, for these purposes, no distinction is justified between convictions now final, as in the instant case, and convictions at various stages of trial and direct review. We regard the factors of reliance and burden on the administration of justice as entitled to such overriding significance as to make that distinction unsupportable." [52] To me this means that the retroactivity of the court's other prospective rulings are to be measured in each instance from the date of the reliance. In other words, I would suggest that in the case of a confession made while in police custody, for example, the warnings required by *Miranda* are required only if the confession was made after the decision in *Miranda* was announced. To make that ruling applicable to pre-*Miranda* confessions just because the case happened to be tried, or retried, after the *Miranda* decision was rendered is, in the language of the Supreme Court in the *Stovall* case, "unsupportable."

Notes

1. *Chic Fashions (West Wales) Ltd.* v. *Jones,* [1968] 2 Weekly L.R. 201. (C.A.).
2. *Id.* at 209.
3. *Id.* at 211.
4. Ten Broek, *Equal Under Law* 16–17 (1965).
5. 353 U.S. 391, 421 (1957) (Emphasis is the Court's).
6. Griswold, *The Fifth Amendment Today,* 9–30, 53–82 (1955).
7. Griswold, *The Right to be Left Alone,* 55 N.W. U.L. Rev. 216, 223 (1960).
8. 380 U.S. 609 (1965).
9. *Tehan* v. *United States* ex rel. *Shott,* 382 U.S. 406, 415 (1966).
10. *Id.* at 416.
11. *Id.* quoting Goldberg, in *Murphy* v. *Waterfront Comm'n,* 378 U.S. 52, 56 n. 5 who quotes *United States* v. *Grunewald,* 233 F.2d, 581–82 (Frank, J., dissenting).
12. Schaefer, *The Suspect and Society* 69–70; (1966 Rosenthal Lectures).
13. 384 U.S. 719, 729 (1966).
14. *Grosso* v. *United States,* 390 U.S. 62, 73 (1968).
15. Cross, *Confessions and Cognate Matters: An English View,* 66 Colum. L. Rev. 79, 80 (1966).
16. *Terry* v. *Ohio,* 392 U.S. 1 (1968).
17. *Sibran* v. *New York,* 392 U.S. 40, 62–63 (1968).
18. *Peters* v. *New York,* reported *id.* at 66–68.
19. 392 U.S. 1 (1968).
20. *Id.* at 11–12.
21. *Id.* at 10–11.
22. *Id.* at 15.
23. *Id.* at 20–22.
24. 384 U.S. 436 (1966).
25. 388 U.S. 218 (1967).
26. 316 U.S. 455 (1942).
27. Schaefer, *The Suspect and Society,* 10 (1966 Rosenthal Lectures).
28. 384 U.S. at 479.
29. *United States* v. *Wade,* 388 U.S. 218 (1967).
30. See generally Wall, *Eye-Witness Identification in Criminal Cases* (1965).
31. Cahn, *Law in the Consumer Perspective,* 112 U. Pa. L. Rev. 1 (1963).
32. Schaefer, *The Suspect and Society,* 41–42 & n. 39 (1966 Rosenthal Lectures).
33. 392 U.S. at 23.
34. *Id.* at 19.
35. *Id.* at 38.
36. *Id.* at 26–27.
37. 384 U.S. at 444.
38. *Id.* at 461.
39. *Id.*
40. *Id.* at 475.
41. *Id.* at 477.

42. *Wolf* v. *Colorado,* 338 U.S. 25 (1949).
43. 367 U.S. 643 (1961).
44. 381 U.S. 618 (1965).
45. *Id.* at 629.
46. Schaefer, *The Control of "Sunbursts": Techniques of Prospective Over-ruling,* 23–24 (Twenty-Fourth Annual Benjamin Cardozo Lectures 1967).
47. 380 U.S. 609 (1965).
48. 382 U.S. 406 (1966).
49. 384 U.S. 719 (1966).
50. 384 U.S. 436 (1966).
51. 388 U.S. 293 (1967).
52. *Id.* at 300–01.

5

The Fourteenth Amendment and Political Rights

Robert B. McKay

The history of liberty, in the United States and elsewhere, has been written mainly in the struggle for political rights. There was a time when religious freedom was a principal cause of national warfare and individual violence. But today, except perhaps in the case of little Israel's standoff of the entire Arab world, religious warfare has rather fallen out of fashion. In the less God-fearing world of the present, the no less considerable contemporary passions spend themselves on issues of political freedom, individual liberty, and equality.

The struggle for political rights has taken many forms throughout history. Prominent examples in the Anglo-American world include the contest for power in medieval England between the barons and their king, from which emerged the free Parliament, and the American War of Independence. Today the issues may seem different when the valiant Czechs struggle without apparent success to win a measure of freedom, or when students storm the barricades in Paris, Mexico City, and on Morningside Heights. Fortunately, the present topic does not require the difficult and perhaps impossible task of determining the relative virtue of the various causes. The point here is only that the rallying cry is always essentially the same: the struggle is waged under the banner of political liberty. For the present we need only note the force of the claim that political rights have been denied.

The issues of political freedom are as varied as the facts of political life. The charge of tyranny is raised against majorities as well as minorities; it is made from the right as well as from the left; and the groups whose authority is challenged range from labor unions and universities to political conventions and legislative bodies. But always the issue is framed in terms

Robert B. McKay is Dean of the New York University School of Law.

of political rights said to have been denied. To a freedom-loving people (as which people is not?) no claim has greater appeal than a threat to political rights.

History assures us that the demand for political freedom is not a modern invention. Aristotle recognized that man is by nature a political animal,[1] and ever since man has spent much of his time proving Aristotle right, often basely in unnecessary warfare, but at least sometimes gloriously in the use of his rational faculties to enlarge political freedom for himself and his fellow man.

This volume commemorates the centennial of one of the most important documents in man's struggle for the realization of political rights. But the Fourteenth Amendment would not have been possible in 1868, nor would the liberating interpretation it has since been given by the Supreme Court of the United States have been conceivable, save in the context of a history that led almost inevitably—at least so it now seems—along this route. Read once more the spare prose and majestic cadence of the principal operative portion of the amendment, the second sentence of the first section:

> No State shall make or enforce any law which shall abridge the privileges or immunities of citizens of the United States; nor shall any State deprive any person of life, liberty, or property without due process of law; nor deny to any person within its jurisdiction the equal protection of the laws.

There were of course other provisions in the original United States Constitution—as there are in other amendments relating to political rights, some indeed far more explicit—but there can be no doubt that this is the most important, the very capstone of the whole structure.

The great historic events that made possible the specific text of the Fourteenth Amendment and its own constitutional growth are illumined by other papers in this volume. It is accordingly necessary now only to develop briefly the main themes of political freedom, particularly as this freedom applies to representative democracy in the United States.

Liberty and equality are the twin antecedents of representative democracy, and they remain today its principal support. The English Revolution of 1688 emphasized the importance of liberty, and the French Revolution of 1789 underscored equality. The essentially unique feature of the Constitution of the United States, as drafted in 1787, was its demonstration that these two abstractions, liberty and equality, could be effectively combined into a single government. The further contribution of American democracy has been the addition of majority rule as a workable doctrine. In 1787 majority rule was more an article of faith than a matter for inclusion in a written constitution. Gradually, however, the concept of political rights developed, to reveal that if liberty and equality were to be effectively guaranteed they required the support of majority rule, tempered always by the restraining hand of the Bill of Rights to protect against majority abuse of the power to govern. The miracle of how the Fourteenth Amendment, in the single sentence already quoted, managed to accomplish both parts of that grand design is the story that is unfolded in this Centennial Celebration.

Three political rights appear in the Constitution of the United States: (1) the right to vote without discrimination on grounds of race, sex, or other factors not rationally relevant to exercise of the franchise; (2) the right to hold public office; and (3) the right to assemble and petition for redress of grievances. Other political rights, perhaps equally important, are not explicitly guaranteed by the constitution, but are now clearly within the constitutional protections as defined by the Supreme Court of the United States: (1) the requirement of substantial population equality among congressional districts, state legislative election districts, and electoral units of local governments; and (2) the power of Congress to define and limit state-imposed qualifications for voter eligibility and to fix standards of legislative apportionment.

The small band of eighteenth century statesmen who charted the initial course of the United States, including the draftsmen of its constitution, were deeply committed to the trinity of principles already mentioned: liberty, equality, and majority rule as limited by the need for protection of minority rights. Thomas Jefferson, for example, commenting on the nature of representative democracy in a letter to a friend in 1819, noted the proper relationship between equality and majority rule in these words:

> Equal representation is so fundamental a principle in a true republic that no prejudice can justify its violation because the prejudices themselves cannot be justified.[2]

James Madison's beliefs about freedom of expression and of conscience are perhaps better known than his views on suffrage, but the latter convictions were no less firm and no less cogently stated. The general rule, he said, was this:

> If we avert to the nature of Republican Government, we shall find that the censorial power is in the people over the Government, and not in the Government over the people.[3]

At one time, Madison had been content with some restrictions on those who could exercise the franchise. But he later repudiated this view, saying that such limitation

> violates the vital principle of free Government that those who are to be bound by laws, ought to have a voice in making them. And the

violation would be more strikingly unjust as the lawmakers became the minority.[4]

Despite the faith of Jefferson, Madison, and others in the principle of enlarged suffrage and equal representation, these notions were at the time almost unknown elsewhere, as was the notion of representative democracy governed by a written constitution. As always, the novel appeared radical, and so it undoubtedly was at the time. It is accordingly not surprising that the political rights so boldly praised were less securely established in practice. Apparently it occurred to no one that the vote should be extended to women, and of course not to slaves. Indeed, Article I, section 4 left to the states primary responsibility for fixing the qualifications of voters; and it was perfectly clear that in most states this meant restriction of the franchise to a handful of property owners.[5] It was not until well into the nineteenth century that property qualifications for exercise of the franchise were generally removed.[6] States were free to impose whatever restrictions they wished, based on age, religion, race, residence, payment of poll tax, or other restrictions later developed with an exquisite sense of how most effectively to discriminate against disfavored groups.

The Constitution of the United States, as drafted in 1787, also showed less than complete faith in even the relatively small group of voters who were given the franchise. While Article I, section 2 specified that members of the House of Representatives should be chosen "by the People of the Several States," [7] section 3 of the same article provided that senators should be chosen by the state legislatures, a matter not changed until the Seventeenth Amendment was ratified in 1913. Also, Article II, section 1 provided then, as it does today (with minor technical changes imposed by the Twelfth Amendment), for indirect election of the President. Incredibly, despite the qualification under these provisions of two minority Presidents and general dissatisfaction with the winner-take-all aspects of the electoral college (among its other defects), Congress has never put to the voters a substitute provision for direct election of the President, or even for a scheme to recognize voter preferences on some proportional basis.[8]

Curiously, in one respect political democracy in the United States was more equalitarian in the late eighteenth century than was to be the case in the middle and late decades of the nineteenth century. Although the constitution in its original form was silent on the subject, the early state constitutions abandoned the English tradition of representation on the rotten borough principle; instead, in general they chose to rely on representation in reasonable proportion to population. In Pennsylvania, for example, the first constitution stated that "representation in proportion to the number of taxable inhabitants is the only principle which can at all times secure liberty, and make the voice of a majority of the people the law of the land. . . ." [9] Ironically, as the franchise was extended in the nineteenth century, the majoritarian principle in state legislatures was gradually eroded until, by the end of the century, legislative malapportionment was more the rule than the exception; [10] and the situation continued to worsen until 1964 when the Supreme Court announced the equal-population principle in the *Reapportionment Cases*.[11]

Before turning to fuller exposition of the impact of the Fourteenth Amendment on state legislative apportionment, some attention should be given to the other political rights already mentioned where the Fourteenth Amendment has operated principally in a supportive capacity. These are the right to hold office and the right to assemble and petition for redress of grievances.[12]

The first thing to be said is that the thrust of these rights is more in the direction of freedom of expression and conscience than in the direction of privileges and immunities, equal protection, and due process, the core concepts of the Fourteenth Amendment. The freedom to hold public office without regard to political or religious belief shows that various constitutional principles often reinforce one another. The right to hold office, unquestionably a political right, is protected against the threats most likely to endanger its exercise, political or religious tests of orthodoxy, by that natural ally of political rights, the First Amendment. However, as will be noted below, the Fourteenth Amendment is also relevant in the large number of instances where the threat to the right is from a state or its officials. Two examples will make the point.

In *Bond* v. *Floyd*,[13] the Georgia Legislature had sought to exlude Julian Bond, a Negro, from the seat in that body to which his constituents had elected him. The state's claim was that his statements in opposition to United States policy in Vietnam were inconsistent with his oath to support the constitution, but the Supreme Court rejected Georgia's argument that a state "is constitutionally justified in exacting a higher standard of *loyalty* from its legislators than from its citizens." [14] Instead, the Court said, the standard for legislators, as for private citizens, requires that "debate on public issues should be uninhibited, robust, and wide-open." [15]

Similarly, when a notary public was denied a commission in Maryland because of his refusal to declare his belief in God, the Supreme Court, in *Torcaso* v. *Watkins*,[16] upset the oath as a test for public office because it violated the freedom of religion guaranteed by the First and Fourteenth Amendments.

These two cases, the Georgia limitation on freedom of expression by legislators and the Maryland demand for religious affirmation, relate to the present topic in two ways. First, these cases show that the protection of political rights is not limited to the Fourteenth Amendment; indeed, the primary source of protection may at times reside elsewhere. Second, even where the primary protection depends on the First Amendment or on other provisions of the Bill of Rights, those vital guarantees would mean much less without the reinforcement of the Fourteenth Amendment, whose due process clause supplies the bulwark against state limitation of the enumerated rights.

The right "of the people peaceably to assemble, and to petition the government for a redress of grievances" is also a political right expressly provided for in the First Amendment and carried forward by the due process clause of the Fourteenth Amendment as a limitation on the states. "The right of peaceable assembly," the Supreme Court said in 1937, "is a right cognate to those of free speech and free press and is equally fundamental. . . . The holding of meetings for peaceable political action cannot be proscribed." [17]

The principle there stated is unquestionably right, and as clearly stated as the uncertain facts typical of sometimes disorderly assemblies permit. But this is unquestionably an area in which American devotion to political freedom and freedom of expression will be increasingly tested in the turbulent days that predictably lie ahead.[18] It may well take all our faith in the values of free expression and political liberty for the nation to survive this period without repressive action that could end in loss of hard-earned liberty.

Voting Rights

The Fourteenth Amendment, for most of its first 100 years, must be counted a failure when measured against the aspirations of its drafters. Professor Commager has told us of the spirit that motivated the drafting and ratification of the Fourteenth Amendment, and Professor Schwartz has emphasized that the purpose was *at least* to secure equal civil and political rights without regard to race, color, or previous condition of servitude. Whether there was a conscious purpose to secure substantial equality among state legislative districts is more conjectural, a matter to which we shall later return. But there can be no doubt that the purpose of the Fourteenth Amendment, as made completely specific in the Fifteenth Amendment, was to assure equal treatment at least in the exercise of the franchise. The measure of its failure is a story on which we need not linger, however dark a chapter in our history. For there is more than a hint of hope in recent decades, particularly in the partnership newly discovered between Court and Congress, in assuring full and free participation in the political process by all Americans without the discrimination that has scarred the past.

To realize how far we have come, however, it is necessary to consider at least briefly how far there was to go.[19] For present purposes, the Fourteenth and Fifteenth Amendments are viewed as having been intended to accomplish extension of the franchise to Negroes, although of course the Fourteenth Amendment was not so limited. The doubts expressed in the period from 1868 to 1870 about the adequacy of the equal protection clause to achieve this end, which were sufficient to prompt adoption of the completely specific Fifteenth Amendment, should no longer be a matter of concern. Present views of the equal protection clause should leave no doubt that no voting rights case would be decided differently if the Fifteenth Amendment should now be withdrawn. The same is surely true also of the Nineteenth Amendment, which seemed in 1920 necessary in order to extend the franchise to all women.[20] But surely, today, not even the most ardent feminist would think that amendment more helpful to any constitutional defense of the rights of the female sex than the equal protection clause.

I hope, then, that I may be forgiven the small heresy of reading out of the constitution (as nonessential) the Fifteenth and Nineteenth Amendments, concentrating instead at this point on the egalitarian aspects of the Fourteenth.[21] I am of course not unmindful of the fact that many of the Supreme Court pronouncements on voting rights have been articulated in terms of Fifteenth Amendment rights; and much of the congressional legislation has relied on section 2, the enforcement section, of the Fifteenth Amendment. What I do suggest is that the equal protection clause would have served equally well as a basis for the judicial interpretations in defense of equal voting rights, and that section 5—the enforcement section of the Fourteenth Amendment—would have provided as secure a base for voting rights legislation as did section 2 of the Fifteenth Amendment.

With that preface, half assertion and half apology, let me review the constitutional protection of voting rights, treated as though the Fourteenth and Fifteenth Amendments were in this context unitary in design and purpose.

Even before ratification of the Fourteenth Amendment, the Radical Reconstruction leaders took power from the white Southern governments and vested control in five military districts. Within a year, more than 700,000 Negroes were registered to vote, slightly more than the number of whites then registered to vote in the same area.[22] For a time, Negroes were a significant influence in the political process in several Southern States:

> Negroes participated in all Southern radical governments, although they exercised control in none of them. . . . No Negro became Governor of any Southern State, although South Carolina, Mississippi, and Louisiana had Negro lieutenant governors. . . . On the national level, the South during this period sent 14 Negroes, six from South Carolina, to the House of Representatives.[23]

But even during this brief period of near-Negro equality, Negro voting and political participation was limited by harassment and exploitation.[24] The whole edifice collapsed after the Compromise of 1877, in which Southern Democrats helped to resolve the disputed Hayes-Tilden election contest by throwing their support to Hayes with an understanding of more favored treatment for the South in the future.[25] With their champions in the national capital silenced, Negroes soon lost their political voice almost entirely in the South and not inconsiderably elsewhere.

For a time—also brief—the law seemed a promising ally to the voting rights claims of the Negroes. The Fourteenth and Fifteenth Amendments were clear enough, or so they seemed. And for a time there was even legislation that sought to assure equal rights, including criminal penalties for violation of those rights.[26]

Those statutes were never adequately enforced; they were not sympathetically received by the courts;[27] and many of the key provisions were repealed, including most of the Enforcement Act in 1894.[28]

By 1910, Negro suffrage in the South had been reduced to an insignificant level, and there it remained for almost half a century. Literacy tests and poll taxes eliminated most of the voters. Where those ostensibly legal[29] restrictions on the exercise of the franchise were thought possibly insufficient, more sophisticated legal artifices were used, including "grandfather" clauses, exemptions for persons of good moral character who understood the obligation of citizenship, and exemptions for those who could understand and interpret a section of the federal or state constitution. Until 1965, when the most egregious of these practices were outlawed,[30] the Supreme Court was remarkably tolerant, forbidding only the discriminatory grandfather clause and the white primaries,[31] while maintaining a discreet silence on all else for half a century.

Congress also remained silent. Between 1871 and 1957, there was no civil rights legislation to protect the exercise of the franchise (or for any other purpose), a remarkable record in the face of well documented—and obvious—voter discrimination.[32] The federal criminal statutes that survived the 1894 retreat were limited in scope, further limited by restrictive interpretation,[33] and rarely invoked.[34] Section 242, which provides criminal penalties for deprivation of constitutional rights under color of state law, was used only once before 1941 to protect the right to vote; and section 241 was used against election frauds, but seldom to punish deprivations of the right to vote on account of race.[35] The civil remedies that survived the 1894 repeal act were seldom used, and less often successful, except in the series of cases that outlawed the white primaries.[36]

When at last Congress acted, its first three efforts to deal with voter discrimination were largely unsuccessful. Whatever merit the Civil Rights Acts of 1957,[37] 1960,[38] and 1964[39] may have had in other respects, they did little to enlarge Negro voter participation. Attorney General Katzenbach reviewed the disappointing record before the Senate Commmittee on the Judiciary in March 1965 in these words:

> [E]xisting law is inadequate. Litigation on a case-by-case basis simply cannot do the job. Preparation of a case is extraordinarily time consuming because the relevant data—for example, the race of individuals who have actually registered—is frequently most difficult to obtain. Many cases have to be appealed. In almost any other field, once the basic law is enacted by Congress and its constitutionality is upheld, those subject to it, accept it. In this field, however, the battle must be fought again and again in county after county. And even in those jurisdictions where judgment is finally won, local officials intent upon evading the spirit of the law are adept at devising new discriminatory techniques not covered by the letter of the judgment.[40]

The Voting Rights Act of 1965 [41] depends for its authority in most of its provisions upon section 2, the enforcement section, of the Fifteenth Amendment. But for present purposes, it could also rely on section 5 of the Fourteenth Amendment. The operative language of both is the same, giving to Congress the power "to enforce" the provisions of the amendment "by appropriate legislation." Accordingly, if the Fifteenth Amendment's proscription of state action that denies or abridges the right to vote on account of race, color, or previous condition of servitude is comparable to the equal protection proscriptions of the Fourteenth Amendment, it should follow that the experience under the 1965 Act, including judicial interpretations, is relevant to the Fourteenth Amendment potential for congressional implementation.

This being so, I find the experience under the Voting Rights Act of 1965 encouraging not only because of the extent to which voting rights have been opened up, but as well for what it foretells of the avenues now open for congressional implementation—enforcement, if you will—of other individual rights and freedoms concededly within the reach of the equal protection or due process clauses of the Fourteenth Amendment.

The point to be emphasized in this connection then is that the 1965 Act has succeeded, not only in the courts,[42] but as well at the ballot box, where the franchise is now for the first time since Reconstruction available to large numbers of Negroes in the South. The striking success of the Act in securing new voter registration is revealed in figures of the United States Commission on Civil Rights:

> Negro registration now is more than 50 per cent of the voting age population in every Southern State. Before the Act this was true only of Florida, Tennessee, and Texas. The biggest gain has been in

Mississippi, where Negro registration has gone from 6.7 to 59.8 per cent. But there also have been important gains in other States. In Alabama, the percentage has gone from 19.3 to 51.6; in Georgia, from 27.4 to 52.6; in Louisiana, from 31.6 to 58.9; and in South Carolina, from 37.3 to 51.2.[43]

Encouragingly, the substantial rise in voter registration has been accompanied by a significant increase in the number of those actually voting, in the number of Negro candidates for elective office, and in the number of those elected to office.[44] Moreover, not surprisingly, the growing Negro vote has been a deciding factor in a number of contests not involving Negro candidates, thus requiring moderation of racist views and elimination of some of the more extremist candidates.

The problems of racial discrimination in voting are far from over. Indeed, new devices are being experimented with to minimize the impact of the newly exercised rights. One of these devices, the racially motivated gerrymander, is scarcely new in the South or the North;[45] but it operates now with new malevolence. The final section of this paper will have something to say about this subject, as it relates to the equal-population rulings that protect against dilution of the vote through improper congressional districting and state legislative apportionment. Before turning to the equal protection aspects of districting and apportionment, however, a further word must be said about the judicial interpretation of the Voting Rights Act of 1965.[46]

Ostensibly the most important Supreme Court case decided under the Voting Rights Act of 1965 is doctrinally the least interesting. In *South Carolina* v. *Katzenbach*,[47] the constitutionality of the 1965 Act was upheld, including the curious bootstrap provisions relating to jurisdiction to which Justice Black objected.[48] But on the *power* of Congress to act the court was unanimous. The tipoff came early in the opinion when Chief Justice Warren, writing for the court, said:

> The Constitutional propriety of the Voting Rights Act of 1965 must be judged with reference to the historical experience which it reflects.[49]

This is familiar doctrine that has been employed to justify congressional implementation of constitutional grants of power ever since Chief Justice Marshall first reminded that it is a *"constitution* we are expounding."[50]

Of course it might be argued that the problem here was different, because in many of the earlier cases the legislation sought to be justified was ordinarily based upon an affirmative grant of power, while here the enforcement provision was being used to enforce a constitutional negative, in support of federal legislation that sought to displace state legislation said to deny or abridge voting rights on account of race. But there were precedents of this kind as well; and Congress had done its homework. The discrimination was laid bare for all to see; and again the precedents were not lacking. If the enforcement clause meant anything, the precedents made clear, Congress could enforce the negative by legislation implementing the prohibitions.[51]

The most important cases arising out of the Voting Rights Act of 1965, in terms of constitutional doctrine, were *Katzenbach* v. *Morgan*,[52] and *Cardona* v. *Power*.[53] Both cases arose under section 4(e) of the act which, unlike other major provisions of the act, was enacted to secure rights under the Fourteenth Amendment. The problem toward which this section was aimed was peculiarly limited. The Court observed that it should be viewed as a measure "to secure for the Puerto Rican community residing in New York nondiscriminatory treatment by government—both in the imposition of voting qualifications and the provision or administration of governmental services, such as public schools, public housing and law enforcement." [54] The statutory device adopted was a provision that no person who has successfully completed the sixth primary grade in a public school in, or a private school accredited by, the Commonwealth of Puerto Rico in which the language of instruction was other than English shall be denied the right to vote because of his inability to read or write English. The difficulty was that this provision, if valid, would supersede that portion of the New York election law that required literacy in English as a qualification for voting, a provision that denied the vote to many of the hundreds of thousands of Puerto Ricans who had migrated to New York City.

The constitutional problem was laid bare in the Supreme Court's reaction to the companion case, *Cardona* v. *Power,* in which the New York law was challenged directly on equal protection grounds. If the majority had felt, as Justices Black and Fortas did in dissent, that the New York law was a violation of equal protection, it would have been easy enough to say that the federal statute was adopted merely to enforce by appropriate legislation this denial of equal protection. However, the majority, in an opinion by Justice Brennan, held that it was not necessary to decide the constitutional issue, which might be moot for the following reason: If appellant could establish that she had completed six years of schooling in a qualified Puerto Rican school (a matter on which the record was silent), she would be entitled to vote in New York under the decision in the *Morgan* case. Without waiting for the answer to that question, the majority explicitly held that Congress has the power to "enforce" the equal protection clause by "appropriate legislation" even if the state action forbidden, standing alone, might not be regarded as a violation of the equal protection clause. Thus, the Supreme Court's inquiry in this case was "limited to determining whether such legislation is, as required by section 5, appropriate legislation to enforce the Equal Protection Clause." [55] Again, as in *South Carolina* v. *Katzenbach,* the Court concluded that the congressional findings were sufficient for this purpose.[56]

The principle formulated in the *Morgan* and *Cardona* cases was limited to state action involving official conduct (that is, the state's election process). A related principle was developed in the same term in *United States* v. *Price* [57] and *United States* v. *Guest* [58] to provide an entirely new perspective on the Fourteenth Amendment. What was said in 1870 more or less at large in *Ex parte Virginia* [59] is now fully realized. The Court there had said of section 5 of the Fourteenth Amendment:

> It is the power of Congress which has been enlarged. Congress is authorized to *enforce* the prohibitions by appropriate legislation. Some legislation is contemplated to make the amendments fully effective.[60]

In *Price* and *Guest*, the court gave new meaning to the civil rights acts surviving from the Reconstruction period and, more important, invited Congress to protect rights guaranteed by the Fourteenth Amendment even against private individuals not acting in an official capacity. Thus, the Supreme Court softened appreciably the proposition always accepted as constitutional gospel: that the Fourteenth Amendment could never be invoked except where state action (however defined) was involved. If that remains a valid proposition when the Fourteenth Amendment is judicially invoked in the absence of enforcing legislation, it is apparently no longer true that Congress is so limited. Six justices, in two separate concurring opinions, made the point precisely. Justice Clark, speaking also for Justices Black and Fortas, stated the new proposition succinctly:

> [T]he specific language of § 5 empowers the Congress to enact laws punishing all conspiracies—with or without state action—that interfere with Fourteenth Amendment rights.[61]

Justice Brennan, speaking also for Chief Justice Warren and Justice Douglas, stated the proposition more fully, but no less emphatically. He said in part:

> A majority of the Court expresses the view today that § 5 empowers Congress to enact laws punishing *all* conspiracies to interfere with the exercise of Fourteenth Amendment rights, whether or not state officers or others acting under the color of state law are implicated in the conspiracy. Although the Fourteenth Amendment itself, according to established doctrine, "speaks to the State or to those acting under the color of its authority," legislation protecting rights created by that Amendment, such as the right to equal utilization of

state facilities, need not be confined to punishing conspiracies in which state officers participate. Rather, § 5 authorizes Congress to make laws that it concludes are reasonably necessary to protect a right created by and arising under that Amendment; and Congress is thus fully empowered to determine that punishment of private conspiracies interfering with the exercise of such a right is necessary to its full protection.[62]

One further point should be made to reveal the broad sweep of the doctrine just outlined. The congressional power to enforce the prohibitions of the Fourteenth Amendment (and presumably of others as well) is enlarged to permit regulation of matters that may lie outside the scope of the judiciary in the absence of such enforcing legislation. However, as Justice Brennan stated specifically in *Morgan:*

> Section 5 does not grant Congress power to exercise discretion in the other direction and to enact "statutes so as in effect to dilute equal protection and due process decisions of this Court." We emphasize that Congress' power under section 5 is limited to adopting measures to enforce the guarantees of that Amendment; section 5 grants Congress no power to restrict, abrogate, or dilute these guarantees. Thus, for example, an enactment authorizing the States to establish racially segregated systems of education would not be—as required by section 5—a measure "to enforce" the Equal Protection Clause since that clause of its own force prohibits such laws.[63]

State Legislative Apportionment

No decision of the Supreme Court of the United States—not even the vital *Brown* v. *Board of Education*[64]—sent more shock waves through the state capitals of the nation than *Reynolds* v. *Sims.*[65] When the states were told they must reapportion both houses of each bicameral legislature (and the single house in Nebraska, the only state with a unicameral legislature) to meet standards of substantial population equality, dire predictions were made that this would mean (in some unspecified way) the end of free government. The Supreme Court, it was said, had at last gone too far in interfering with the rights of the states; and efforts were mounted to limit the jurisdiction of the federal courts to handle reapportionment cases, to reverse the decision by amending the United States Constitution, and even to change the method of amending the constitution to make amendment more responsive to transient expressions of popular opinions.[66] These efforts all failed, perhaps through the fortuitous combination of two circumstances. In the first place, important resistance to the various proposals, particularly those to limit jurisdiction of the federal courts, came from those who instinctively resist all efforts to limit the independence of the judiciary. Second, this group ultimately found surprising support from the general public. It soon developed that the reapportionment decisions were popular with the majority of the people, many of whom had been in part disenfranchised by long-endured malapportionment. The voters were largely unimpressed with the concern of incumbent legislators who saw in the decisions a threat to their own legislative authority.[67]

The surprising fact is that the equal-population principle was so quickly digested. Within four years after *Reynolds* v. *Sims* adjustment was made in the apportionment formula of every state where a challenge was raised. Even under a strict view of the degree of population equality required, at least two-thirds of the states were already in full compliance,[68] and the remainder seemed to be waiting only for more definitive guidelines from the Supreme Court before making the final adjustment. This must be counted a stunning success for the Supreme Court and, more important, a triumph for political rights where, in unusual degree, the component elements of liberty, equality, and majority rule merged into the single principle of substantial population equality in legislative representation.

Whatever constitutional doubts there may have been initially about the soundness of *Reynolds* and its companion cases arose out of what at first seemed a troublesome question. Justice Harlan, the most articulate spokesman in dissent, thought there was nothing in the text or in the history of the Fourteenth Amendment to justify this ruling. Certainly it was true that this case was not like *Brown* v. *Board of Education* in which it was possible to find in the animating purpose behind the Fourteenth Amendment a strong desire to eradicate all the barriers to full civil equality between white and black.[69] However, if there were aspirations among the drafters of the Fourteenth Amendment to require population equality in legislative representation, they were, in Professor Commager's phrase, no more than "dimly perceived."[70]

The question thus sharply raised is not new to constitutional jurisprudence in the United States. It is a part of the century-and-a-half-old dispute between the strict constructionists and those who see in the Constitution a charter adequate for a largely undetermined future, and flexible enough to meet challenges not yet fully understood. Over the years the latter view has in general prevailed. In 1966, Justice Douglas reviewed the issue in connection with the equal protection clause in *Harper* v. *Virginia Board of Elections* [71] and concluded in these words:

> [T]he Equal Protection Clause is not shackled to the political theory of a particular era. In determining what lines are unconstitutionally discriminatory, we have never been confined to historic notions of equality, any more than we have restricted due process to a fixed catalogue of what was at a given time deemed to be the limits of funda-

mental rights. . . . Notions of what constitutes equal treatment for purposes of the Equal Protection Clause *do* change. [72]

Justice Harlan's point is, however, somewhat more insistently maintained, not only in the *Reapportionment Cases,* but as well in *Carrington* v. *Rash* [73] (invalidating a Texas constitutional provision preventing a person who had entered military service in another state from acquiring voting residence in Texas, while remaining in military service); and *United States* v. *Mississippi* [74] and *Louisiana* v. *United States* [75] (invalidating so-called literacy tests under the Fourteenth Amendment where Justice Harlan thought it possible only under the Fifteenth); and *Harman* v. *Forssenius* [76] (invalidating a state poll tax under the Twenty-fourth Amendment, Justice Harlan limiting his concurrence to that point, avoiding any inference by the majority that the same result could have been achieved under the Fourteenth Amendment). His thesis throughout has been that history proves that the Fourteenth Amendment, especially section 2, "expressly recognize[s] the States' power to deny 'or in any way' abridge the right of their inhabitants to vote for 'the members of the [State] Legislature.' " [77] If he were right in this assertion of the meaning of the relevant history, doubt would be cast on many of the Court's voting rights decisions and the decisions bearing on the right to equal legislative representation, clearly the two most important political rights that have been held secured by the Fourteenth Amendment.

The historical record has been combed many times for enlightenment as to the meaning of due process and equal protection, but until Justice Harlan undertook his lonely search, the historical review had not focused directly on the point he raises. That history has now been painstakingly reviewed once more by Professor William W. Van Alstyne, who had these precise questions in mind when he made the search. His conclusion, fully supported by the evidence he cites, provides the complete answer to Justice Harlan on the reapportionment issue.

> The application of the Equal Protection Clause to practices of state legislative malapportionment is unexceptionable in terms of the inconclusive legislative history of the Fourteenth Amendment. It is neither precluded by any remedy exclusively provided in § 2, nor at variance with the language or any original and declared limitation on the Equal Protection Clause itself. Under these circumstances, it is difficult to believe that the decision in *Reynolds* v. *Sims* should have been foreclosed solely on the strength of the legislative history of the Fourteenth Amendment.[78]

On the question whether section 2 of the Fourteenth Amendment precludes use of the equal protection clause as a basis for invalidation of state voter qualification restrictions, Professor Van Alstyne finds the evidence less conclusive, but certainly open to the interpretation taken by the majority. He says:

> The sum of the record respecting § 2, then, seems insufficient to support an inference that even though its language is utterly noncommittal on whether Congress could exercise authority flowing from other constitutional provisions to broaden the franchise, it was nonetheless clearly understood at the time to preempt any such authority or preclude the exercise of that authority. Whether such authority might have been elsewhere in the Constitution or in the Fourteenth Amendment itself, in §§ 1 and 5, must consequently be a function of the language and understanding of those sections—an issue not foreclosed by § 2.[79]

If these interpretations are historically verifiable, which appears to be the case, they are certainly constitutionally appealing. The last decade of American constitutional law development has brought more significant advance in the protection and advancement of political rights than all the rest of our constitutional history put together, most of it made possible by re-examination of the reach of the Fourteenth Amendment. Review once more the record: voting rights have been vastly enlarged, to the great advantage of Negro and Puerto Rican minority groups, and to the great benefit of the nation. Poll taxes have been eliminated, first in federal elections by the Twenty-fourth Amendment, and then in state elections on equal protection grounds. Literacy tests that were used for discriminatory purposes have been ruled invalid.

Perhaps most important of all, the distortions in the governing process caused by minority-controlled legislatures have been put aside as malapportionment becomes a matter of history rather than a fact of present contention.

There are, to be sure, unanswered questions, but not as many as usually follow in the wake of great constitutional upheavals. Now that the Supreme Court has held that the equal-population principle applies to local government bodies of a legislative character,[80] as well as to state legislatures, there remain only two important questions that still require an answer.

1. *How equal is substantial equality?* The issue has been widely and, one suspects, in some cases deliberately misunderstood. In *Reynolds* the Supreme Court stated that precise mathematical equality is not required.

> We realize that it is a practical impossibility to arrange legislative districts so that each one has an identical number of residents, or citizens, or voters. Mathematical exactness or precision is hardly a workable constitutional requirement.[81]

Local factors in justification of population deviation were mentioned approvingly, including reliance on local government boundary lines which might also be useful to prevent a gerrymander if the line-drawing function should be left entirely at large.

By 1967, the Court was ready for the next step, holding in *Swann* v. *Adams* [82] that the burden rested with the state to justify population deviations among the various districts. Then, in 1969, when pressed to define the limits of variations permissible on a *de minimis* theory, the court declared:

> We can see no nonarbitrary way to pick a cutoff point at which population variances suddenly become *de minimis*. Moreover, to consider a certain range of variances *de minimis* would encourage legislators to strive for that range rather than for equality as nearly as practicable. [83]

Justice Brennan warned also that justification for deviations was necessary, "no matter how small," in the absence of a showing of "a good-faith effort to achieve *precise* mathematical equality." (Emphasis supplied.) [84]

It may also be that Congress, using its authority under section 5 of the Fourteenth Amendment, already adverted to, could give policy guidance on this subject. But Congress, of course, could not specify deviations inconsistent with the equal protection requirement as defined by the Supreme Court. Accordingly, in balance it may be preferable to leave the matter where it is, for resolution out of the cases.

2. *The Gerrymander.* Malapportionment was itself a gerrymander of the most egregious kind. With the population gerrymander essentially eliminated by adoption of the equal-population principle, some thought the problem ended. Not at all. The focus has merely shifted to more subtle forms of discrimination. When legislative representation district lines could be drawn without regard to population equality, it was often easy enough to favor the dominant political party or to discriminate against racial, ethnic, or socioeconomic groups without seeming to do more than favor geographic areas, particularly rural. But now the equality requirement tends to lay bare the motivation behind the more obvious maneuvers.

To make the equal-population principle a fully effective support for representative government, it will probably be necessary to strike down at least the most blatant distortions of the process, whether the gerrymander is designed along racial, partisan, or socioeconomic lines.

The Supreme Court has thus far avoided the gerrymander thicket. In 1960 it acknowledged, in *Gomillion* v. *Lightfoot*, [85] that the racial gerrymander in that case (redrawing of a city's boundaries to eliminate the Negro vote) could be prohibited under the Fifteenth Amendment as a denial of the right to vote. But since that time the answer has been different where the allegation has been only that the lines were shifted to the disadvantage of particular groups, allegedly in violation of the Fourteenth Amendment. Thus, in *Wright* v. *Rockefeller*,[86] where the complaint alleged that New York's 1961 congressional districting statute "segregates eligible voters by race and place of origin," the suit was dismissed by the Supreme Court for lack of proof. Subsequently, the Court has persisted in its avoidance of that vital issue,[87] which is particularly regrettable since the need for redistricting will again become necessary in every state after completion of the 1970 census.

The hard questions of political democracy require more attention. Americans have never really examined the question whether election districts should be homogeneous or diverse. It is sometimes suggested that lines should be drawn to preserve enclaves of racial grouping or political strength, to assure specific representation for those interests. But I am doubtful.

Legislative representation lines are never neutral. The work of the line-drawers does have consequences for the representative process. Accordingly, the democratic ideal is best served by standards that will, as nearly as possible, objectify the process and protect it against the conscious or unconscious bias of the line-drawers. In fulfillment of this purpose, districts should be compact and contiguous, and their boundaries should coincide as nearly as practicable with political subdivision lines, natural barriers such as mountains or rivers, or man-made barriers such as highways, parks, and community centers.

The problems of democracy are not easy, and no one should expect them to be so. Much progress has been made. The search will continue, as it must.

Notes

1. Jowett (ed.), *Dialogues of Plato: Politics* 3 (rev. ed., 1900).
2. Letter to William King. Jefferson Papers, Library of Congress, vol. 216, p. 38616.
3. Annals of Congress. 3rd Congress (Nov. 27, 1794) 934.
4. Madison, *Notes of the Debates in the Federal Convention of 1787*, at 619, 622 (app. VII, n. 2). For more complete discussion of this point, see Brant, "The Madison Heritage" in Cahn (ed.), *The Great Rights* 15, 27–37 (1963).
5. When the Constitution was ratified, probably not more than a quarter of the adult males were entitled to vote. See McKinley, *The Suffrage Franchise in the Thirteen English Colonies in America* 488 (1905).
6. In New York State, for example, property qualifications for white voters were removed in 1826 for the election of state officials, but not until 1874 for Negro voters. 1821 Const. Art. II, Sec. I, as amended in 1826; 1846 Const., Art. II, Sec. I, as amended in 1874. Even today there remain some property ownership restrictions on the exercise of the franchise in New York. The New York Legislature has imposed property qualifications as a condition for voting in certain local referendums; and they have been upheld. *Spitzer* v. *Village of Fulton*, 172 N.Y. 285 (1902). See discussion in 4 *New York Temporary State Commission on the Constitutional Convention*, "The Right to Vote" 33–38 (1967).
7. It was not until 1964 that this seemingly innocuous phrase was held to require substantial equality among the congressional districts within each state. *Wesberry* v. *Sanders*, 376 U.S. 1 (1964).
8. There has been no lack of criticism. See, e.g., Wilmerding, *The Electoral College* (1958); Kirby, *Limitations on the Power of State Legislatures Over Presidential Elections*, 27 Law and Contemp. Prob. 495 (1962); Roche, *The Founding Fathers: A Reform Caucus in Action*, 55 Am. Pol. Sci. Rev. 799 (1961); *Electing the President: Recommendations of the American Bar Association's Commission on Electoral College Reform*, 53 A.B.A.J. 219 (1967).

    In 1966 a group of voters filed an original proceeding in the Supreme Court of the United States, alleging that the present system violates the equal protection of the laws and the due process clauses of the Fourteenth Amendment. But the Supreme Court denied leave to file the bill of complaint. *Delaware* v. *New York*, 385 U.S. 895 (1966).
9. McKay, *Reapportionment: The Law and Politics of Equal Representation* 18 (1965).
10. *Id.* at 23–29.
11. *Reynolds* v. *Sims*, 377 U.S. 533 (1964).
12. For a full discussion, see Schwartz, *A Commentary on the Constitution of the United States:* "Rights of the Person" 777–82 (Part III, Vol. II, 1968).
13. 385 U.S. 116 (1966).
14. *Id.* at 135.
15. *Id.* at 136, quoting from *New York Times Co.* v. *Sullivan*, 376 U.S. 254, 270 (1964).

16. 367 U.S. 488 (1961).
17. *De Jonge* v. *Oregon,* 299 U.S. 353, 365 (1937).

    In earlier cases the clause had been more narrowly construed, as though it read: "the right of the people peaceably to assemble in order to petition the Government." See, e.g., *Cruikshank* v. *United States,* 92 U.S. 542 (1876). More recently, however, the Court has found in the First Amendment a right of association. See, e.g., *Shelton* v. *Tucker,* 364 U.S. 479, 485 (1960); Rice, *Freedom of Association* (1962). As Professor Bernard Schwartz has noted, "Such right means little if it does not include a right to meet for any peaceful and lawful purpose. We may consequently state today that there is a broad right to assemble . . . in order to petition the Government that is specifically contained in the amendment and was narrowly construed, as seen in the *Cruikshank* case." B. Schwartz, *A Commentary on the Constitution of the United States:* "Rights of the Person" 781 (Part III, Vol. II, 1968).

18. The Court has suggested a stopping place in relation to some kinds of assembly in such cases as *Adderley* v. *Florida,* 385 U.S. 39 (1966). Compare *Cox* v. *Louisiana* (No. 1), 379 U.S. 536 (1965) with *Cox* v. *Louisiana* (No. 2), 379 U.S. 559 (1965).

19. The historical sketch that follows draws heavily upon the following: Franklin, *Reconstruction: After the Civil War* (1961); *1968 Report of the Commission on Civil Rights Political Participation* (1968); Christopher, *The Constitutionality of the Voting Rights Act of 1965,* 18 Stan. L. Rev. 1 (1965).

20. In 1875, after the adoption of the Fourteenth Amendment, the Court had upheld a statute restricting the franchise to male citizens. *Minor* v. *Happersett,* 88 U.S. (21 Wall) 162 (1875). That result would be inconceivable today even without the Nineteenth Amendment.

21. Apart from the immediate topic, is it not also true that the privileges and immunities clause of Article IV, section 2, clause 1 ("The Citizens of each State shall be entitled to all privileges and Immunities of Citizens in the several States"), is made unnecessary by the equal protection clause of the Fourteenth Amendment? The commonly accepted interpretation of the privileges and immunities clause, as it appears in Article IV, is that it does no more than forbid any state to discriminate against citizens of other states in favor of its own, without, of course, forbidding reasonable classifications. See *Whitfield* v. *Ohio,* 297 U.S. 431 (1936); *Chambers* v. *Baltimore and Ohio Railroad,* 207 U.S. 142 (1907).

22. Franklin, *Reconstruction: After the Civil War* 42 (1961).

23. *1968 Report of the United States Commission on Civil Rights, Political Participation* 2–3.

24. *Id.* at 3–5.

25. See Woodward, *Reunion and Reaction: The Compromise of 1877 and the End of Reconstruction* (1951).

26. The Enforcement Act of 1870 required election officials to give all citizens equal opportunity to perform any act prerequisite to voting. Act of May 31,

1870, ch. 114, 16 Stat. 140. In addition, the act made it a federal crime to violate state laws governing the election of federal officers, to interfere with the exercise of a citizen's right to vote, or to commit fraudulent acts in connection with registration of voters or counting of ballots. In 1871 the act was amended to establish a system of federal supervision of elections. Act of Feb. 28, 1871, ch. 99, 16 Stat. 433.

27. See, e.g., *United States* v. *Cruikshank*, 92 U.S. 542 (1876); *United States* v. *Reese*, 92 U.S. 214 (1876); *James* v. *Bowman*, 190 U.S. 127 (1903). But cf. *Ex parte Yarbrough*, 110 U.S. 651 (1884); *Guinn* v. *United States*, 238 U.S. 347 (1915).

28. Act of Feb. 8, 1894, ch. 25, 28 Stat. 36. Five sections escaped: a declaration of each person's right to vote without regard to race or color (now 42 U.S.C. § 1971(a)(1) (1964)); two sections creating civil liability for interference with a citizen's right to vote (now 42 U.S. §§ 1983, 1985 (1964)); and two sections imposing criminal sanctions for comparable wrongs (now 18 U.S.C. §§ 241, 242 (1964)).

29. The poll tax was upheld in *Breedlove* v. *Suttles*, 302 U.S. 277 (1937), but was overruled in *Harper* v. *Virginia Board of Elections*, 383 U.S. 663 (1966). Literacy tests were upheld in *Lassiter* v. *Northampton Board of Elections*, 360 U.S. 45 (1959).

30. *United States* v. *Mississippi*, 380 U.S. 128 (1965); *Louisiana* v. *United States*, 380 U.S. 145 (1965). Cf. *South Carolina* v. *Katzenbach*, 383 U.S. 301 (1966), discussed *infra*.

31. *Guinn* v. *United States*, 238 U.S. 347 (1915) and *Lane* v. *Wilson*, 307 U.S. 268 (1939) (grandfather clause); *Terry* v. *Adams*, 345 U.S. 461 (1953) and *Smith* v. *Allwright*, 321 U.S. 649 (1944) (white primaries).

32. See, e.g., *Report of the President's Committee on Civil Rights* (1947).

33. See, e.g., *United States* v. *Cruikshank*, 92 U.S. 542 (1876); *United States* v. *Reese* 92 U.S. 214 (1876).

34. See 1961 *Civil Rights Commission Report:* "Voting" 75, 81.

35. Christopher, *The Constitutionality of the Voting Rights Act of 1965*, 18 Stan. L. Rev. 1, 3 (1965).

36. See *Terry* v. *Adams*, 345 U.S. 461 (1953); *Smith* v. *Allwright*, 321 U.S. 649 (1944); *Nixon* v. *Herndon*, 273 U.S. 536 (1927).

37. 71 Stat. 634 (1957), 42 U.S.C. §§ 1971, 1975d (1964).

38. 74 Stat. 86 (1960), 42 U.S.C. §§ 1971(c), (e), 1974(e), 1975(h) (1964).

39. 78 Stat. 241 (1964), 42 U.S.C. §§ 1971, 1975 a-d, 2000 a to h-4 (1964).

40. *Hearings on Voting Rights Before the Senate Committee on the Judiciary*, 89th Cong., 1st Sess., Pt. 1, at 14 (1965). See also Christopher, *The Constitutionality of the Voting Rights Act of 1965*, 18 Stan. L. Rev. 1, 4–9 (1965).

41. 79 Stat. 437 (1965), 42 U.S.C. § 1973 (1964 ed., Supp. III).

42. See *South Carolina* v. *Katzenbach*, 383 U.S. 301 (1966); *Katzenbach* v. *Morgan*, 384 U.S. 641 (1966); *Cardona* v. *Power*, 384 U.S. 672 (1966).

43. *1968 Report of United States Commission on Civil Rights.* "Political Participation" 12.

44. *Id.* at 14–17.
45. Compare *Connor* v. *Johnson,* 256 F. Supp. 962 (S.D. Miss. 1966), aff'd, 386 U.S. 483 (1967), with *Wright* v. *Rockefeller,* 376 U.S. 52 (1964).
46. Commentary includes Bickel, *The Voting Rights Cases,* 1966 The Supreme Court Review 79.
47. 383 U.S. 301 (1966).
48. *Id.* at 355.
49. *Id.* at 308.
50. *McCulloch* v. *Maryland,* 17 U.S. (4 Wheat.) 316, 407 (1819). See also *Heart of Atlanta Motel* v. *United States,* 379 U.S. 241, 258–59, 261–62 (1964); *Everard's Breweries* v. *Day,* 265 U.S. 545, 558–59 (1924).
51. *United States* v. *Raines,* 362 U.S. 17 (1960); *Louisiana* v. *United States,* 380 U.S. 145 (1965); *United States* v. *Mississippi,* 380 U.S. 128 (1965); *Hannah* v. *Larche,* 363 U.S. 420 (1960); *United States* v. *Thomas,* 362 U.S. 58 (1960). Cf. *Ex parte Virginia,* 100 U.S. 339, 345–46 (1880).
52. 384 U.S. 641 (1966).
53. 384 U.S. 672 (1966).
54. *Katzenbach* v. *Morgan,* 384 U.S. 641, 652 (1966).
55. *Id.* at 649–50.
56. *Id.* at 652–56. Justices Harlan and Stewart dissented in a single opinion directed to both *Morgan* and *Cardona. Id.* at 659.
57. 383 U.S. 787 (1966).
58. 383 U.S. 745 (1966).
59. 100 U.S. 339 (1880).
60. *Id.* at 345.
61. *United States* v. *Guest,* 383 U.S. 745, 762 (1966).
62. *Id.* at 782.
63. *Katzenbach* v. *Morgan,* 384 U.S. 641, 651–52 n. 10 (1966).
64. 347 U.S. 483 (1954).
65. 377 U.S. 533 (1964).
66. These challenges to the Court have been widely discussed, including the following: On the proposal to change the amending process (an issue that began before the decision in *Reynolds* v. *Sims*), see Black, *The Proposed Amendment of Article V: A Threatened Disaster,* 72 Yale L.J. 957 (1963). On the confrontations aimed squarely at the *Reapportionment Cases,* see Dixon, *Democratic Representation* 387–435 (1968); McKay, *Court, Congress, and Reapportionment,* 63 Mich. L. Rev. 255 (1964).
67. For a discussion, see McKay, *Reapportionment Reappraised* (Twentieth Century Fund Pamphlet 1968).
68. *Id.* at 14. The same was true in even larger measure in the related case of congressional districting (*id.* at 13–14) where the Supreme Court had required substantial population equality under the authority of Article I, section 2. *Wesberry* v. *Sanders,* 376 U.S. 1 (1964).
69. Professor Commager has made the point eloquently in his paper on "The Fourteenth Amendment: Historical Perspective." See also, from the wealth of commentary on this point, Ten Broek, *The Antislavery Origins*

of the Fourteenth Amendment (1951); Bickel, *The Original Understanding and the Segregation Decision,* 69 Harv. L. Rev. 1 (1955).

70. *Supra* p. 14.
71. 383 U.S. 663 (1966).
72. *Id.* at 669.
73. 380 U.S. 89, 97 (1965).
74. 380 U.S. 128, 144 (1965).
75. 380 U.S. 145, 156 (1965).
76. 380 U.S. 528, 544 (1965).
77. *Reynolds* v. *Sims,* 377 U.S. 533, 589, 594 (1964) (Harlan, J., dissenting).
78. Van Alstyne, *The Fourteenth Amendment, the "Right" to Vote, and the Understanding of the Thirty-Ninth Congress,* 1965 The Supreme Court Review 33, 85.
79. *Id.* at 68.
80. *Avery* v. *Midland County,* 390 U.S. 474 (1968). Cf. *Sailors* v. *Board of Education,* 387 U.S. 105 (1967); *Dusch* v. *Davis,* 387 U.S. 112 (1967).
81. *Reynolds* v. *Sims,* 377 U.S. 533, 577 (1964).
82. 385 U.S. 440, 445 (1967).
83. *Kirkpatrick* v. *Preisler,* 394 U.S. 526, 531 (1969).
84. *Ibid.*
85. 364 U.S. 339 (1960).
86. 376 U.S. 52 (1964). See also *Honeywood* v. *Rockefeller,* 376 U.S. 222 (1964).
87. See *Wells* v. *Rockefeller,* 394 U.S. 542 (1969); *Connor* v. *Johnson,* 386 U.S. 483 (1967); *Fortson* v. *Dorsey,* 379 U.S. 433 (1965).

6

Religion and the Law

Harvey G. Cox

The late Perry Miller devoted much of his scholarly career to the task of demonstrating how central a place religion has played in the history of the American nation. Our identity and sense of purpose stem from our early conviction that we were a people with "an errand in the wilderness," with a task to perform in history. Also, Miller argues, in the period after the Revolution, the evangelical awakenings provided the basis for a set of character traits that lasted throughout the nineteenth century. These early values and traits, though considerably modified, remain today.

It is of course not unusual that our religion should have played a central role in shaping the character of our culture. The same is true of many civilizations. What is unusual, however, is that in the American experience, this happened for the first time without legal establishment of any particular religion but with the equal protection of all religious beliefs and practices. Many were opposed both to disestablishment and to equal protection for all religions. But despite the misgivings of New England theocrats and Vatican integralists, religion in America did not disappear without establishment; it thrived. It thrived so well in fact that we now take the non-establishment equal protection formula almost for granted. We should not. In other societies quite different views of the legal status of religion obtain. In some societies the law is used to enforce a particular religion as predominant, for example, Ceylon, Spain and Israel. In others, the law encourages one particular religion or denomination as in England and West Germany. In still others, such as the USSR, the law is used to harass religion. In many, it remains carefully neutral. So far in American history, the effort to balance a calculated refusal to honor any religion with the careful protection of all has succeeded remarkably well.

The formula, however, is a precarious one. Historical developments, both in religion and in law, make it impossible ever to consider the balance of

Harvey G. Cox is Professor of Divinity at the Harvard Divinity School.

non-establishment and protection settled once and for all. Religion, despite what some theologians seem to claim and what some avid secularists would like to believe, is neither eternal nor inert. Religions not only change and develop, but in recent years the effort *consciously* and *purposely* to modify religious practices has gained widespread acceptance at least in some faiths. This was certainly the significance of Vatican II and the meaning of the word "aggiornamento." Also, we no longer believe that all laws are made for eternity. "New occasions teach new duties; time makes ancient good uncouth," as James Russell Lowell put it. We must constantly raise the question of the adequacy and justice of the present relation of religion to law in our society. Are we moving toward the danger of "establishing" a religion, as is claimed by critics of tax support for parochial school children, poverty funds for church-sponsored community action programs, federal loans to church colleges, or tax exemption for religious institutions? Or are we failing to protect the full range of religious expression—as would be claimed by Black Muslim minister Mohammed Ali, by imprisoned Jehovah's Witnesses who will make war only in the final battle of Armageddon, or by conscientious objectors to particular wars?

Hardly a month goes by in which the issue is not raised in one way or another. The indictment of Yale chaplain William Sloane Coffin, Jr. for allegedly violating the Selective Service Law explicitly mentions his participation in a worship service at Boston's historic Arlington Street Church, as does the indictment of Harvard graduate student Michael Ferber. If these indictments on the one hand cheered ministers by proving that at least *someone* listens to sermons attentively, even if it is only the FBI agent in the third pew, still the practice of arresting ministers partly because of what they say from pulpits is not something we customarily condone in America. As a teacher in America's oldest institution for theological education, I was surprised and disappointed that so little notice was given to this serious departure from American tradition.

There are other things going on which raise serious questions about the adequacy of our present protection of religious expression. The laws against advising persons to violate the draft law, for example, raise serious questions for pastoral counselors, especially since the present law is a highly discriminatory one—allowing conscientious objector status to pacifists but not to selective objectors. The law in effect discriminates in favor of Quakers, Mennonites and other total pacifist groups, and against Lutherans and Catholics whose religious tradition teaches them to distinguish between just and unjust wars.

It also seems strange, somehow, to find judges deciding what is, or is not religious. From Protestant Paul Tillich to Catholic Leslie Dewart, and for centuries before them, many Christian theologians have been hesitant to speak of God as "a being," supreme or otherwise. Some non-Western religions have gotten along for eons without a "supreme being." Yet for years, in our country, whether or not one believed in a supreme being became the test of whether one was "religious" in cases regarding conscientious objection.

We can never rest assured that either the separation of church from state or the constitutional protection we extend to religion needs no surveillance. Vigilance and change are always needed. Even as we maintain this vigilance, however, it is appropriate that we ask another question: *why* does the law protect religion?

At one level the answer to this question seems self-evident. We believe the right of religious freedom stands among those liberties which the founders held were "inalienable." We protect religion because we protect the individual.

That, however, is a somewhat individualistic conception of religious freedom. It smacks of its Lockean roots in bourgeois-enlightenment thought. As such it may not provide today a completely adequate intellectual basis for the guarantee of equal protection of religion under the law. Another danger of subsuming religious freedom under private rights is that public expressions of religion can be excluded. To subsume religious freedom under individual rights suggests a Protestant, individualistic notion of religion—itself not at all "neutral." Granted that the individual must be protected, are there other philosophical reasons, reasons in line with a more corporate view of the polity, for protecting religious expression? We cannot avoid the philosophical issue.

Again our ancestors had an answer. They saw religion as the bedrock of public morality. Religion provided the grounds for the values of the republic. With such noble exceptions as Thomas Paine, most of them thought atheism was the first step toward anarchy. Our anticlerical tradition in America tends, in contrast to that of France or the USSR, to be deist with Jefferson or transcendentalist with Emerson, not atheist as with Voltaire or Bakunin. Religion has often been seen as the stabilizer of society and the bastion against excess. It should be protected, it was held, as a precaution against revolution and moral deterioration.

This attribution of a conservative social function to religion has shown a remarkable persistence through American history. This persistence is the more remarkable when one notices that the facts have frequently contradicted theory. Recent historical studies of the American Revolution strongly suggest that the Calvinist preachers played a significant role in fomenting it. Religious leaders and religious rhetoric were in dramatic evidence during the abolitionist struggle. When we witness instances of "symbolic sanctuary" in churches today, it is hard not to recall the illegal auctions of contraband slaves in Boston churches during the period after the *Dred Scott* decision. That tradition continues today. It would be hard to persuade the parishioners of Fr. Philip Berrigan or Fr. James Groppi that religion serves a quieting, pacifying function, though many of them fondly wish it would. The fact is that, in American history, religion has played a somewhat ambiguous role. Though it has most often sanctioned the *status quo* and sanctified traditional values, it has sometimes supplied the motor for social change. Men of faith have voted Whig, Republican, Socialist and "Know-Nothing." They have died for the flag, burned it, and refused to salute it. They have not always been a conservative force, but have provided a very unpredictable input into the polity.

But what now? Our society today is probably sufficiently removed from the danger either of theocracy or of atheist tyranny that we can ask, once again, just what religion can and should contribute to its future. Why, from the perspective of good social policy, should religion be protected and even encouraged in a secular, scientific post-industrial age?

In responding to this question, let me refer to a highly improbable source: the recent decision of a United States District Court to refuse to dismiss a narcotics indictment against Mrs. Judith H. Kuch, a Boo-Hoo, or minister, of the "Neo-American Church" which claims that LSD and marijuana are its sacraments. This church should not be confused with the "Native American Church," an Indian church which already makes use of peyote in its worship. Although Mrs. Kuch insisted that her indictment violated her constitutional right of free exercise of religion, the judge disagreed. He said that,

> after reading the "so-called Catechism and Handbook" of the Church containing the pronouncements of the Chief Boo-Hoo, one gains the inescapable impression that the membership is mocking established institutions, playing with words, and [is] totally irreverent in any sense of the term. . . . the "Catechism and Handbook" is full of goofy nonsense, contradictions, and irreverent expressions.
>
> [For examples, the judge pointed out that the church symbol is a three-eyed toad, and its official songs are "Puff, the Magic Dragon" and "Row, Row, Row Your Boat."] *United States* v. *Kuch,* 288 F. Supp. 439, 444 (D.C. 1968).

Now there can be little doubt that the Neo-American Church is a little goofy and irreverent. And I doubt if a major civil liberties battle will shape up around Mrs. Kuch, though perhaps it should. Still, if "goofiness" and "irreverence" exclude a group from being counted as a religion, we begin to move onto shaky ground. Anyone who has perused Luther's polemics on the papist antichrist or tuned in on the Rev. Billy Joe Hargis' opinions about the National Council of Churches will have winced at their irreverence. It has always been so. The early Christians were accused by the Romans of being "atheoi," atheists. Pompey was shocked at the irreligion of the Jews when, upon striding into the inner court of the Temple in Jerusalem, he found it devoid of statues. Polemical sects have appeared by the thousands in religious history, and the irreverance of their language makes the tone of the Neo-American Church seem pious by comparison.

Or what about "goofiness?" If religions are to be refused recognition and protection by the law because they seem goofy, then there are a number of candidates anyone of us could nominate for exclusion from equal protection. Is it goofy to believe the angel Moroni gave Joseph Smith some golden tablets on a hill in New York State? Hundreds of thousands of Mormons do believe this. Is it goofy to fast, go without sleep or talking, wear a hairshirt, sprinkle babies with water, climb St. Peter's steps on your knees? Is it goofy to believe a man opened a path through the Red Sea, or came to life from the dead? How do we determine what is goofy and what is sensible in religion? Do we count how many people believe it? That would be hard on minority faiths. Do we ask how long the belief has existed? That would rule out new religious movements. Oddly enough, if numbers and age had anything to do with the legitimacy of a religious belief, Mrs. Kuch's marijuana cult has very ancient precedents, at least as far back as the Bacchae, and probably as many sympathizers as some of the smaller among the three hundred or more odd sects now thriving in America.

My point here is not to argue for the Neo-American Church, but to ask for a more generous attitude toward goofiness, even, or perhaps especially, when it appears in religious form. It was, after all, the soberest of souls, St. Paul, who wrote to the Church at Corinth that "the foolishness of God is wiser than the wisdom of men." Religion, though it often functions as a stabilizing force, also provides the context within which some valuable forms of deviant behavior are protected. I say "valuable" because a changing society always needs to be experimenting with new values, new life styles, new visions. Otherwise it grows sterile and flaccid. Freud may have been right that religion is a form of neurosis, but a certain amount of neurosis is needed to move the growing edge of the culture and to raise questions about what we mean by such words as "normal" and "sane." It is the very oddness and intractability of religious behavior, even its weirdness at times, which must be protected by the law.

Any society can protect decent, upstanding churchgoers in their worship. Only a confident, open, creative society can protect visionaries, ecstatics, seers, and fanatics. But it is precisely they who need the protecting, in part from the churchgoers. Nor can we mask our cultural religious orthodoxy under rubrics of mental health. In the old days, we imprisoned heretics and gave adulterers icy dips in the dunking chair. If today we confine people whose religion seems bizarre or give them electric shock treatments, we may see the difference, but we can hardly blame the heretic if he fails to appreciate the distinction.

Society should protect religion, not just because the Ten Commandments help, or once helped, to keep people moral. We should protect it because an open society needs to cultivate forms of personal and corporate existence which, though they may seem "goofy" to us now, could appear emminently sane to our descendants.

In the past, religion has generally been seen as one of the great stabilizing and conserving forces in the culture. But in some ways, our society neither needs that conserving force nor can be stabilized by it. Secularization and pluralism have done their work. Our major institutions now proceed without benefit of clergy and according to values which no longer have their explicit grounding in religion. Yet religion somehow remains, and for many people, it is becoming more a matter of personal style than a badge of ethnic background. If it is not quite what Whitehead described, that is, "what a man does with his solitude," it is at least becoming more and more idiosyncratic. Even those who belong to one of the great historic denominations have their own, often somewhat eccentric, views on what its doctrines mean. Therefore the protection of religion becomes the protection of the heretical, the schismatic, the excommunicate. By protecting these people, the law holds open one of the few but valuable places where men can exercise real individuality.

It may well be that we stand at a period in which profound and perplexing changes will occur in religion. Nietzsche once made a distinction between apollonian forms of religion (those characterized by restraint, severity, and wisdom) and dionysiac forms (characterized by ecstasy, emotion, and excess). We may be leaving an apollonian period in the history of Western religion and entering a dionysiac religious epoch. There is evidence that this is already happening. Traditional authority structures are crumbling, both in religion and civil society. Fond beliefs are criticized, ancient ethical practices are questioned. Yet, despite the crepe hangers, religion does not seem in any sense to be dying. There seems to be widespread evidence of a renaissance in religion, an interest in meditation, a rediscovery of festivity, a searching for ecstasy and vision, a quest for nonmaterial values. The renaissance however goes far beyond normal ecclesiastical boundaries and—a fact that judges should recognize—its forms can sometimes appear rather bizarre.

After a century of equality before the law, we cannot assume that religion is adequately protected just because we protect what we have recognized and accepted as religion in the past. This kind of protection would have failed to protect Buddha, Jesus, Mohammed and every real religious innovator since Abraham. In the years to come, the law will be faced, time and again, with movements claiming to be religious and therefore claiming the protection of the law. The temptation will be to judge these new movements in terms of existing models. Is it too much to hope that the law can learn to be a little more imaginative and flexible? The role of religion is not only to link us to the traditions of the past, but to open us to the hopes for the future. It calls us not just to the memory of the Passover, but to the expectation of the Messianic Era. Christianity not only recalls the lives of Jesus and his Apostles, but proclaims the coming Kingdom of God. The goofiness and irreverence of today have sometimes proven to be the sanity and piety of tomorrow.

7

Free Speech in an Age of Violence

Merlo J. Pusey

Freedom of expression is not the first principle enunciated in the Bill of Rights, but it was the first Bill of Rights guarantee transfused into the Fourteenth Amendment. That distinction should surprise no one, for the constitutional mandate that "Congress shall make no law . . . abridging the freedom of speech, or of the press" is one of the first essentials of a democratic society. It holds a very special relationship to our whole constitutional system.

In a very real sense, freedom of expression becomes a part of many other rights. Religious freedom, which was placed first in the Bill of Rights, would be meaningless without the right of men to speak what their consciences dictate. "The right of people peaceably to assemble" would be a sham if they could not freely communicate to one another their hopes, fears, aspirations, and ideas when they come together. And the right "to petition the Government for a redress of grievances" is merely a specific application of the larger right of free expression.

The amazing thing is that this essential lubricant of all the processes of democracy should have been so recently applied to state and local governments. When the Bill of Rights was in the process of formation by the First Congress, James Madison, its principal author, sought to make guarantees of freedom of speech and of the press, freedom of conscience, and the right of trial by jury in criminal cases binding against the states. The Senate rejected that proposed limitation on state power. Nearly eight decades elapsed before the Fourteenth Amendment was adopted, following the Civil War, and then Congress was thinking chiefly about guaranteeing the rights of the freed slaves. It did not go back and spell out the freedoms that Madison would have protected against state action. Today we can be

Merlo J. Pusey is Associate Editor of the *Washington Post*.

thankful that it used language broad enough to embrace the great freedoms in the First Amendment, but it took the Supreme Court more than half a century to find these hidden treasures of freedom in the Fourteenth Amendment's command that no state shall "deprive any person of life, liberty, or property, without due process of law."

The story of this discovery is now a familiar one, but it merits emphasis and reemphasis on this centennial of the great Fourteenth Amendment. Until the 1930's, punishment of men for speech and publications deemed dangerous to law and order was relatively common. The principle of freedom of expression was recognized, but those who went beyond the prescribed bounds of restraint could be penalized for what was regarded as abuse of that freedom. The Supreme Court in 1920 upheld a Minnesota statute forbidding the advocacy of pacifism.[1] Although Justice Brandeis dissented, he saw "no occasion to consider" whether this limitation on freedom of speech violated the Fourteenth Amendment. When the Supreme Court upheld the Missouri Service Letter Law in 1922, it said flatly: ". . . neither the Fourteenth Amendment nor any other provision of the Constitution of the United States imposes on the States any restrictions about 'freedom of speech' or the 'liberty of silence'. . . ."[2] Justices Holmes and Brandeis concurred.

The Supreme Court seemed to look in the other direction in 1923, when it struck down Nebraska's law forbidding the teaching of the German language.[3] Curiously, it was Justice James C. McReynolds who spoke for the court in that defense of free expression against arbitrary state action. Justices Holmes and Sutherland dissented. Two years later, the first specific transfusion of First Amendment rights into the Fourteenth Amendment by way of the due process clause was achieved in the *Gitlow* case.[4] At the time, however, the significance of the ruling was muffled because the court merely assumed "for present purposes" that "freedom of speech and of the press—which are protected by the First Amendment from abridgment by Congress—are among the fundamental personal rights and 'liberties' protected by the due process clause of the Fourteenth Amendment from impairment by the States." The effect of the ruling, moreover, was to uphold New York's statute forbidding the advocacy of criminal anarchy and to punish Gitlow for writing a pamphlet calling for a Communist revolution. Similar conclusions were drawn in several other cases. The great transfusion was not immediately helpful to the cause of free expression because the court insisted that the state had an overriding right to punish abuse of free expression "by utterances inimical to the public welfare, tending to corrupt public morals, incite to crime, or disturb the public peace."[5]

Some years earlier, Justice Holmes had enunciated his "clear and present danger" test to mark the dividing line between permissible and forbidden speech in *Schenck* v. *United States*[6] and had subsequently elaborated his formula in numerous dissents [7] in collaboration with Justice Brandeis. His subsequently famous thesis was:

> The question in every case is whether the words used are used in such circumstances and are of such a nature as to create a clear and present danger that they will bring about the substantive evils that Congress has a right to prevent. It is a question of proximity and degree.[8]

As the third decade of the twentieth century came to a close, however, the court was a long way from following Holmes and Brandeis in their efforts to evolve a realistic formula to determine the bounds of free expression.

A dramatic turn came when in 1930 Charles Evans Hughes succeeded William Howard Taft as Chief Justice of the United States. Hughes emerged as a powerful champion of free expression in several notable opinions he handed down for the Supreme Court in the spring of 1931. In *Stromberg* v. *California* [9] he led the court in upsetting the conviction of a 19-year-old girl who had taught children to salute a red flag in a Communist camp. For the new Chief Justice, it was a clear case of unconstitutional suppression of free expression. There was no evidence of any incitement to violence or crime, or threat to overthrow organized government by violent means. Hughes used the occasion to proclaim the heavy reliance of democracy on freedom of expression:

> The maintenance of the opportunity for free political discussion to the end that government may be responsive to the will of the people and that changes may be obtained by lawful means, an opportunity essential to the security of the Republic, is a fundamental principle of our constitutional system. A statute which, upon its face, and as authoritatively construed, is so vague and indefinite as to permit the punishment of the fair use of this opportunity is repugnant to the guarantee of liberty contained in the Fourteenth Amendment.

Hughes had a deep distrust of formulas, shibboleths, and court-made doctrines used as short cuts to judicial conclusions. The court's task, he had noted before he ascended the bench the second time, was to seek "a correct appraisal of social conditions and a true appraisal of the actual effect of conduct." [10] He preferred to measure actual conduct against the direct language of the great charter and the basic principles which its authors had sought to establish. In these he found ample authority to sustain the rights of free expression against repressive laws of either the nation or the states.

In another major free-expression case Chief Justice Hughes spoke for the court in consigning Minnesota's press-gag law to limbo.[11] It was the first time the Fourteenth Amendment's guarantee of liberty had been used completely to obliterate a state law. Over the vigorous opposition of Justices Butler, Van Devanter, McReynolds, and Sutherland, the court laid down a formidable barrier against the suppression of newspapers for criticism of public officials.

Hughes did not embrace the semantic illusion that freedom of the press is an "absolute right." The government, he reasoned, could forbid the publication of the sailing dates of troop ships and prevent the obstruction of recruiting in wartime; it could protect community life against incitements to violence and uphold the requirements of decency. But it could not close up a newspaper, even a scurrilous sheet deemed a "public nuisance," to stop criticism of public officials.

Near v. *Minnesota* struck with special force against prior restraint of a newspaper for what was deemed to be an offense against public policy. Tracing the abuses of prior restraint of the press in England, Hughes found in Minnesota's imitation of that practice "the essence of censorship." It made no difference that the object of Minnesota's suppression was a vicious little scandal sheet. "The fact that the liberty of the press may be abused by miscreant purveyors of scandal," the court said, "does not make any the less necessary the immunity of the press from previous restraint in dealing with official misconduct." Minnesota had presumed to suppress a newspaper which was deemed to be malicious without even requiring proof of malice. The Supreme Court took full advantage of a flagrant case to underwrite freedom of the press in more positive and sweeping terms than had ever before come from the high bench.

The scope of freedom for hated expression was further spelled out a few years later in the Herndon case.[12] An Atlanta Communist named Angelo Herndon had been convicted and imprisoned, under a Georgia law, because he had in his possession a pamphlet urging a revolutionary struggle for power aimed at the achievement of self-determination for the Black Belt. The court, with Justice Roberts as spokesman, could find no evidence of unlawful incitement to insurrection in the pallid facts of the case. It struck down the statute as "a dragnet which may enmesh anyone who agitates for a change of government if a jury can be persuaded that he ought to have foreseen his words would have some effect in the future conduct of others."

In 1936 the same court, with Justice Sutherland as spokesman, struck down Huey Long's tax on the gross receipts of the large Louisiana newspapers that were opposing him.[13] Freedom of the press from arbitrary and punitive taxation was thus firmly established. Chief Justice Hughes spoke for the court once more in extending the doctrine of *Near* v. *Minnesota* to handbills, circulars, and tracts. In this case, *Lovell* v. *City of Griffin*,[14] the court swept away an ordinance which, in flagrant defiance of constitutional rights, prohibited the distribution of any pamphlet or "literature of any kind" without permission from the city manager. The Supreme Court emphatically repudiated the idea that freedom of the press is a special privilege granted to newspapers and magazines:

> The liberty of the press is not confined to newspapers and periodicals. It necessarily embraces pamphlets and leaflets. These indeed have been historic weapons in the defense of liberty, as the pamphlets of Thomas Paine and others in our own history abundantly attest. The press in its historic connotation comprehends every sort of publication which affords a vehicle of information and opinion.

Freedom of assembly was recognized as a closely related right. People congregate together to make more meaningful their liberty to speak their minds on political, religious, economic, or occupational subjects. Freedom of speech would indeed be a farce if it were not accompanied by the right to assemble listeners, and the right to petition the government for the redress of grievances. The Supreme Court put a new floor under freedom of assembly by striking down Oregon's conviction of Dirk De Jonge for helping to organize and conduct a peaceful Communist meeting.[15]

The opinion of Chief Justice Hughes in this case expressly recognized, however, that freedom of expression may be abused by incitements to violence or crime. The states could protect themselves against such abuses, the court said, but "the holding of meetings for peaceful political action cannot be proscribed."

The Supreme Court in 1940 extended the safeguards of the First and Fourteenth Amendments to another vital area of free expression—labor union picketing. In this case, Justice Murphy spoke for a majority of eight. The effect was to strike down an Alabama statute which sought to penalize picketing and loitering. The aim of the law was to deny labor unionists the right to make known their views of a labor dispute by walking near their employer's place of business carrying signs, regardless of how peaceful the picketing might be. The court would countenance no such abridgment of free expression. It did not doubt that the state could regulate picketing and similar activities for the protection of life and property. "But," it concluded, "no clear and present danger of destruction of life or property, or invasion of the right of privacy, or breach of the peace can be thought to be inherent in the activities of every person who approaches the premises of an employer and publicizes the facts of a labor dispute involving the latter." [16]

The bounds of free speech in the labor-management area had another outward push in *Thomas* v. *Collins*.[17] Texas had punished a labor leader for contempt of court for violating an order which forbade him, under the terms of a state law, to solicit union membership without having first registered and obtained an organizer's card. A majority of five concluded that this was an invasion of Thomas's right to make a speech in support of a lawful movement. In vain the state protested that it was regulating conduct, the solicitation of membership, but the action involved was so intimately intertwined with speech that the majority was unwilling to permit any interference with it in the circumstances.

There was a time (1949) when the court's profound respect for freedom of expression seemed to blind it to some other values in our system. In *Terminiello* v. *Chicago*,[18] a majority upset the conviction of a suspended Catholic priest for disorderly conduct, even though he had aroused two mobs (one inside and the other outside the building in which he spoke) into a frenzy that resulted in the hurling of missiles, use of stench bombs, breaking of windows, and attempts to smash the doors. The disorders appeared to be directly related to Terminiello's appeal to racial hatreds and his free indulgence in what is known to the law as "fighting words." The Illinois courts upheld the conviction because of this use of "fighting words," but the Supreme Court rejected that judgment on the theory that free speech may best serve its high purpose, as Justice Douglas said in the majority opinion, "when it induces a condition of unrest, creates dissatisfaction with conditions as they are, even stirs people to anger." [19] The opinion shows little awareness of the danger that speech which becomes an integral part of violence may contribute to massive disorders and to the substitution of brute force for reason and discussion. "No mob," Justice Jackson declared in his dissent, "has ever protected any liberty, even its own." He went on to warn his brethren that "if the Court does not temper its doctrinaire logic with a little wisdom, it will convert the constitutional Bill of Rights into a suicide pact." [20]

Two years later, the court seemed to take a very different view of speech intertwined with disorder. It upheld New York's conviction of a man who had assembled a crowd by means of sound amplifiers, delivered a fiery speech, and urged Negroes to rise up in arms to secure equal rights.[21] The arrest had been made as a preventive measure after the audience became restless and threatening, but before any outbreak of violence had occurred. In this case the court may have permitted curtailment of free expression too soon—before it was necessary in order to keep the peace.

In recent years, the Supreme Court has become generally unresponsive to demands for the protection of speech that is associated with violence or threats. In 1967 it refused to review a case in which a group of civil rights workers had been convicted for making speeches on the steps of the Greenville, Mississippi, courthouse, because of the danger that such conduct might interfere with the processes of justice.[22] In another case,[23] the court affirmed the convictions of demonstrators who had sought to protest the imprisonment of a group of students at the Tallahassee, Florida, jail. Their rights to freedom of expression and peaceful assembly did not save them when they trespassed upon jail property, in violation of a statute designed to protect the penal system. No one can say with finality where future lines will be drawn between protected speech and forbidden conduct, but it is clear that the right to free expression carries with it no license for violence.

For many years, the court used Justice Holmes's "clear and present danger" phrase to mark the point at which the state could interfere with freedom of expression. In general the concept seemed to work well, as Dr. Edward G. Hudon has pointed out, in relatively minor cases involving infractions of anti-picketing laws, anti-soliciting ordinances, or the jailing of an editor for contempt. [24] However, the Communist cases of the early 1950's brought a realization that this over-worked phrase offered no magic solutions. As the court mulled over these cases, it became clear to a majority of its members that they could not ask the United States Government to stand helpless in the face of a determined and aggressive world Communist movement, actuated by revolutionary doctrines, until the conspirators were ready to strike.

Under the leadership of Chief Justice Vinson, the court upheld the non-Communist affidavit requirement of the Labor-Management Relations Act of 1947.[25] In effect, it simply gave more weight to the security of the nation than it did to the labor union claim of freedom from the signing of loyalty oaths. Then came the *Dennis* case, [26] in which officials of the Communist Party were convicted under the Smith Act for concerted action in teaching the doctrines of Marxism-Leninism. Under the terms of the clear and present danger test, as it had traditionally been applied, the convictions could not have been upheld, as the Government readily admitted. But the majority did not feel at liberty to apply a formula devised to measure isolated encroachments on freedom to a menace of international proportions, which posed an unmeasurable threat to all freedom and democratic government. Writing for a bloc of four, Chief Justice Vinson seized upon Judge Learned Hand's shrewd refashioning of "clear and present danger" to the needs of the hour.[27] The Government need not wait for a *putsch* to begin. The freedom protected by the First Amendment was not freedom to advocate and teach destruction of our constitutional system in a setting where the perils of subversion were readily apparent. Since Justices Frankfurter and Jackson wrote separate concurring opinions and Justices Black and Douglas dissented, the law was left in a state of confusion, but the danger of immobilizing the nation with a shibboleth in time of danger had passed.

Out of this experience evolved a new theory for the resolution of First Amendment claims in collision with the seeming demands of security. "Clear and present danger" was in tatters. Justice Black's contention that freedom of speech, press, and religion are absolutes had never won the support of his brethren. Indeed, the Douglas dissent in the *Dennis* case showed how far the Black thesis was from acceptance. Justice Douglas made clear that he would have voted to uphold the convictions if the Communist leaders had sought refuge in the First Amendment in order to teach the technique of sabotage, the assassination of the President, the theft of public documents, or the planting of bombs. Devoted as he was to the ideal of free expression, he would not risk the destruction of constitutionalism itself on the ragged edges of an overextended idea, and the majority was much further away from doing so. The Communist cases seemed to push a majority of the Supreme Court toward an open-ended theory that First and Fourteenth Amendment freedoms could be reconciled with the right of the state to protect itself only by a "balancing of interests." In effect, it said, the right of the individual to freedom of speech must be weighed against the right of the state to security and the maintenance of law and order. But this attempt to devise a formula that would guide the court through First and Fourteenth Amendment cases was no more successful than previous attempts had been.[28]

In one sense the court balances one set of values against another in every case that is presented to it. That is the nature of the judicial process. But recognition of this fact tells us little about what ought to guide the Supreme Court in the process. Chief Justice Warren has pointed out that when the security of the Nation and freedom of an individual litigant are the weights put into the scales, "it is not surprising that the balance is usually struck against the individual." He went on to say: "If balance we must, I wonder whether on the individual's side we might not also place the importance of our survival as a free nation. The issue, as I see it," he added, "is not the individual against society; it is rather the wise accommodation of the necessities of physical survival with the requirements of spiritual survival." [29]

Certainly Chief Justice Warren's emphasis on the weights that go onto the scales is all important. Freedom is not merely a bauble or luxury graciously granted to the individual for his convenience or his peace of mind. "Free trade in ideas," [30] to use Justice Holmes's term, is the genius of a progressive society. Loss of it would threaten the survival of our constitutional system, no less than subversion by a skillful and ruthless enemy.

What Chief Justice Warren seemed to be saying is that the court must do its utmost to uphold both of these great principles—freedom of expression and security in our physical environment—and to keep the encroachments of one upon the other at a minimum when a collision between them has to be resolved.

The great difficulty with the balancing theory, as it has sometimes been enunciated in the past, is that it seems to leave the Supreme Court too much license to press its own hand down on the scales. No formula was ever devised that would give each segment of the constitution a weight quotient in every given situation. The theory may well have served as a useful escape hatch from the unsustainable thesis that the First and Fourteenth Amendment freedoms are absolute. But it seems to offer little as a guide to the future.

There is no misfortune in the failure of the Supreme Court to find a pat formula for determining how far freedom of speech and press may go, before the government may interpose some restraints in the interests of an orderly society or national survival. No such enduring formula is likely to be found, for the simple reason that problems vary from generation to generation. The great genius of the constitution is that it affords flexibility in meeting the demands of both liberty and order. Guided by precedent and a sensitive national conscience, the Supreme Court can be trusted to etch out the bounds of freedom in new circumstances as they arise, and it is more likely to be successful if it does not try to devise semantic strait jackets for situations that cannot now be foreseen. There is much virtue in returning repeatedly to the pure fountain of the Bill of Rights itself instead of relying upon some verbal concoction which may seem popular at the moment, but which may become an excuse for not thinking about new constitutional problems as they arise.

For the most part the court has done well in its case-by-case approach to questions of free expression. It has been scrupulous in upholding the rights of the individual against encroachments by governments, in a great variety of situations. One of the most significant landmarks in this area in recent years is the *New York Times* case in which the Supreme Court made it extremely difficult for public officials to silence their journalistic critics by means of libel suits. Speaking for the court, Justice Brennan took note of "a profound national commitment to the principle that debate on public issues should be uninhibited, robust, and wide-open, and that it may well include vehement, caustic, and sometimes unpleasantly sharp attacks on government and public officials." [31] Even if the criticism involved "defamatory falsehood" about an official's conduct, the court ruled, the official could not recover damages unless he proved "that the statement was made with 'actual malice'—that is, with knowledge that it was false or with reckless disregard of whether it was false or not."

The Supreme Court has also provided a generally effective shield for editors against misuse of the power of judges to punish for contempt. The general rule is that "freedom of the press must be allowed in the broadest scope compatible with the supremacy of order." [32] Judges may use their contempt powers to punish disorder in the courtroom, but not to penalize an editor who assails the performance of the court in print. The essentials of orderly judicial proceedings can be protected without tolerating a backlash that could reach into newspaper offices. [33]

There was some fear a few years ago that the court's heavy accent on free expression and the so-called right to privacy might result in curtailment of the investigative functions of Congress and the state legislatures. In 1957 the court, without a majority behind any one opinion, reversed the conviction of a witness before the House Un-American Activities Committee who had refused to testify as to whether he had known certain individuals as members of the Communist Party.[34] Speaking for himself, and for Justices Black, Douglas, and Brennan, Chief Justice Warren intimated that First Amendment rights had been jeopardized and concluded that the resolution authorizing the committee did not meet constitutional standards. But the pendulum soon swung in the other direction with Justice Clark writing for a different majority in the *Barenblatt* case.[35] Once more a conviction for refusal to testify before the Un-American Activities Committee was at stake, but this time the court took a broader view of the investigative powers of Congress and found no encroachment upon First Amendment rights. Similar conclusions were reached in *Wilkinson* v. *United States* [36] and *Braden* v. *United States*,[37] and the court refused to interfere with New Hampshire's probing into allegedly subversive activities in a summer camp.[38] If it were a question of approving or disapproving many of the things the Communist-hunting committees have done, there would be much sympathy with the restrictive view of the Supreme Court's activists in this sphere. But the right of the people to know what is going on in their country, including the right of Congress to spread the facts on the record, is no less vital than uninhibited discussion to the survival of a free society.

In the troublesome realm of obscene expression, the Supreme Court has taken a moderate course. The *Roth* case, decided in 1957, established for the first time that "obscenity is not within the area of protected speech or press." [39] Though the court has been understandably reluctant to sustain findings of obscenity, except in the most flagrant cases, a majority upheld the obscenity convictions of Ralph Ginzburg [40] and Edward Mishkin [41] in 1965 and ruled that the manner in which a defendant merchandizes obscene material may be taken into account in determining its character. Again, in 1968, the court upheld the conviction of a luncheonette operator who sold two "girlie" magazines to a 16-year-old boy in violation of a New York statute designed to protect minors against the dissemination of pornography. Writing for a majority of six, Justice Brennan concluded that, since obscenity is not protected expression, it may be suppressed "without a showing of the circumstances which lie behind the phrase 'clear and present danger' in its application to protected speech." [42] The court let the protective New York statute stand because it concluded that "it was not irrational for the legislature to find that exposure to material condemned by the statute is harmful to minors"—even though it was not obscene by adult standards.

Near the end of its 1967 Term, the Supreme Court also spoke with a clear and unequivocal voice against the idea that unlawful conduct can be shielded by a cocoon of protected speech. The Court of Appeals for the First Circuit had held that a 1965 amendment to the Selective Service Act forbidding the knowing destruction or mutilation of a draft card was an unconstitutional abridgment of freedom of speech. The reasoning was that Congress had singled out for special punishment those servicemen who engaged in public protests, and that the measure was therefore a special blow at free expression.

Chief Justice Warren cut through this spongy conclusion by showing that the act applied to private, as well as public, destruction of draft cards, and that its effect was to support an orderly administration of the Selective Service System. David Paul O'Brien's claim that his draft-card-burning ceremony was protected "symbolic speech" fared no better. "We cannot accept the view," the chief justice wrote, "that an apparently limitless variety of conduct can be labeled 'speech' whenever the person engaging in the conduct intends thereby to express an idea." [43]

With only Justice Douglas dissenting, the court went on to lay down an important rule for dealing with intermingled "speech" and "nonspeech" elements. In such cases, the opinion said,

> a sufficiently important governmental interest in regulating the nonspeech element can justify incidental limitations on First Amendment freedoms. To characterize the quality of the governmental interest which must appear, the Court has employed a variety of descriptive terms: compelling; [44] substantial; [45] subordinating; [46] paramount; [47] cogent; [48] strong. [49] Whatever imprecision inheres in these terms, we think it clear that a government regulation is sufficiently justified if it is within the constitutional power of the government; if it furthers an important or substantial government interest; if the governmental interest is unrelated to the suppression of free expression; and if the incidental restriction on alleged First Amendment freedom is no greater than is essential to the furtherance of that interest.

To many who have come to think of the First and Fourteenth Amendments as shields for violence and illegal conduct, Chief Justice Warren's opinion may seem to take an unnecessarily narrow view. But these people are trying to transform freedom of expression into something quite different from its historic, traditional, and legal meaning. Not satisfied with the results of unfettered discussion, they are trying to distort the constitutional underpinning for that great principle into a license for coercion and disruption of the orderly processes of government. Clinging to the language of free speech, they seek to debase the concept by stretching it over inexcusable conduct. They seem to assume that this could be a logical way of expanding free expression, but it would more likely undermine the whole basic principle.

In my opinion, the Supreme Court has rendered a great service to the cause of free expression by divorcing it from violence, obscenity, and illegal conduct. The greatest threat to freedom today is coming, not from an oppressive government, but from individuals and groups who seek use of freedom as a mask for intimidation and anarchy. The court has said in unequivocal language that the First and Fourteenth Amendments are not to be used for this purpose. As Justice Abe Fortas aptly puts it, these amendments guarantee "freedom to speak and freedom of the press—not freedom to club people or to destroy property." [50]

The underlying truth is that these precious freedoms are gems in a constitutional setting. Removed from the framework of an orderly society, they would count for nothing. When everything has been said about the "absolute" nature of these First and Fourteenth Amendment freedoms, the fact remains that the entire Bill of Rights is an appendage to a still more basic charter of government. Individual rights cannot be interpreted in such a way as to cripple the legitimate and essential operations of that government, without exposing the whole structure to the perils of disintegration. And if the structure should give way, the freedoms that we prize so highly would be nothing more than empty words on a piece of parchment.

The right to dissent and to protest against policies favored by the majority is the hallmark of a free society. It must be protected with patience, fairness, and a sincere effort to understand the views of the dissidents or the minority group. But this right to dissent does not carry with it a license to impose the minority view upon the majority. It does not carry with it the privilege of taking the law into one's own hands, of obstructing the processes of governement, of trampling upon the rights of others, or of resorting to violence when persuasion and petitions for redress of grievances fail. Even in an age of sweeping social and political transitions, freedom of expression remains freedom of expression. It is not changed, through some alchemy of wishful thinking, into freedom to do anything a fertile imagination may contrive to make the protests or demands effective.

It will not be surprising if many of the so-called free-expression cases which get into the courts in the next few years involve abuses or distortion of this freedom that cannot be sustained under the constitution. Many judges may find it necessary to do what the Supreme Court did in the draft-card-burning case. If so, some statistical-minded critics may soon be assailing the courts for a reactionary record in handling free-expression cases. Actually, however, the cause of freedom is served as faithfully by rejecting claims that lawless conduct and violence are protected forms of speech, as by striking off the muzzles that some officials like to apply to citizens. The courts must be alert to the evils of anarchy and uncurbed violence, if for no other reason than that such conduct often leads to tyranny and oppression.

Freedom of expression is a dynamic and timeless concept reserved for people who love order and stability as well as liberty. We have reason to be eternally grateful to the men who wrote this principle into the First Amendment and to those who made possible its transfusion into the Fourteenth. But the task of making it a living reality in our day falls entirely upon the present generation. Let us not suppose that we can leave the job solely to the courts, without sorting out the differences between speech and physical coercion in our own minds. Freedom of expression starts with a willingness to live and let live—to argue with words only and not with fists, or bricks, or guns, or knives, or matches. On this centennial of the Fourteenth Amendment, there is no more vital task to which we can dedicate ourselves than the restoration of free expression as a way of life, cleansed from malice and intimidation as well as from lawless actions and violence.

Notes

1. *Gilbert* v. *Minnesota*, 254 U.S. 325 (1920).
2. *Prudential Insurance Co.* v. *Cheek*, 259 U.S. 530 (1922).
3. *Meyer* v. *Nebraska*, 262 U.S. 390 (1923).
4. *Gitlow* v. *New York*, 268 U.S. 652 (1925).
5. *Ibid.*, p. 667.
6. 249 U.S. 47 (1919).
7. See especially *Abrams* v. *United States*, 250 U.S. 616 (1919).
8. *Schenck* v. *United States*, 249 U.S. 47, 52.
9. 283 U.S. 359 (1931).
10. Hughes, *The Supreme Court of the United States*, 165–166 (1928).
11. *Near* v. *Minnesota*, 283 U.S. 697 (1931).
12. *Herndon* v. *Lowry*, 301 U.S. 242 (1937).
13. *Grosjean* v. *American Press Co.*, 297 U.S. 233 (1936).
14. 303 U.S. 444 (1938).
15. *De Jonge* v. *Oregon*, 299 U.S. 353 (1937).
16. *Thornhill* v. *Alabama*, 310 U.S. 88 (1940).
17. 323 U.S. 516 (1945).
18. 337 U.S. 1 (1949).
19. *Ibid.* p. 4.
20. *Ibid.* p. 37.
21. *Feiner* v. *New York*, 340 U.S. 315 (1951).
22. *McLaurin* v. *Greenville*, 385 U.S. 1011 (1967).
23. *Adderley* v. *Florida*, 385 U.S. 39 (1966).
24. Hudon, *Freedom of Speech and Press in America*, 173 (1963).
25. *Communications Ass'n* v. *Douds*, 339 U.S. 382 (1940).
26. *Dennis* v. *United States*, 341 U.S. 494 (1951).
27. 183 F. 2d 201, 212.
28. Hudon, *Freedom of Speech and Press in America*, 174.
29. Chief Justice Warren's James Madison lecture at the New York University School of Law, see *The Great Rights*, 109 (Cahn, ed., 1963).
30. *Abrams* v. *United States*, 250 U.S. 616, 630 (1919) (dissenting opinion).
31. *New York Times Co.* v. *Sullivan*, 376 U.S. 254, 270 (1964).
32. *Bridges* v. *California*, 314 U.S. 252 (1941).
33. See also *Wood* v. *Georgia*, 370 U.S. 375 (1962).
34. *Watkins* v. *United States*, 354 U.S. 178 (1957).
35. 360 U.S. 109 (1959).
36. 365 U.S. 399 (1961).
37. 369 U.S. 431 (1961).
38. *Uphaus* v. *Wyman*, 360 U.S. 72 (1959).
39. *Roth* v. *United States*, 354 U.S. 476, 485 (1957). See Justice Douglas's note No. 4 in his dissenting opinion in *Ginsberg* v. *New York*, 390 U.S. 629, 653 (1968).
40. *Ginzburg* v. *United States*, 383 U.S. 463 (1966).
41. *Mishkin* v. *New York*, 383 U.S. 502 (1966).
42. *Ginsberg* v. *New York*, 390 U.S. 629 (1968).
43. *United States* v. *O'Brien*, 391 U.S. 367 (1968).

44. *NAACP* v. *Button,* 371 U.S. 415, 438 (1963); see also *Sherbert* v. *Verner* 374 U.S. 398, 403 (1963).
45. *NAACP* v. *Button* at p. 444; *NAACP* v. *Alabama ex rel Patterson,* 357 U.S. 449, 464 (1958).
46. *Bates* v. *Little Rock,* 361 U.S. 516, 524 (1960).
47. *Thomas* v. *Collins,* 323 U.S. 516, 530 (1945).
48. *Bates* v. *Little Rock,* 361 U.S. 516, 524 (1960).
49. *Sherbert* v. *Verner,* 374 U.S. 398, 408 (1963).
50. *Reader's Digest,* September, 1968, p. 39.

8

The Amendment and Equality Under Law

Abe Fortas

The 100th anniversary of the Fourteenth Amendment comes at a moment in our history when its substance is again at stake in the seething, roaring conflict of our society.

I do not mean by this that the existence or the words of the Great Amendment are in danger of assault. There are few Americans who would launch a frontal assault upon the century-old text. There are few Americans who would openly declare war upon the basic principle which animates it: the principle that people are entitled to fundamental rights, and they are entitled to them equally.

But as lawyers, judges and historians we know that this is not the level upon which the battle is fought. The battle is fought, as always, as a conflict over the meaning of the great phrases of the amendment—due process, equal protection of the laws, and privileges and immunities of citizens of the United States; and it rages as a controversy over the respective powers of the national and state governments.

The Fourteenth Amendment lends itself to this conflict because it is written in mortal words, and because it was the product of life and of the democratic process. Throughout its century of existence, the Fourteenth Amendment has meant many things to many men. Men of equal integrity, of equal devotion to freedom and liberty and patriotism, have arrived at fundamentally different interpretations of its words and principles. No one familiar with the judicial opinions or the scholarly literature can assert the contrary.

Unhappily, it is not true that the words of the Fourteenth Amendment are clear and precise guides to conclusions and decisions. They are, indeed, as Cardozo put it, "of the greatest generality." [1]

Abe Fortas is a former Associate Justice of the United States Supreme Court.

The broad outline of the intention of the amendment is clear. The first eight amendments to the Constitution—our Bill of Rights—had set forth the great principles of human freedom. But in 1833, the Supreme Court had held that these amendments limited only the federal government and did not apply to the life of the individual as it was affected by the basic agencies of government—the states.[2]

In the Fourteenth Amendment, for the first time, the states were commanded to respect and implement the great principles of human freedom. The amendment carefully and specifically provided not merely for state protection of those rights, but also for national power to secure those rights.

In the Fourteenth Amendment, also for the first time, it was made clear that "the people" of the United States whose rights were protected by the constitution included not just the gentry, not just the white people, but all of the people—at least, that it could not and did not exclude some of the people because they were Negroes. I make this qualification because women and most Indians remained (and to some extent still remain today) constitutional non-persons to whom the Fourteenth Amendment has not been fully extended.

The Fourteenth Amendment was indeed a Revolution. It seemed to mean that the Civil War had achieved its professed humanitarian objective —a goal that most wars profess but rarely attain.

There can be no doubt that those who drafted the Fourteenth Amendment a century ago fully realized that they were writing words of vast scope and comprehensive thrust. They intended to secure fundamental rights for all; they specifically intended that freedmen should enjoy all rights of citizens, equally with those of white persons. So much was firmly, even grimly, certain and clear in their minds. Beyond that, they neither achieved nor claimed perfection. Whatever the motives and purposes of the drafters, the words of the amendment were the product of conflict and compromise of views among diverse legislators. They were a prescription in capsule form—designed by practical men to win acceptance in the political process, however ambiguous the meeting of the minds might be. The sponsors were unyielding on only one point: they were committed to strike at a vast, pervasive and virulent disease—the denial by the former Confederate States of the fundamental and equal rights of the freedmen. To achieve this end, they recognized the need for compromise. It was as a document, full of compromise and uncertainty, that the amendment was candidly presented.

A century of living-experience shows that the technical quality of their work had the virtues of its vices and the vices of its virtues. Its generality and ambiguity invited the erosion and partial nullification that came. They also permitted, however, growth and adaptation to life's changing facts and ethical standards. For as history shows us over and over again, a constitutional precept has the quality of greatness only in proportion to its capacity for growth and development. It has the quality of greatness not because it commands the future, but because it inspires it; because it directs the future towards man's noble aspirations and lays out the guides toward their achievement.

The Fourteenth Amendment is, in fact, the prime example of the famous observation of Justice Holmes:

> [W]hen we are dealing with words that also are a constituent act, like the Constitution of the United States, we must realize that they have called into life a being the development of which could not have been foreseen completely by the most gifted of its begetters. . . . The case before us must be considered in the light of our whole experience, and not merely in that of what was said a hundred years ago.[3]

The growth of this "life of its own," so far as the Fourteenth Amendment is concerned, has included some surprises. An example is, of course, the Supreme Court's inclusion of corporations as beneficiaries of the equal protection and due process clauses—a vital decision which first took the form of a blunt announcement by Chief Justice Waite from the bench in the course of an argument.[4]

At the same time that the court was engaged in this major expansion of the amendment's scope on behalf of the propertied interests, it was involved in a drastic curtailment of its scope with respect to the amendment's intended beneficiaries—the Negroes or freedmen. The story is known to all of us. It has been admirably summed up by Justice Brennan.[5] To many scholars, the surgery seems totally unjustifiable in terms of permissible judicial techniques.

From today's storm-tossed point of history, we can hardly avoid a sigh of regret for what might have been: If the Supreme Court had not emasculated the amendment; if Justice Miller had voted the other way in the *Slaughterhouse* cases [6] and thereby turned the majority around; if the elder Harlan's lone dissent in the *Civil Rights* cases [7] had prevailed; if, as Justice Brennan tells us, the Fourteenth Amendment had not lain substantially dormant as a document of human freedom until at least the 1930's . . . If, on the other hand, the amendment had been faithfully applied as it was intended: to insure by governmental action, national and local, that all men were secure—and secure equally—in their fundamental rights to life, liberty and property; if this had been the course of history, perhaps we would not today be paying a fearful price for the decades of neglect—for the decades of erosion of the Thirteenth, Fourteenth and Fifteenth Amendments.

If this had been the course of history, it is not inconceivable that there would have been a gradual, decent evolution of a *modus vivendi* among free people, instead of the present explosive struggle. But this was not to be. A quiet but pervasive national nullification of the philosophy of those amendments began within a few years of their adoption. Only in the last 30 years, and really only in the past 15 years, has that course been reversed in the direction of reviving the original thrust and intent of the Civil War amendments.

It is indeed paradoxical, in view of the position of the most vociferous critics of today's Court, that the recent decisions with respect to Negro rights are not a departure from, but a return to the original purpose of the amendments. But I think most scholars would agree that this is so. And just as nullification of the Fourteenth Amendment was, I think, a broad national decision, so the move towards revitalization has been made by a wide spectrum of our society. Action has been taken not just in the courts, but by successive presidents, by the Congress, and by a number of state and local governments.

The process has not been confined to validation of the rights of Negroes. The rights of all persons in the nation have been strengthened in accordance with the great prescription of the Fourteenth Amendment. Aliens, women, juveniles, all persons who must rely on welfare payments—all of these have been among the specific beneficiaries.

The rights and privileges of persons caught up in the criminal process of the states have been asserted, largely by means of incorporation in the due process clause of most of the basic standards of the federal Bill of Rights. The rights, privileges and immunities of persons to speak and publish and criticize public officers—to combine and assemble and petition —have been confirmed as fundamental and comprehensive, secure against the states and private persons as well as the federal government.

Perhaps of the greatest importance has been the powerful thrust towards insisting upon equality under law. Equality, of course, in a constitutional or legal sense, means more than the specific provision guaranteeing equal protection of the laws; equality includes, for example, the right of an indigent person to counsel—vindicated under the due process clause of the Fourteenth Amendment. It includes services which the state must make available to the indigent to guarantee him a fair trial—such as a transcript of evidence.[8] These cases affirm that in order to achieve a major due process objective—for example, the right to counsel—the state must furnish the indigent free facilities which it will not furnish to the non-indigent.

Indeed, until the last 15 years, the major progress towards equality in law has not taken place under the equal protection clause, but by force of other provisions. Regrettably, perhaps, the privileges and immunities clause of the Fourteenth Amendment has not been available for this process because of the drastic surgery perpetrated on it in the *Slaughterhouse* cases.

As a result of that surgery, the guaranty to all citizens of the privileges and immunities of citizens of the United States became nothing more than a shadow and appendage of the supremacy clause, rather than a guaranty, as many supposed, that all of the states would protect the "fundamental" or "natural rights" of all citizens within their borders.

The due process clause has, until recently, been the principal instrument for achieving equality. The practical application of the due process clause to ban coerced confessions has, in a sense, tended to raise the rights of the poor and friendless to the standard long assured better-off—or better advised—citizens. Indeed, not only the Fourteenth Amendment, but also the First Amendment, has been invoked in situations where the effect was to equalize the rights or bargaining power of the disadvantaged in our society. In the picketing cases, in the group litigation cases, and in the many cases involving the protection of the rights of religious sects to engage in door-to-door solicitation, the court has been immediately concerned not with equality but with other constitutional values, but the effect of its decisions has been to help those with less political, economic and social power.

There is still much to be done. But, without doubt, the last 15 years— since 1954—have witnessed a great thrust towards the realization of equality of right for all in this nation. The causes of this forward thrust are not to be found in the personnel of the Supreme Court, nor do they consist solely or even primarily of the decisions of that tribunal. The drive for equal rights is a product, a part—a subtly interrelated part, to be sure—of a pervasive social movement. The social causes, I think, are to be found in the developing idealism of our people; in the consciences and the ethical and religious training of the people of this country and their maturing appreciation of the political and humanistic ideals of our institutions; in the achievement by Negroes of some progress through the measure of education and opportunity our society has made available to them; and in the levelling effect of military service. Other factors that have powerfully stimulated the process include the example of the African liberation movements, and the successful onslaught upon white colonialism; the economic dislocations of the rural areas of this country, and, particularly, of the poorest part of the rural population, largely Negro; and the urban migration of the Negro. It has also been of great importance that, for the first time, forceful organization and leadership arose among the Negroes themselves; and for the first time, effective, expert, and specialized legal representation was available—mostly through the NAACP and its lawyers of whom I would especially mention Mr. Thurgood Marshall—now Justice Marshall.

This broad movement goes beyond legal rights. It is a drive towards realization of full equality of position in all respects. The drive for equality is a basic theme in the story of man. In 1835, in de Tocqueville's famous commentary, he said that the passion for equality in democracies is "ardent, insatiable, incessant, invincible." "The nations of our time," he said, "cannot prevent the conditions of men from becoming equal. . . ." De Tocqueville, however, emphasized a point which needs emphasis today. He said that "it depends upon [men] themselves whether the principle of equality is to lead them to servitude or freedom, to knowledge or barbarism, to prosperity or wretchedness." [9]

Today, in this nation, this is a real not theoretical choice. There is the danger that the fierce struggle for equality will seriously damage the very institutions which prompt and permit the aspiration itself—that equality, if it is achieved, will be equality in a crippled and degraded society; or— more likely—that the struggle itself will be so fierce that it will set in motion counter forces of repression and reaction. This is the formidable danger that we face.

We must, I emphasize, clearly distinguish between the concept of equality, or egalitarianism, in its total and awesome generality, and equality of right as a constitutional doctrine. Our constitution insists upon equality of right—equal rights under law; equal protection by law; equal access to public facilities and equal opportunity to participate in government. These are the principles—the basic commands. The specific form, shape and content of the institutions and practices of society that carry out those commands are not constitutionally mandated. Elements in society other than the courts should determine these institutions and practices—provided (and it is a big proviso) that they faithfully, truly and honestly incorporate the basic principles made mandatory by our constitution. The judicial task is and should be essentially negative, to protect fundamental principle. The courts, I think, properly refuse to prescribe *how* the constitutional commands shall be carried out *except* where the legislatures have so completely failed to act that the courts, in effect, must cope with a default situation—a bankruptcy.

These defaults, when they occur, are a breakdown not only of the substantive scheme of the Constitution of the United States—a failure to protect human rights. They are also neglects of constitutionally defined institutional responsibilities. They place upon the courts a responsibility which they should not have for, as I have said elsewhere, courts are not the only repositories of responsibility for constitutional principle. They are its ultimate guardians; but the duty of faithfulness to constitutional command in shaping the institutions and practices of society—the obligation to fulfill in practice the promise of the constitution's "great generalities," in Cardozo's phrase—rests initially and pervasively upon the shoulders of the legislative and executive branches of our government. It is indeed sad and regrettable when their refusal or inability to conform with basic constitutional principles compels the courts, in effect, to exercise receivership powers in order to secure compliance with constitutional mandate.

Long ago, we were committed to the attainment of equality for all. This is a choice that was made centuries ago in our religious heritage. It is a choice that was renewed in the struggle that produced Magna Carta, in the long battle of the English to win acceptance of the rule of law and its applicability equally to all men, and for the independence of the judiciary.

The philosophical lineage of the doctrine of the equal rights of men traces to the Bible; to Zeno and the Stoics; to Cicero and Seneca; and most of all, to John Locke. The choice was reaffirmed by the founders of our government, and incorporated in our Declaration of Independence and our Constitution. The French Revolution gave it a further dimension; and then finally, the choice was again written into our institutions in the indelible blood of the Civil War. This took the form of the great reconstruction enactments: constitutional amendments, civil rights laws and laws giving the federal courts vast new powers to see that the federal constitution and laws were enforced.

But men utter and use the words of equality within the framework of their own moral and political conceptions. The recital in the Declaration of Independence is marvelously inspiring: that all men are created equal and that they are endowed by their Creator with certain inalienable rights among which are life, liberty and the pursuit of happiness. But the sad truth is that for that age, "all men" did not mean *all* men. It did not include slaves. It did not really include all freedmen, or women, or Indians. I doubt that it was really a declaration of attitude towards paupers or vagabonds or aliens.

The Articles of Confederation were a bit more precise. In the "privileges and immunities" clause, the draftsmen were careful to limit coverage to the "free inhabitants of each of these States," and expressly to exclude "paupers, vagabonds and fugitives from justice."

Rhetoric again overwhelmed fact in the drafting of the constitution itself. The United States Constitution, as you know, recited that it was established by "the people" in order to "secure the Blessings of Liberty to ourselves and our Posterity." But clearly, the people did not mean all of the people. It clearly was not a commitment to liberty for slaves or indentured servants. Certainly, as a look at any of the Slave Codes of the 18th and 19th century shows—even the one covering the District of Columbia, the federal enclave—the marvelous guarantees of the Bill of Rights (although many of them were phrased in terms of "persons" or "people") did not apply to slaves. They were non-persons. They were property or "things," not persons. They were not among "the people" who had the right peaceably to assemble and to petition for a redress of grievances, or the right to be secure in their persons, houses, papers and effects against unreasonable searches and seizures, or the right to due process of law, counsel, jury trial, and so on.

There was no doubt that the outcome of the Civil War commanded a change in this basic conception. But what change? The Thirteenth Amendment, effective December 18, 1865, abolished slavery and involuntary servitude. But the denial of equality in law to the slaves and the freedmen continued; and so the Fourteenth Amendment was drafted, submitted by Congress to the States, ratified, and became effective July 28, 1868. Then, in order to protect the voting rights of the freedmen, the Fifteenth Amendment was proposed, and was ratified as of March 30, 1870.

It seems to me that the core of the great constitutional amendments may be simply stated: in various and, so it would seem, entirely comprehensive ways, it was sought to assure that all "persons" would be treated equally under the law; that the rights of life, liberty and property would be safeguarded; and that the Congress, as well as the states, would have the power and the duty to enact laws necessary to secure these ends. But equality was not to come for many years.

Wars and social revolutions produce perishable fruit; and so, a few years after adoption of the great amendments, there began the long and discouraging history of erosion to which I have referred—an erosion based upon state refusal to implement the amendments and upon Supreme Court decisions, beginning with the *Slaughterhouse* and *Civil Rights* cases, that cut away the bone and sinew of the amendments.

For most of the members of that Court, and through the following decades, the passions of the abolitionist movement and of the Civil War had cooled. A great moral, political and ethical point had been made, and it had been won on the battlefield. The catharsis of the victory of the cause of Union and Emancipation was succeeded by the often sordid and petty politics of Reconstruction.

It is not surprising that these events ended in a sharp swing against vigorous assertion of the principles and policy of the Reconstruction Amendments. So, until about 1935, the history of the equal protection clause shows a general retrenchment from the advanced posts of the framers of the constitution.

The process of judicial erosion of the great amendments is a fascinating study. A bold stroke, in the *Slaughterhouse* cases, cut the heart from the privileges and immunities clause and reduced it to little more than a shadow and appendage of the supremacy clause. Another bold stroke, in the *Civil Rights* cases, reduced to a whisper the mighty words of Section 5 of the Fourteenth Amendment authorizing the Congress to enforce it. It was held that the rights involved—essentially, those to life, liberty and property—were derived only from the states; that it was only in the state's police power that constitutional authority to protect them could be found; and that the federal government had no power to legislate to carry out the purposes of the amendment: for example, to require equal accommodation of blacks and whites in public places. Even the more or less explicit prohibitions of the amendment—prohibitions against denying equal protection or due process—it was held applied only where state, as distinguished from private, action was involved.

This process reduced to a limited office the equal protection as well as the due process clauses. State action could be challenged in the courts; but the possibility of such challenge was more theoretical than real because of the attitude of the courts, and because of the unavailability of skilled counsel willing and able to litigate the issues.

Even in the full cry of retreat from the intended thrust of the amendment, however, there was fairly general agreement that equality was, indeed, its basic objective. In *Plessy* v. *Ferguson* (1896),[10] the Court stated:

> The object of the amendment was undoubtedly to enforce the absolute equality of the two races before the law. . . . But in the nature of things it could not have been intended to abolish distinctions based upon color, or to enforce social, as distinguished from political equality, or a commingling of the two races upon terms unsatisfactory to either. Laws permitting, and even requiring, their separation in places where they are liable to be brought into contact do not necessarily imply the inferiority of either race to the other, and have been generally, if not universally, recognized as within the competency of the state legislatures in the exercise of the legislative power even by courts of States where the political rights of the colored race have been longest and most earnestly enforced.

Accordingly, in the Court's view, "absolute equality before the law" had been established. But it was not quite absolute. *Plessy* indicated that Negroes might have an equal right to the use of public highways and common carriers, but not to their undifferentiated use.

Similarly, the jury cases established at an early date that Negroes could not be forced to defend themselves before a jury from which, by statute or systematic action of state officials, Negroes were excluded. It soon developed, however, that absent a statute, or an overt pattern of official action excluding Negroes from jury service, the Supreme Court was rarely prepared to find a denial of equal rights to Negroes.

I think that most modern scholars agree with the conclusions stated by Robert J. Harris, that "the opinion of the Court in *Plessy* v. *Ferguson* is a compound of bad logic, bad history, bad sociology and bad constitutional law." "Prior to the *Plessy* case," Harris says, "the Court uniformly regarded all racial discrimination perpetrated by a state or its agencies as invidious and void regardless of its alleged reasonableness." [11] Harris concludes that when *Plessy* was reversed 58 years later, in *Brown* v. *Board of Education*,[12] it might properly have been overturned not merely on the ground that time had washed out its foundation, but also on the basis that it was itself a departure from precedent and wrong when made.

Congress, encouraged by the Court's hostile decisions, ignored the implied command of the Civil War amendments that it enact legislation to enforce their provisions. Indeed, substantial parts of the post-Civil War legislation were repealed, while surviving provisions went largely unenforced.

Then, finally, the tide began to turn. Beginning with the great depression, and with the Nazi exploitation of racism, profound changes in our national attitude toward racism occurred. The change was first manifest in the criminal law.

When the Scottsboro prosecutions came along in the 1930's, the Court and the Nation were ready to move forward. Perhaps, it would be more accurate to say that they were ready to move backward, towards the original purpose of the Fourteenth Amendment and the equal protection clause.

The Scottsboro prosecutions inspired nationwide awareness of the gross denial of justice to Negroes that sometimes occurred in criminal cases. In 1932, Justice Sutherland wrote the opinion in one of the Scottsboro cases: *Powell* v. *Alabama*,[13] a landmark case on the right of counsel. Later cases involved the exclusion of Negroes from juries. Along with them, however, other cases involving the right to counsel and coerced confessions disclosed brutal mistreatment of Negroes. The Court had begun the use of the due process clause of the Fourteenth Amendment to insist upon fair and equal treatment of Negro defendants.

However, it is not surprising that vast social changes should first appear in the criminal process. As Winston Churchill reminded us many years ago: "The mood and temper of the public in regard to the treatment of crime and criminals is one of the most unfailing tests of civilization of any country."

Here is the point at which the violence, the unrest, the unsatisfied demands, the hidden vices of a society come to surface. Here is the point at which the strength of a society and its commitment to civilized values are under greatest pressure. Here is the point at which there is the constant test of whether the society is willing to and can solve its problems of discipline and order by civilized and decent methods. And here is the point at which the surge of a society's progress towards justice, equality and humanity may first become evident.

But these early criminal cases involving Negro defendants were important far beyond the criminal law. They reflected a change in the Court's approach to the equal protection problem; and they were a sort of workshop which led lawyers and groups including the NAACP to go beyond the criminal process to mount a litigation attack on other forms of inequality.

Apart from the criminal law cases, the early judicial milestones along the road to equal rights were achieved in the 1940's: the primary election cases in 1944; [14] the restrictive covenant cases beginning in 1948; [15] the cases breathing life into unrepealed but dormant sections of the early civil rights legislation; [16] and the cases forbidding segregation on public conveyances in interstate commerce, first, on statutory grounds. [17]

Hand in hand with these specific decisions, there had been basic changes in doctrinal statements by the Supreme Court and individual Justices. As early as 1921, Chief Justice Taft, in *Truax* v. *Corrigan*, [18] had uttered the words, then more prophecy than description, that due process "tends to secure equality of law in the sense that it makes a required minimum of protection for everyone's right of life, liberty, and property, which the Congress or the legislature may not withhold," and that the equal protection clause was a guaranty against "undue favor . . . or class privilege . . . and [against] hostile discrimination or the oppression of inequality."

Then, in the 1940's the Court affirmed the power of the Congress to enforce the Fourteenth and Fifteenth Amendments, in contrast to the old *Civil Rights* cases. The definition of the state action necessary to bring discrimination within the scope of the Fourteenth Amendment was eased.

Indeed, the story of the post-1935 period has been captioned by one writer, echoing the conclusions of many others, as The Court Returns to the Constitution. [19]

Inevitably and inexorably, then, the Supreme Court and the nation approached the watershed. In the nation, Negro demands for equality of right—an end to discrimination on the basis of race—were being asserted more and more vigorously and effectively. New and more aggressive leaders were arising. More and more, their demands met with sympathetic response and corrective action. The Second World War and the Korean conflict, in which Negro soldiers participated in large numbers, provided powerful impetus. President Truman ordered desegregation of the armed forces.

Eventually, the crisis point came in the public school cases. Contrary to the general impression, the death of *Plessy* v. *Ferguson* was not sudden. In reality, *Plessy* was not killed by *Brown*. *Brown* administered the *coup de grace* to a badly wounded doctrine.

The first wounds were at normally conservative hands. In 1938, Chief Justice Hughes wrote the Supreme Court's 7–2 opinion in *Missouri* ex rel. *Gaines* v. *Canada*. [20] In 1950, Chief Justice Vinson wrote for the unanimous court in *Sweatt* v. *Painter* [21] and in *McLaurin* v. *Oklahoma State Regents*. [22] These cases carefully avoided overruling *Plessy*, but they made its end inevitable. They ruled that separate facilities for Negroes could be justified only if they were actually equal, but the determination as to equality was to be made on the basis of careful and realistic factual analysis, taking into account, not the customs of the area, but both tangible and intangible factors. For example, in *Sweatt* v. *Painter,* the denial of equality was confirmed by the presence at the white law school, but not at the school for Negroes, of a chapter of the Order of the Coif; by the existence of a law review; by comparing the size and consequence of the faculty and the alumni. And the *McLaurin* case made it clear that if Negroes were admitted to the white facility, discrimination against them (by segregation in class) would not be permissible.

So when the school segregation cases came before the Court during the 1952 Term, the result had been foreshadowed. The message of *Sweatt* and *McLaurin* was that the career of the "separate but equal" doctrine was, in reality, at an end. The end came in 1954 in *Brown* v. *Board of Education.* The unanimous court held that segregation in public schools violates the equal protection clause. The Court did not claim to rely on the specific intent of the framers of the Fourteenth Amendment, which it called "at best . . . inconclusive." [23] It did not even call as its witness early precedents which the 1896 decision in *Plessy* ignored. Instead, it relied primarily upon the vastly changed conditions: equal protection of the educational rights of the Negro in 1954, it held, requires something more than would have been necessary in 1896, when educational facilities were relatively elementary and when sophisticated education itself was not essential to the State and the individual as it is today. On this candid basis, the Supreme Court, through Chief Justice Warren, concluded that "in the field of public education the doctrine of 'separate but equal' has no place. Separate educational facilities are inherently unequal." [24]

Closely analyzed, *Brown* might seem to be nothing more than a judicial rejection of the method of compliance approved by *Plessy,* with the Fourteenth Amendment's command that the States must furnish Negroes equal rights in public education. However, of course its significance was far greater. It rejected the basic premise upon which the white and especially the Southern establishment had rebuilt its life and institutions after the Civil War. It struck its blow against the institutions of the South and the white establishment at its most sensitive point—the physical separation of the races.

So, the revitalization of the principles of the three great amendments was in full swing. Equality—in the full sense of the *Brown* case—for all public facilities was constitutionally required. Equality of access to the polls and to full participation in the governmental process at all levels, was compulsory.

Congress joined in, with the Civil Rights Act of 1957, the first civil rights legislation in more than 70 years (that is, since 1875), and then with the Civil Rights Acts of 1960 and of 1964, the Voting Rights Act of 1965, and the Civil Rights Act of 1968.

Churches, the military, hundreds of private employers, all joined the move for equal access and equalization of opportunity. At times, it seemed that there was under way a vast national crusade to reverse a century of neglect and discrimination, and finally to achieve the protections and equality of rights to which this nation solemnly pledged itself 100 years ago.

But the bitter and formidable opposition was and is there. The revolution of principle was vast and thoroughgoing; but the revolution of fact is still at the threshold.

Indeed, at this moment in our celebration of the Fourteenth Amendment, one cannot avoid thinking that perhaps there is a sad parallel between then and now: Is the curve of events, this time, to retrace that which followed the Civil War? The great amendments were followed by a few years of fulfillment and many years of negation. Within a few years after 1868, the Fourteenth Amendment's commitment to fundamental and equal rights for all was reduced to a feeble promise of maybe, sometimes and in some respects.

Beginning most dramatically in 1954, our generation, like that of the post-Civil War period, has reaffirmed the principle of equal rights for all —including Negroes. The promise of equality of treatment has again been made—by Congress, by institutions of our society and by the courts.

Will this new commitment—repeated after a century of negation—be kept? Will it remain and flourish, or will it, too, become words of limited value, currency of dubious worth?

The surge for revitalizing the principle of equal civil and political rights for the Negro has affected a substantial area of national interests beyond those of the Negro. The new forward surge of constitutional concern for the rights of all people, and not just the fortunate, has been reflected in legislation and court decisions designed to assure equality of rights to the defense and fairness in the criminal process: the right to counsel, despite poverty; the indigent's right to appeal a conviction, equally with his more fortunate fellow; and the right to some measure of protection in the interrogation process, that the modest *Miranda* [25] procedures and other cases in the field provide.

Then came the reapportionment or so-called one-man-one-vote cases, as another product of the awakening of the giant force of the Fourteenth Amendment's command for equal rights. Again, the basic premise of these cases is simple and indisputable, and it had long been reflected in court decisions. No duly qualified citizen may be deprived of his vote, and each man's vote is entitled to equal weight.

However, there have grown up in this nation hundreds of arrangements which have the effect of giving different consequences to individual votes. Usually these take the form of the creation of election districts or units, each of which is entitled to one representative in the legislative body, although they differ substantially in the number of people composing the units. In the famous case of *Baker* v. *Carr,* [26] decided in 1962, the Court, in the name of the constitutional mandate for equal rights, sounded the end for these schemes. Its reasoning, it may be said, is based upon the court's statement in *Yick Wo* v. *Hopkins,* [27] decided in 1886, that the political franchise is "a fundamental political right, because preservative of all rights." If equal rights are to be guaranteed, as the Fourteenth Amendment commands, then, the Court reasoned, each man's vote must be of equal weight, and its equal force must not be impaired by districting, by the county unit system or any other device.

It has been suggested that the use of the equal protection clause of the Fourteenth Amendment in the representation cases must be considered in quite a different light from its revitalization and use in the cases involving discrimination on the basis of color. The racial decisions, it is said, are clearly within the original and specific purpose of the amendment. On the other hand, the representation cases, however appropriately decided, are not within the specific purpose of the framers of the amendment. In short, the rotten-borough system, they say, was not one of the evils to which the framers specifically addressed themselves.

I think that is correct. The voting representation cases reflect another aspect of constitutional jurisprudence: that the words and the principle of a constitutional provision have direct impact and application, apart from the specific object of the provisions. Like the use of the clause in the interest of corporate property, or perhaps in cases involving aliens or Mexicans or members of the armed forces, the representation cases demonstrate this fact. The point, of course, recalls again Justice Holmes's observation that the words of a constitution call "into life a being, the development of which could not have been foreseen completely by the most gifted of its begetters."

The revitalization of the Fourteenth Amendment that has occurred in the past generation or so has been an intensely interacting part of a gigantic social movement. It has been a contributing cause, as well as an effect of the mighty accomplishments of our time. The great command of the Fourteenth Amendment—equality under the rule of law, protecting the fundamental rights of humanity—is, after all, basic in our religious and ethical ideals.

Each forward thrust towards its full realization is progress on the long road of man to a truly civilized state. The road is not easy; it is bitterly obstructed by those who lift their eyes not upward with high devotion and hope, but backwards and downwards with hate and prejudice.

Today there is every indication that the century's anniversary of the Landmark of Liberty will usher in a new and savage struggle between freedom's believers and its destroyers. I have faith that freedom will survive. I have faith that the Fourteenth Amendment's great principles will flourish. But they will resist impending onslaught only as we have the courage to understand and acknowledge their meaning; only as we have the courage to acknowledge their ambiguities and uncertainties as well as their positive commands; only as we understand our history; and only as we have the faith and the courage to defend freedom and justice and equality, and to stand, steadfastly and unmoving, against those who, in whatever guise, seek nullification of the great principles of our American Constitution.

Notes

1. *Selected Writings of Benjamin Nathan Cardozo* 137 (Hall ed. 1947).
2. *Barron* v. *Baltimore,* 7 Pet. 243 (U.S. 1833).
3. *Missouri* v. *Holland,* 252 U.S. 416, 433 (1920).
4. *Santa Clara County* v. *Southern Pac. R. Co.,* 118 U.S. 394, 396 (1886).
5. *Supra* p. 2.
6. 16 Wall. 36 (U.S. 1873).
7. 109 U.S. 3 (1883).
8. *Gideon* v. *Wainright,* 372 U.S. 335 (1963); *Griffin* v. *Illinois,* 351 U.S. 12 (1956).
9. Tocqueville, *Democracy in America* 102 (Bradley, ed., 1954).
10. 163 U.S. 537, 544 (1896).
11. Harris, *The Quest for Equality* (1960).
12. 347 U.S. 483 (1954).
13. 287 U.S. 45 (1932).
14. *Smith* v. *Allwright,* 321 U.S. 649 (1944).
15. *Shelley* v. *Kraemer,* 334 U.S. 1 (1948).
16. Culminating in *United States* v. *Guest,* 383 U.S. 745 (1966).
17. *Morgan* v. *Virginia,* 328 U.S. 373 (1946).
18. 257 U.S. 312, 332–3 (1921).
19. Jackson, *The Struggle for Judicial Supremacy* 197 (1941).
20. 305 U.S. 337 (1938).
21. 339 U.S. 629 (1950).
22. 339 U.S. 637 (1950).
23. 347 U.S. at 489.
24. *Id.* at 495.
25. *Miranda* v. *Arizona,* 384 U.S. 436 (1966).
26. 369 U.S. 186 (1962).
27. 118 U.S. 356 (1886).

9

Constitutional Developments
in Britain

Lord Denning

It is a privilege for me to come to this important centenary and to speak for England, which is, as the poet says, a land where:

> A man may speak the thing he will,
> A land of settled government,
> A land of just and old renown,
> Where Freedom broadens slowly down
> From precedent to precedent.

When I think of the criticism which is sometimes directed at the Supreme Court of the United States today, I recall the incident in my own Court in London when a lady threw books at us. As she was urged towards the door she was heard to say: "I congratulate your Lordships on your coolness under fire." So today I would say: "I congratulate the Justices of the Supreme Court on their coolness under fire."

At home I have a book called "Sources of our Liberties" which I value. It was given to me by the President of the American Bar Association. It gives the historic documents on which the American Constitution is based. It starts over 750 years ago, with the Great Charter which was sealed at Runnymede. It finishes 100 years ago, with the amendment which we celebrate today. It traces the steps by which we gained our freedom. Yet this freedom of ours is not a freedom which allows everyone to do as he likes. Freedom is poles apart from license. Freedom, to be worth anything, is freedom under the law. The emphasis throughout our constitutions is not only on the liberty of the subject. It is also on the rule of law. If our society is to survive, law and order must be maintained. It must be maintained by the will of all right-thinking folk.

Lord Denning is Master of the Rolls.

On October 2, 1968, I went to Westminster Abbey at the opening of the Legal Year. As the prayer was said for the judges, I felt that we had remembered that part which asks that judges should "clear the innocent" but we have forgotten the part which adds that they should "convict and punish the guilty." When we see mobs of students, or others, acting in lawless fashion, disrupting the lives of thousands, I would recall the words of Rudyard Kipling:

> Whenever mob or monarch lays
> Too rude a hand on English ways,
> A whisper wakes, the shudder plays
> Across the reeds at Runnymede.

Those words are for you as for me, for the Great Charter is our joint inheritance. It was on Monday June 15, 1215, that John, King of England, met the barons in "the meadow which is called Runnymede between Windsor and Staines." It is there that one of my predecessors, as Master of the Rolls, wrote down in the Latin script the words that have come down the centuries. Its effect on succeeding generations has been due, not so much to the specific remedies which it provided, but to the language in which it was couched. Here we have set down the guarantee of freedom under the law:

> No freeman shall be taken, imprisoned, disseised, outlawed, banished, or in any way destroyed, nor will we proceed against him or prosecute him, except by the lawful judgment of his peers and by the law of the land.

Immediately following it in the Charter is the guarantee of the impartial administration of justice:

> To no one will we sell, to no one will we deny or delay, right or justice.

Sir Edward Coke, 400 years later, gave this commentary on the Charter:

> Upon this Charter, as out of a root, many fruitful branches of the Law of England are sprung. . . . As the gold-finer will not out of the dust, threads, or shreds of gold, let pass the least crumb, in respect of the excellency of the metal; so ought not the learned reader to let pass any syllable of this law, in respect of the excellency of the matter.

It was in Coke's time that your forefathers set foot here and brought the laws of England with them, including the Great Charter and all the others. They upheld its principles far better than we who were left behind, and 100 years ago, in an amendment to the constitution, they used words redolent of the Charter itself—words which we recall with gratitude today:

> Nor shall any State deprive any person of life, liberty or property
> without due process of law, nor deny to any person within its jurisdic-
> tion the equal protection of its laws.

Just a few simple English words, but full of meaning. Much study has
been spent upon them—much said, much written. I will not venture to
comment here on the very important decisions that have been given
on those words. All I would do is to show how these selfsame principles
have been developed in England. We are perhaps fortunate in that we
have no written constitution. Parliament can change any law. It can do
anything, we say, except make a man a woman or a woman a man. We
have had to change our most fundamental concepts in order to meet the
needs of the time. It has been done by Parliament, not by the judges, for
we think that judges should not get involved in political controversy. It
was Lord Macaulay who said: "The history of England is emphatically
the history of progress. It is the history of a constant movement of the
public mind, of a constant change in the constitutions of a great Society."

Let me give some illustrations by looking at the past and then at the
present. First, the rule of law itself. Lord Coke, 360 years ago, stood firm
for the rule of law against the encroachments of the King. It is recorded in
the 12th volume of Coke's reports, page 63, in the case of "Prohibitions
del Roy." It was on a Sunday, November 10, 1608, that King James I
called the judges together and claimed the right to decide cases himself in
his royal person. He called to witness Bancroft, Archbishop of Canter-
bury, in his support. The Archbishop said: "This is clear in divinity; such
authority, doubtless, belongs to the King by the word of God in the
Scripture." To which it was answered by Coke, in the presence and with
the clear consent, he says, of all the judges of England: "The King in his
own person cannot adjudge any case, but this ought to be determined in
a Court of Justice, according to the law and custom of England." The
King replied, "My lords, I always thought, and by my soul I have often
heard the boast, that your English law was founded upon reason. If that
be so, why have not I and others reason as well as you the Judges?" To
which Coke replied:

> True it is, please Your Majesty, that God has endowed Your Majesty
> with excellent science as well as great gifts of nature: but Your Majesty
> will allow us to say, with all reverence, that you are not learned in
> the laws of this your realm of England. The law is an art which re-
> quires long study and experience before that a man can obtain to the
> cognizance of it. The law is the golden met-wand and measure to try
> the causes of Your Majesty's subjects, and it is by the law that Your
> Majesty is protected in safety and in peace.

King James was greatly offended by being thus answered. He said: "Then I am to be under the law. It is treason to affirm it." Coke, in reply, quoted Bracton, a judge in the reign of Henry III. "Thus wrote Bracton: 'The King is under no man, save under God and the law.'" That one sentence is the watchword under which Parliament and the lawyers waged the Civil War.

It is said that, despite the resistance of Coke, King James did try a case himself and afterwards said: "I could get on very well after hearing one side, but after hearing both sides, I know not what way to decide."

Yet, the statement of Bracton, "The King is under no man, save under God and the law," remains true today: except that it reads, "The executive Government is under no man save under God and the law." This was shown by a recent case when the government departments claimed to have a special privilege—Crown Privilege—by which they could prevent the courts from looking at departmental papers. A police cadet was accused of theft by his superior, the Police Superintendent. He was acquitted by a jury. He then sued the superintendent for malicious prosecution. The reports which the superintendent had made were of the greatest relevance to prove or disprove malicious prosecution, but the attorney-general came to the Court and forbade the superintendent to produce them. However, the House of Lords held that the judges could look at them to see if they should be produced or not. The House looked at them and ordered them to be produced. In so doing, they had to depart from an earlier precedent in the House itself—thus mitigating the rigour of the doctrine of *stare decisis*— and they also held that the government departments were under the rule of law. They were forced to produce the documents.

Now for another illustration. Time was when there were grand juries in England. These were made up of the gentlemen of the county. They considered the evidence against every man accused of serious crime, and decided whether he should be put on trial or not. The oath told them their task. It endured through the centuries in words which impressed all who heard them: "You shall diligently inquire and true presentment make, of all such matters and things as shall be given you in charge or shall otherwise come to your knowledge. The King's counsel, your fellows', and your own you shall keep secret: You shall present no person from envy, hatred or malice; nor shall you leave anyone unpresented through fear, favour, affection or reward, or the hope or promise thereof; but you shall present all things truly, as they come to your knowledge, according to the best of your skill and understanding. So help you God!"

So the Grand Jury were there to see that the law was enforced. Those who offended were to be brought to trial. But at the same time no man was to be unjustly accused. Your forefathers rated it so highly that they wrote it down in the Constitution of the United States that "No person shall be held to answer for a capital, or otherwise infamous crime, unless on a presentment or indictment of a Grand Jury."

In England, grand juries have disappeared. I recall them coming back into court and returning "A true bill" or "No true bill." But they have been abolished these 40 years, for they had outlived their usefulness. The enforcement of the law is now left to the police. The chief constable decides whether or not a person should be accused of an offense. His officers take the statements from the witnesses and place them before an examining magistrate. The magistrate decides whether the person is to be committed for trial or not. Hardly ever is there a private prosecution.

A great responsibility is thus placed on the police, raising grave constitutional issues. Are they the servants of the executive government? Can a minister of the Crown give them directions whether to prosecute or not for an offense? The answer is emphatically no. The police force is independent of the executive. It is for them to investigate offenses. It is in their discretion whether to prosecute or not, but how can we be sure that they do their duty? How can we know that they "present all things truly" as they ought to do? The question was asked and answered by the Court of Appeal in 1968. Gaming clubs were springing up where men played roulette with a zero, and other games for high stakes. London was becoming a gambler's paradise, more notorious than Las Vegas. The promoters made huge profits. Grave evils were attendant on it. Thugs and strong-arm men used violence. Even murder was known to follow. Yet the police did not prosecute the clubs, they stood idly by. A private citizen complained to the courts. He sought a *mandamus* against the Commissioner of Police commanding him to do his duty. The commissioner admitted that he had issued orders that, as a matter of policy, the police were not to keep observation on clubs unless specially authorized. The commissioner said that the law was too uncertain for him to take action. The Court of Appeal held that it was the duty of the police to investigate and to prosecute when the evidence justified it, and that this duty could be enforced by the Courts of Law. This constitutional principle is thus established: The police are independent of the executive, but they are subject to the law. We can say to them, as we said to the Grand Jury: "You shall present all things truly, as they come to your knowledge, and you shall in no wise fail therein." In consequence, many of the clubs have been prosecuted and convicted. Their illegalities have been curbed. The rule of law may yet prevail.

Take next, trial by jury. At the time when my forefathers—and yours—came to settle here, they brought with them the most English institution of all—trial by jury. No man was to be found guilty except by the verdict of 12 of his fellowmen. Whenever a man was arraigned for felony and pleaded Not Guilty, the Clerk of Assize asked him: "How will you be tried?" He replied "By God and my country." Then he was put in charge of the jury. The clerk said to them, "To this charge he has pleaded Not Guilty and put himself upon his country, which country you are." When the jury came to give their verdict, it had to be unanimous. The clerk asked them, "How say you? Do you find the prisoner Guilty or Not Guilty?" If the foreman replied "Guilty," the clerk followed with the question, "Is that the verdict of you all?" The foreman answered, "It is." Likewise with civil actions. At common law these were all tried by a judge with a jury, and the verdict had to be unanimous. Unanimity was settled just 600 years ago. When the Judges of Assize went to Northampton, the jury were divided, 11 to 1. The judge told the one that he would commit him to prison unless he agreed with the others. He replied: "I would rather die in prison than give a verdict against my conscience." Thereupon the judge accepted the verdict of the 11. But the case was taken before all the judges in London. They held that the verdict of the 11 was no verdict, because no man was bound to give a verdict against his conscience. They added a word of advice to the judge. They said that he ought to have carried the jurors with him round the circuit in a wagon until they were agreed! That last sentence shows how the judges used to ensure unanimity. They kept the jury without food or drink until they were agreed. It also shows how they ensured that there was no bribery or corruption of the jurors. The jury were kept together from the beginning of the case till the end. No one was allowed to talk to them except the bailiff, and he only to ask them whether they were agreed or not.

The judges also used strong measures against jurors. They claimed to be able to commit the jurors to prison if they gave a perverse verdict, or if they disobeyed the directions of the presiding judge on a point of law. However, that claim was defeated by the jurors who tried William Penn and William Meade, the Quakers. You will know it better than I do. The Quakers were charged with unlawful assembly because they had preached before 200 people at Gracechurch Street in the City of London. The Recorder directed the jury that the Quakers were guilty. They refused so to find them. He kept them that night without food or drink or candlelight. He kept them the whole of the next day, and the next night. Still they refused to find them guilty. On the morning of the third day, he required each of the jurors to give his verdict separately. The foreman, Edmund Bushell, gave his first. He found the Quakers "Not Guilty." So did they all. The Recorder was furious. He said they had been guilty of contempt of court, because they had disobeyed his direction in point of law. He fined them 40 marks apiece. And when they did not pay, he committed them to prison. They brought their writ of *habeas corpus* before the King's Judges. They held that no judge had any right to fine or imprison a jury for disobeying his direction in point of law, because every case depended on the facts; and of the facts the jury were the sole judges. So Edmund Bushell and his fellow jurors were set free. And William Penn came over to Pennsylvania to find freedom here.

No wonder that those who came from England believed in trial by jury! No wonder, when the States declared their independence, they regarded it as fundamental! I take as an instance the Declaration of Rights made by the Representatives of the Good People of Virginia on June 12, 1776. It says that "in all capital or criminal prosecutions, a man had a right to a speedy trial by an impartial jury of his vicinage, without whose unanimous consent he cannot be found guilty." Furthermore "that in controversies respecting property, and in suits between man and man, the ancient trial by jury is preferable to any other and ought to be held sacred." These sentiments still stand, I believe, here in the United States and are embodied in the constitution.

In England, a great change has been wrought. Trial by jury has virtually disappeared in civil actions. Nearly every case is tried by a judge sitting alone. No litigant has a right to trial by jury; it is in the discretion of a judge. How should a judge exercise this discretion?

The question was asked and answered by the Court of Appeal in 1965. An Army sergeant had been very seriously injured in a motor accident. He claimed trial by jury. The court held that in personal injury cases, no matter how serious the injuries, the trial should normally be by judge alone. The reason is because a judge is much more suitable to assess the damages. When by accident a man's mind is destroyed, so that he can no longer think, or his body is paralysed from the neck down, no money can compensate him for the loss. The damage must be a conventional sum based on experience. The judges know the general run, whereas jurors do not. The damages in one case should be in line with sums awarded in other cases; else there is dissatisfaction as between one plaintiff and another. The damages also should be able to be predicted so that cases can be settled reasonably, without recourse to the Courts. Let me add, too, another reason. Trial by jury takes much longer, it leads to great delay. Delay of justice is a denial of justice. So we have abandoned trial by jury in civil cases.

Trial by jury has suffered a transformation in criminal cases too. The jury need no longer be unanimous. A man can now be found guilty by a majority of 10 to 2. The reason for this was the onset of bribery and corruption. The offense was known to your forefathers as Embracery. In the old days it was averted by keeping the jury together, from the beginning of the case to the end, without food or drink, or pay. In modern times, however, the jurors are well treated. They are allowed to separate for meals. They are allowed to go home at night. They are paid an expense allowance and compensation for their time. Yet it means that there is opportunity for the accused man or his friends to bribe or corrupt them, or even to threaten them. It has been known to happen. One or two jurors have stood out, and refused to find an accused guilty, so that the jury have had to be discharged —after weeks of trial—without giving a verdict. To prevent such happenings, in serious cases the jurors had to be given police protection. Their houses were guarded against intruders. The situation was so intolerable that we have had to introduce majority verdicts. It went much against the grain, but by all accounts it is working well.

An even more radical suggestion has been made, and by no less a person than the Lord Chief Justice of England. It is to abolish trial by jury altogether in some criminal cases. Financial frauds and conspiracies are difficult to unravel. Thousands of documents have to be read, and scores of witnesses to be called. Cases may last for weeks or months. No ordinary 12 men can be expected to understand them. Skilled counsel can raise all sorts of complexities and say, "Are you satisfied beyond reasonable doubt?" And they, for want of understanding, will say "Not Guilty." There is a strong case for trial by a judge with expert assessors.

So we see how one of the most English institutions—trial by jury—is being eroded. At the time when the founding fathers came here, it was regarded as the keystone to liberty. So did the settlers who went from England to other great territories overseas—to Canada, to Australia, and to New Zealand—but not elsewhere. It did not take root in India or Pakistan, nor in many other territories. It does not suit countries where there are deep racial or religious or tribal differences. It may not suit the multi-racial communities of the future. Time alone will show.

Now another instance. Time was, when a man accused of crime was not allowed to give evidence on his own behalf. It was supposed that he had such an interest in the case that no one could believe a word he said. He was not even allowed counsel to speak for him; all he could do was to make a statement from the dock. Many a man was quite incapable of saying anything useful to him. If he was charged with a capital offense, such as stealing a sheep, he would be well advised to learn by heart the first verse of the 51st psalm. It runs, you remember:

> Have mercy upon me O God according to thy loving kindness: According unto the multitude of thy tender mercies blot out my transgressions.

If he could repeat that verse, out of his own head, or with the aid of a compassionate prompter, he could claim benefit of clergy—so that he would not be hanged but transported for life.

That is all changed now. Every man is entitled to give evidence on his own behalf. In the United States you have had the call of Gideon's trumpet.

Every man accused of a serious offense is entitled to have counsel to defend him. If he has been denied it, the conviction will be set aside. In England we have had a revolution too, but we have done it differently. A man has long been entitled to have counsel to speak for him, but it was until recently subject to this proviso: that he must have some money to pay the fee, or some friend must find it for him. If he had a lot of money, he could employ eminent counsel. If he had only a little, he could ask for a "dock brief." He could pick any counsel in the Court (although he could only see the backs of their wigs) and ask him to defend him. The fee in my day was £1: 3s: 6d., now it is £2: 4s: 6d. On payment of that nominal sum, counsel was bound to act for him. That was a very makeshift system, and it has now been replaced by a modern system of Legal Aid. Every person who is accused of crime and is unable to pay, himself—as most are not able—is defended at the expense of the State. He is allowed solicitor and counsel, who are paid the fees which they could reasonably ask a paying client.

It is sometimes suggested that the cause of crime is poverty and squalor, and that so long as thousands of people are ill-housed, ill-clad and ill-nourished, we cannot hope for improvement. In our experience, that is simply not true. There is no poverty in England now to speak of. There is no squalor worth mentioning. There is good education for all. And yet the rate of crime has risen greatly, as it has done throughout the world. The criminal courts are full to overflowing. Often enough the young men who appear have been earning good wages, and yet they commit crimes in their spare time. They live in society, but they are enemies of it. They have no respect for law and order. What is the remedy? I know of none, save to see that the law is enforced justly and efficiently, and to bring up our people to hold law in respect and to condemn wrongdoing.

Here the police forces have an important part to play. I often think that in England the police are criticized too much, and thanked too little. They are, or should be, the friends of the law-abiding citizens. Remember that when society is under attack—as it is under attack by criminals—the police are the only people that we can look to for our defense. Judges or lawyers cannot do it. They are only in the second line. The front line is held by the police. Society for its defense needs a well-led, well-trained, well-disciplined force of police whom it can trust, and enough of them to be able to prevent crime before it happens—or, if it does happen, to detect it and bring the accused to justice. The police must, of course, act properly. They must obey the rules of right conduct. They must not extort confessions by threats or promises. They must not search a man's house without warrant. They must not use any more force than the occasion warrants. And so forth. But so long as they act honestly and properly the judges and lawyers should support them to the uttermost. There is nothing more detrimental to the rule of law than for the guilty to get off scot-free. There is nothing more discouraging to the police than to see a known criminal —whom they have at last succeeded in tracking down—acquitted owing to some technical rule of law. The Courts have done well to lay down rules so as to protect an innocent person. But those rules must not be so used as to throw open doors for all the criminals to escape.

I trust that in England the judges have kept the balance. Many criminals are convicted on their own confessions—which have been given freely to the police—or on searches which have been lawfully made. Even if the police, out of excess of zeal, have overstepped the mark, yet we admit in evidence, real evidence, such as stolen property that has been found in the possession of the accused. And when an accused man gives evidence, if he casts imputations on the prosecution or on the police, we allow him to be cross-examined as to his record. We do, that is, if the Judge in his discretion thinks it fair. Also, all trials should be done speedily. In England we aim at every criminal being tried within eight weeks of his arrest, and this is nearly always achieved. It is right, again, to provide for a system of appeals. Every trial court is liable to err, so let its decision be reviewed. Let it be done speedily, however, and finally. In England we aim at one appeal to the Court of Appeal within two or three months, and no further appeal except with special leave in cases of public and general importance. This is only fair to the accused man and to society. No man should be kept in suspense—or allowed to stave off punishment—for years by long drawn-out legal machinery.

Now may I turn to another great problem of our times. It is race relations. At common law, we were able to secure for every man his personal freedom—irrespective of race, religion or colour—but we were unable to secure for him equal treatment in other respects. That has had to be done by statute, whereas you have done it by the judges. Let me tell you just how the common law developed. I go back to the case over 200 years ago, to the days of slavery, when it was lawful, in our British colonies, for men to own slaves as if they were chattels. In about 1776, the owner of a slave called Somerset brought him from Jamaica to England, and was about to return with him to Jamaica. The slave did not want to go. The owner had him in irons on a ship in the Thames. Somerset brought his writ of *habeas corpus* before Lord Mansfield in London—the great writ which protects the freedom of the individual from any unjust imprisonment. Lord Mansfield then declared in his memorable words:

> Every man who comes to England is entitled to the protection of our laws, whatever the colour of his skin or whatever oppression he may heretofore have suffered. The air of England is too pure for any slave to breathe—let the black go free,

and he was set free. Now this freedom was established by your constitution and it is in the universal declaration of human rights, "no one shall be held in slavery or servitude." It was established in England by the decisions of the judges. No country, no people, ever did more for the abolition of slavery than did the English people; men like Samuel Wilberforce and the others.

But now, let me go on a little with the history of racial relations. Let me take an instance which you may remember in recent years, when there were more coloured people coming into England. There was, in the Nottinghill district of London, a riot in which youths set upon coloured people in the streets. They were only about 17 years of age, these white boys. In the ordinary way, the judge might not have sentenced them to imprisonment of any long term, probably not more than six months, but the judge sent these to prison for long periods of years. This is what my colleague, Mr. Justice Salmon, said:

> On the night of the 24th of August, you nine men formed yourselves into a gang, and set out on a cruel and vicious manhunt. You armed yourselves with iron bars and other weapons. Your quarry was any man, providing there were not more than two of them together, whose skin happened to be a different colour from your own. Two of them were lucky enough to escape before you were able to inflict other than comparatively minor injuries. The other three you left senseless and bleeding upon the pavement.

And he went on:

> Everyone, irrespective of their colour, is entitled to walk our streets, safely, with their heads erect and free from fear. This is one of our proudest traditions, and one which the law will unfailingly uphold. If anyone seeks, as you have done, to trample on those rights, the law will be swift to punish you, the guilty, and to protect the victims.

You may ask, "What are the objects of punishment?" The judge sentenced those youths to five, six and seven years, whereas in the ordinary way for such an assault it would not be more than six or nine months, and they might even be on probation. The objects of punishment are not confined to deterrence or to reform. Another object is to show the emphatic denunciation by a community of a crime. Those sentences by that judge did indeed achieve what was desired. Thereafter, all right-thinking people in England would have nothing whatever to do with racial violence. Yet those decisions dealt only with personal freedom. They did not ensure equality. The common law allowed racial discrimination, whereas you prohibited it by the great amendment which you celebrate today—with the highly important interpretation of it by the judges. Let me tell you something of our alterations in the law of race relations. First, the law as it was before the new Acts. Shortly after World War II, a newspaper, in the North of England, in Lancashire, published an article which was very critical of the Jews, saying they had been active in the black market. It was such as to be calculated to instil hatred of the Jews. That newspaper was prosecuted for seditious libel before one of my colleagues, Lord Birkett, who directed the jury that in order that there should be seditious libel, there has to be incitement of violence, and here there was none. There is no such thing as group libel in English law. The jury, after deliberation of 20 minutes, found the newspaper not guilty. That law has now been altered. In 1965 we passed the Race Relations Act. It is an offense for any person to publish or distribute written matter if it is calculated or likely to stir up hatred against any section of the public, distinguished by colour, race, ethnic, or national origin. Or, indeed, if he uses such words in a public place or at a public meeting, it is an offense. So now, if any person, or a newspaper, publishes words such as to instil hatred against any race on account of their colour, or indeed on account of their race, such as Jews, that is a criminal offense. But it can only be prosecuted at the instance of the Attorney-General. Furthermore, there shall be no discrimination in any place of public resort, hotel, or other places whatsoever; if there is, an injunction can be obtained from the courts against the hotel or proprietor in order to prevent him from practicing any discrimination. Likewise with covenants, if any covenant in an agreement seeks to prohibit the disposal of premises to any person on account of his race or colour or nationality, it is invalid. There is now a bill before Parliament to strengthen the law against discrimination. There is to be no discrimination in education, in employment, in housing, and many other things. A Race Relations Board is to be set up to institute proceedings. All this has been done by Parliament. But you have done it by the judges.

Yet we must remember that there is a tremendous social problem involved. We cannot overlook the fact that many people of different colours and nationalities come to England. It is, after all, a very good place to be. There is freedom there—there is equality—there are high wages. However, we haven't room for everyone. Often those who come have different standards of housing, of health, of morals. We can't be overwhelmed, lest our own standards suffer in the process. Therefore, as you may have seen, the Governments of England have found it necessary to impose considerable restrictions on immigration. And I am sure that would accord with the views of every ordinary person in England. We, after all, must maintain our standards, and one of those standards is freedom for all, irrespective of race or nationality; but it must be freedom under the law.

Finally let me turn to one of the most disturbing features of our times —the resort to demonstrations by mobs. The demonstrations are all very well if they are held peacefully and in accordance with law. But once they deteriorate into violence and intimidation, into sit-ins and sit-downs, then they are contrary to law. And all right-thinking persons should condemn them. I know the arguments to the contrary. They are demonstrations in aid of a good cause. Their end is a good one—so they say—and hence the means is justified. That is a most pernicious doctrine. They make themselves the arbiter of the goodness of the end. Even if the end is good, a good end can never justify a bad means. Only too often it is impossible to distinguish between the means and the end. Violence is contrary to law, whatever the end that is sought. The aims of the coloured people and of students may very well be good in themselves, but they must be achieved peacefully by discussion and the influence of opinion. If Black Power or Student Power becomes an end in itself, then it must be resisted. For it would threaten the very existence of our society.

The above discussion has traced some of the changes which have taken place in the Constitution of England in recent years, keeping it, as I hope, in accord with the times. The law cannot stand still. If law is to obtain the respect of the people it must do justice. You may ask, "What is justice?" It is a question which has been asked for thousands of years by people far wiser than you and me. Socrates asked it 2,000 years ago, and never got a satisfactory answer. Justice isn't something temporal—it is eternal—and the nearest approach to a definition that I can give is, "Justice is what the right-thinking members of the community believe to be fair." We, all of us responsible people, represent the right-thinking members of the community, attempting to do, as best we can, what is fair, not only between man and man, but between man and the State. It is best expressed, perhaps, in the oath which every judge in England, and I am sure, here too in shortened form, takes on his appointment. This is how it runs—it is worth recalling every word of it.

> I swear by Almighty God that I will do right to all manner of people after the laws and usages of this realm without fear or favour, affection or ill-will.

Take each phrase of that oath:

"I swear by Almighty God"	Thereby he affirms his belief in God, and hence in true religion;
"that I will do right"	that I will do justice, not I will do law;
"to all manner of people"	rich or poor, capitalist or communist, Christian or Pagan, black or white, to all manner of people I will do right;

"after the laws and usages of this realm"	it must, of course, be according to law;
"without fear or favour, affection, or ill-will"	without fear of the powerful, favour of the wealthy, without affection to one side or ill-will to another, I will do right.

It is very like the words of the Queen herself, at her coronation, when the archbishop asks her, "Will you to your power cause law and justice, in mercy, to be executed throughout your Dominions," and the Queen answers, "I will." The judges are the delegates of the Queen for the purpose. They represent her to execute law and justice, in mercy. How shall they be merciful unless they have in them something of that quality which, as Shakespeare said, "droppeth as the gentle rain from heaven upon the place beneath."

Those are the attributes of justice. Those are the attributes which, in all the changing times of life, we, the lawyers, must strive to uphold, while keeping them, as in the instances I have given, in accord with the needs of the times, but subject always to the rule of law.

10

Constitutional Developments in Western Europe during the Last Century

André Mathiot

The difficulties of presenting with some accuracy in a general survey the constitutional and political evolution that has taken place in Western Europe since ratification of the Fourteenth Amendment are obviously enormous and numerous.

In addition to the usual problems of comparative government (which can only be studied by considering geography and economy, the particular traditions of the different nations, and the differences in environment and relations to other nations), one encounters here the huge difficulty of putting together political evolutions that occurred at different moments and that, consequently, may have different meanings. Moreover, as often pointed out, the institutions of government which bear the same name can be completely dissimilar in their actual functioning, even (or particularly) on the same small European continent. This is especially true, for example, of what is called "parliamentary regime," "judicial power," "local government," to say nothing of extremely vague principles, such as "separation of powers" or "sovereignty of the people," which may furnish a theoretical justification for quite different institutions and rules.

At first sight, when considering the various European countries and their evolution, what is most striking is *how profoundly they differ* from one another. What kind of resemblance can exist between quiet Switzerland, which has apparently succeeded in reconciling government and liberty and in continuously preserving her democratic institutions, and the

André Mathiot is Professor at the Faculty of Law and the Institute of Political Studies at the University of Paris.

turbulent French nation, highly specialized in revolutions and constitutional changes and almost unequalled in the field of political divisions? The main principles of democratic government have been unquestioned in numerous European countries, but Germany had a totalitarian dictatorship for twelve years and, in Italy, the fascist State lasted from 1922–1924 until 1943. The Scandinavian countries, the Netherlands and (until recently) Belgium have always taken their democratic constitutions for granted, while, in Portugal and Spain, particular forms of personal government have been operating since 1933 and 1939, with only slight changes in the institutions and trends of the Franco regime.

All these contrasts—and still others will be underlined—are not surprising. For each of the different countries, (1) the *starting-points* were different; (2) in the course of time, every country has had its particular *evolution* and (3) each pursued its way in accordance with various *political trends*.

(1) The *starting-points* were noticeably different. In the late nineteenth century, striking divergencies between the European countries appeared with regard to their systems of government, as well as their political situations or economic development.

Except in Switzerland, where a democratic form of government had been established for centuries in some cantons, and for years in others and in the Confederation, some regimes were far from being democratic. In Germany, the imperial constitution of April 16, 1871, masked behind a constitutional façade an authoritarian government and Prussian supremacy. In France, after the adoption of the constitution of 1875, the opposition between monarchists and republicans remained a fundamental division; the republican victory was not consolidated before 1884 and political democracy still had to face later vigorous attacks. Victor-Emmanuel III, king of Sardinia-Piedmont, had been proclaimed king of Italy in 1861 and seemed to be in a position comparable to that of the British king, but the electoral franchise was still restricted (in 1870, there were about 500,000 voters), the elections were not free, and the king retained in fact important personal powers enabling him to control policy rather frequently. In Austria-Hungary, the Habsburg monarchy was not democratic. In Northern Europe, the Netherlands under the constitution of 1814, and Belgium after 1831 had gradually established parliamentary systems on the strong basis of old provincial and local institutions, but the political class was long able to maintain oligarchical influences. The same is true of the Scandinavian countries, where the monarchy had been constitutionally limited early in the nineteenth century, but where effective political democracy developed slowly through the years.

Moreover, these various constitutional frameworks reflected (or were supposed to reflect) different political data or circumstances which were, of course, far from unimportant. In France, for example, the three constitutional "laws" of 1875 were the result of a number of compromises and were based on no single or very simple principle. They were nevertheless marked by a strong distrust of imperial institutions, plebiscites, presidential government, or any form of executive supremacy. The fact that national unification was so recent in Germany and Italy made it very difficult to accept a true and liberal federalism in the former, or any important decentralization in the latter. In Switzerland, on the contrary, the growth of centralized power was hindered by the traditional autonomy of the old cantons. The fact that Sweden and Norway were once united for approximately a century and, for almost 100 years prior to 1905, shared the same king, contributed to develop some similarities, but also to create a strong feeling of nationalism among the peoples of both countries and to favor different lines of political development. It should also be noted that the monarchies of Northern Europe were more inclined than other countries to copy the British model.

The starting-points were also different in the field of economic development. This fact is important, since there is an obvious connection between the success of liberal democracy and equality of opportunity, competition, freedom of business activities, and promotion of economic prosperity. It has been pointed out that the establishment of parliamentary government in Western Europe did, in fact, approximately coincide with the institution of the capitalistic system, that establishment having been delayed, for special reasons, in France until 1830, in Italy until 1850, in Sweden until 1910–1914, in Norway until 1900–1920. It is striking that Germany, between 1871 and 1914, was not able to pass beyond the stage of a limited monarchy, that in the countries of Central Europe, with only embryonic capitalistic structures, the attempts to introduce parliamentary government fell through and that, in Italy after the first World War, the economic and financial crisis—together with other reasons—resulted in a parliamentary crisis and the triumph of fascism.

(2) Naturally enough, these different starting points resulted in *different evolutions*. In addition, in the course of time, different circumstances and influences played their part.

The policy of neutrality of some countries contributed to the preservation and stability of their institutions, while the two World Wars had important governmental consequences for the belligerents, either in strengthening the victorious regimes or in bringing about the collapse or liquidation of institutions that were held responsible for military defeats, or governments that collaborated with the enemy.

In several countries, the personality of a number of men of high political stature was an important factor: de Valera, Marshal Petain, General de

Gaulle, de Gasperi, Adenauer, to say nothing of Salazar and General Franco.

Obviously, the influence of socialism has been closely related to the specific characters of the different socialist parties. The stability of government and the continuity of politics in Sweden and Norway are largely due to the strength and efficiency of the labor and social democratic party in these countries, while the tendencies and divisions of the Socialists in France and Italy made the formation of stable coalition governments often or permanently difficult.

In some countries, anticommunism is and has always been strong; in other countries, such as the Scandinavian countries, Belgium, and the Netherlands, there is a communist party, but one with narrow popular support and unable to trouble the functioning of the regime. Quite different is the political situation in France and Italy. These countries have a multiplicity of parties, among which a strong communist party is able to poll from 20 to 25 percent of the votes at all general elections. Whether or not these parties have really renounced revolutionary action is a debated question; what is sure is that they have contributed much to reduce the efficiency of the regimes, making it often difficult to find a majority in parliament and to govern, indirectly leading to a shift to the right or to dishonest electoral manipulations.

Another reason why European regimes have evolved differently is that their political inspiration came from different sources.

Strange as it may seem, continental Europe has scarcely considered the American system of government as an enviable model. In Switzerland, the constitution of 1848 and its revision in 1874 were largely based on the American pattern, but only in regard to the general lines of federalism. In Austria and the Federal Republic of Germany, up to a certain point, the same inspiration appears. As for the process by which the president is elected and to some extent his political influence, the Republic of Finland and the Fifth French Republic also remind us of some features of the American presidency.

In actual fact, the political evolution in Western Europe has been imbued with a basic faith in the virtues of parliamentarianism, and may be summarized as a series of attempts to copy British institutions. But there are many ways to "parliamentary government" and it is very difficult to discover the secrets of the British "constitution" without some keys, such as the working of a strong two-party system, a powerful and organized opposition, a vigorous public opinion, a real confidence in representative government, and a passionate desire for liberty. The transplantation to Northern Europe has, on the whole, been encouraging, but in the other parts of the continent, the attempts have never resulted in more than partial success.

(3) Finally, in accordance with the popular will in each country, *political trends,* which of course varied greatly in the course of time and from one country to another, also contributed to shape some governmental features. For example, a public policy of promotion of the general welfare, with the necessity of planning, programming and controlling the economy, almost automatically brings on "big government," centralization, and bureaucracy, and may also develop new forms of popular participation in determining and executing policy. Some devices for protecting or restricting liberty may appear or disappear. The part played by the courts in the control of administrative action may be significant or ineffectual. Above all, nations have different ways of doing the same thing.

Despite these discouraging diversities, which have to be taken into account, on the whole, *some common features* seem to characterize most of the political regimes of Western Europe, so that general outlines are recognizable in the constitutional developments almost everywhere. They appeared gradually, sometimes with difficulty, mostly since the end of the nineteenth century.

Any summary description is bound to be misleading. Every system of government has maintained its own distinctive forms and tendencies, resulting from a complex combination of many different factors.

Nevertheless, it is possible to summarize the various and successive developments that have taken place in modern times by considering the three essential points. These seem to be: I. The progress and, almost everywhere, the establishment (or re-establishment) of democracy; II. The vicissitudes of liberalism; III. The growth of the executive.

I. Establishing Democracy

Here, as in other domains, Switzerland may be considered as a peculiar case, since, religious and linguistic differences notwithstanding, that small country has developed a strong sense of national unity and, with the exception of the period of the French domination (1798–1815), has always been devoted to democracy. After 1830, the power of the oligarchies that had survived or revived in some cantons had been entirely destroyed, and representative institutions of a popular character were universally introduced. In 1848, Switzerland had been transformed from a confederation into a federal state, and in 1874 the revised constitution laid the foundations for the modern political system, which is not only democratic, but also extensively based upon the instruments of direct popular government.

The other countries had been (or still remained) under the rule of absolute monarchs, who more or less kept the government of the country in their own hands.

The political developments of the late nineteenth century and the twentieth century have, on the whole, permitted or confirmed, though sometimes with terrible ordeals or dramatic setbacks, a twofold movement.

The first stage of progress had been, either by revolutionary means or through a gradual evolution, the transition from various forms of absolute monarchy or government to different forms of limited monarchy or constitutional government.

At once or, more often, in a later stage, government of the people, by the people and for the people was realized, usually by the introduction or improvement of a variant of the parliamentary system.

1. From absolute monarchy or government to limited monarchy or government.

In Great Britain, the struggle against absolute monarchy had two centuries earlier resulted in the transfer of effective political power from the king to parliament and in the emergence of the cabinet and the office of prime minister. In continental Europe, similar developments occurred in different ways and at different times.

In Sweden, the transformation was spontaneous and was realized as early as 1809. In almost all other countries, the process developed in imitation of the British system of government.

Denmark and Norway did not establish their limited monarchies as early as Sweden did. In Norway, however, which had been ceded to the king of Sweden by the king of Denmark in 1814, a limited monarchy was established on August 14 of the same year, the state being proclaimed independent in a personal union with Sweden, which was abrogated on October 26, 1905. (The constitution of 1814, as revised in 1905 and later, is still in force.) In Denmark, the Royal Law of 1665 had established against the aristrocracy an absolute monarchy, which was not constitutionally limited until 1866.

In the Netherlands and Belgium, constitutional monarchy was established at about the same time. After the United Provinces were freed from French domination in November, 1813, the Congress of Vienna joined the Belgian provinces to the northern Netherlands, and the first constitution for that sovereign state was promulgated in 1814. The union was dissolved by the Belgian revolution of 1830. After the secession, a constitutional representative and hereditary monarchy was established in Belgium by the constitution of 1831. After the treaty of London of 1839 had recognized Belgium as an independent state, the constitution of the Netherlands was revised in 1840, maintaining a constitutional and hereditary monarchy. In both countries, the legislative power was (and theoretically still is) vested in the Crown and Parliament.

France had a long and tortuous history. After the First Empire and the constitutional Charter of 1814, the revolution of 1830 was a liberal reaction against personal government, and the new Charter of 1830 was an attempt to establish the parliamentary system. (The French Charter largely inspired Belgium and the Netherlands.) During the last years of the Second Empire, its authoritarian character was altered and, in 1875, the constitutional laws of the Third Republic were a new attempt to promote liberal government, but it was by no means certain that the republican regime or parliamentary system would last for long.

As for Italy and Germany, it has already been pointed out that the Albertian *Statuto,* which had been granted to Piedmont by the king and later extended to the united nation, had been modelled upon the conservative lines of the French charter and Belgian constitution of 1831 and did not establish a true parliamentary regime, while, in Germany (until 1910 at least), the Bismarckian constitution actually created a monocratic organization: that is, the Reichstag remained powerless and the Reich chancellor could retain his office so long as he enjoyed the confidence of the Emperor. The parliamentary system was only introduced by the Weimar constitution, and it, unfortunately, could not produce confidence in democracy.[1]

The process of limitation has rarely been a continuous one. In several countries, the principle of limited government itself has been dramatically challenged for years and its significance is still extremely reduced in Portugal and Spain, but its broad acceptance, equally with that of representative government, generally involved three important features, as follows.

A. All the Western European countries have proclaimed or admitted a principle somewhat similar to the British rule of law, usually called the principle of legality or the sovereignty of law. It implies more than compliance with the law on the part of the citizenry: it also imposes limitations on the powers of government and the administrative authorities and is quite incompatible with any kind of arbitrary rule.

The first consequence is the supremacy of the constitution, which holds the nature and course of government within prescribed limits. In this field, all the countries of continental Europe have rejected the British system of a flexible constitution. Not only have the principles, objectives and rules of government been defined in precise terms in written constitutions, but also all are more or less rigid and their strength is supposed to be ensured through the difficulties of the process by which the constitution can be amended. Consequently, all the ordinary laws passed by parliament are subordinate and must comply with the constitutional rules. Some nations have added to the constitution a declaration, preamble or Bill of Rights. The practical importance of the supremacy of the constitution is, of course, considerably increased when fundamental rights are declared binding on legislation, administration and judiciary (Bonn Basic Law, art. 1, par. 3) or when the ordinary courts (rarely) or a special constitutional tribunal are empowered to pass on the conformity of statutes to the constitution (Austria, Italy, Germany). In France, the present Constitutional Council has been created to see that parliament remains within its own prerogative, but the principle of legality is enforced either by the ordinary courts or by the administrative courts and the Conseil d'Etat.

Another consequence of the sovereignty of law is the existence of control over the legality of executive and administrative action in different ways (as will be indicated later in this paper), but, in fact, the continental systems are probably closer to the common law systems than may appear at first sight.

B. Evolution during the past century tended to bring about recognition of a minimum of separation of powers, which seems to be another main feature.

Very early in every country, the necessity of preventing abuses of power resulted in keeping the legislative or executive and the judicial functions separate or carefully defined. As for the separation between executive and legislative functions, it is obviously not to be found either in our parliamentary systems or in Switzerland, but the two branches of government that have to collaborate with each other have been granted different powers —even though the legislature is or has become the dominant organ (as in Switzerland, in France under the Third and Fourth Republics, and in Italy), even though the evolution has reached the stage of Cabinet government or a kind of presidential rule.

C. It is also striking that the establishment of a limited monarchy or government coincided with a gradual transformation of political representation, consisting, as in Great Britain, in the decline of the aristocracy and the growing influence of the middle classes, at a time when the principle of the sovereignty of the people was not really accepted. That transformation, by the way, was directly connected with the twilight of upper chambers that has occurred throughout Europe.

These developments led to the democratization of governments.

2. Progressive democratization.

As long as a king or chief executive may rule without being obliged to act in accordance with the will of the people, as expressed directly in general elections and indirectly through parliament in the intervals between elections, there may be a constitutional government, but there is no true democracy. This paper will summarize (A) how limited governments were transformed into parliamentary governments in most countries; (B) how these governments were, generally in another phase, based upon the will of the people; and (C) will finally consider the result of this evolution.

A. Except when new independent states were created at a time when democracy could be immediately established (which happened for the republics of Finland and Austria, and for the Irish Republic), there has usually been an interval between the establishment of a limited government and the adoption of all the general characteristics of parliamentary government: namely, a politically non-responsible and neutral head of state, a cabinet which is politically responsible to parliament and must resign if it fails to command a majority and, more often than not, the power of dissolution.

As has been underlined, the Swiss political system is an exception.[2]

All the other Western European countries, either continuously or at important moments in their history, have modelled their institutions on those of Great Britain, or tried to reproduce its political system. Except perhaps in Belgium, where the constitution of 1831 already provided for ministerial responsibility, parliamentary government was progressively introduced. In other countries, in the course of time, the individual and criminal responsibility of ministers gradually became collective and purely political, and the king or president was deprived of the power to determine any political issue on his own initiative or even to give up political neutrality.

The following table points out that a rather long time often elapsed between the appearance of constitutional government and the recognition (either by a revision of the constitution, or in actual practice) of the essential characteristics of parliamentary government.

Countries	Constitution (limited government)	Parliamentary government established
Belgium	1831	1831
Denmark	1866	1901
France	1830; 1875	after 1877
Germany	apparently 1871	1919 (Weimar)
Italy	1848–1870	20th century
Netherlands	1814	1848, 1870
Norway	1814	1884, 1895, 1920
Sweden	1809	1876, 1914

(The third column indicates that, in some countries, all the parliamentary rules were not accepted at the same time.)

In most countries, the head of the state retained some personal powers (particularly the power to choose and to dismiss the prime minister) long after the responsibility of the cabinet to parliament had been accepted.[8]

B. Parliamentary government is not synonymous with democracy. Democratization implied the expansion of the electorate and the organization of free elections, so that the parliament, and through parliament the executive, might become a reflection of the popular will.

Of course, the establishment of universal suffrage does not mean democratic government,[4] and all governments, even dictatorships, recognize the need to take public opinion into account, but the democratization of parliamentary government can only be achieved by the extension of the franchise and the final granting of universal suffrage, so that political power rests ultimately with the nation, expressing the will of the people in free elections.

In all countries except France and Germany, the vote was given to all men after (or long after) parliamentary government had been established: in Belgium, 1919–1921; Denmark, 1915; Italy, 1919; the Netherlands, 1919–1922; Norway, 1913; Sweden, 1907. Women were granted the right to vote on the same terms as men in most countries after the first World War, but in France and Italy, after the second World War only.

More often than not, the electoral system evolved gradually in response to changing circumstances and alterations in the social structure, as a result of the action of parties of the left and in connection with the characteristics of the particular party system.

C. The consolidation of the Western European democracies, generally with parliamentary institutions, or the restoration of parliamentary government in Italy and Germany after the collapse of the fascist and nazi regimes, the re-establishment of republican government in France after the Vichy interlude and the Liberation, have confirmed that democracy is, in Europe, as one author has said (and as the evolution of Spain, Portugal and Greece will probably demonstrate), the system "to which every civilization turns or returns."

After different evolutions, either continuous or sometimes marked by pauses or sudden changes, the different democratic regimes may be considered as connected with three types of government, which have developed in accordance with the party systems or because of specific political circumstances.

First, a number of regimes may be compared (cautiously) with the British one. They have been able to model their institutions and political life on the pattern of a kind of cabinet government, because they have almost succeeded in establishing a kind of two-party system, or because in these countries minor parties (particularly extremist groups) remained powerless, in such a way that one well-organized party could be strong enough to obtain popular support for its policies and to govern, either alone, or without enduring the evils of true coalition governments. The dominant party usually follows a middle-of-the-road policy, in order to avoid internal splits and to draw its supporters from several sections of the population.

This is the situation in Sweden. The Swedish parties are six, but the Social Democratic party has been in power for 36 years, with a majority either in both chambers or in one chamber, and Tage Erlander has been prime minister for 22 years. On September 15, 1968, partly because of the international situation, but also because of the large acceptance of the Swedish welfare state, the coalition of the "bourgeois" parties could not prevent the socialists from increasing their support.

In Norway, the situation has been similar in the past. There are six parties, five of which have an important representation in the *Storting*. The labor party has been able to get a majority of seats and to govern, for example, between 1945 and 1961 (with the Gerharden, Torp and Gerharden cabinets).

In the Irish Republic, where only five prime ministers have been in power since Eire became independent, the Fianna Fail party, though facing serious difficulties, could retain at the 1966 elections the same narrow and precarious majority as it had in the previous Dail.

Austria has, in fact, a two-party system: the two major parties are the "people's party" (Christian-Democrat) and the socialist party, and there is also a small Freedom party. From 1945 until 1966, coalition governments associated the two major parties. In April, 1966, the Christian-Democrats having won the absolute majority, Mr. Klaus decided to form an all-conservative cabinet after failure to reach an agreement with the socialists concerning the conditions of a renewed coalition.

The situation is different in Germany, though the party system has evolved in an encouraging manner since 1949. At the time the Bonn basic law was adopted, about 15 parties had political activities, of which four were minor parties. Minor parties have gradually disappeared; two (the neo-nazi S.R.P. in 1952 and the communist party in 1956) were declared illegal by the federal Constitutional Tribunal and the others could not be represented in the Bundestag because they failed to poll five percent of the votes. So, only seven parties were represented after the elections of 1953, four in 1957, and only three since 1961 and 1965. The tendency to bipartism has often been pointed out. Moreover, the Christian-Democrats (C.D.U.-C.S.U.) won a narrow majority in 1953 and a rather large one in 1957. Yet, even with an absolute majority and though largely the first party in 1961 and 1965 as it had been since the beginning, the C.D.U.-C.S.U. (Christian Democratic Party) preferred to form coalitions (with the liberal F.D.P. (Free German Party) since 1961) and Germany had the same chancellor, Dr. Konrad Adenauer, during 14 years. However, because of the internal differences within the christian-democracy and of some difficulties with the F.D.P., Adenauer himself had to face some problems and to compromise. In 1966, the classic coalition collapsed, was replaced by the so-called "great coalition" with the socialist

S.P.D. (Social Democratic Party), a rival party, and this is a quite different formula.

Nevertheless, in all these countries, the functioning of parliamentary government is, on the whole, satisfactory. National divisions are not alarming. Very often, homogeneous minority cabinets were formed and could govern rather easily with the permanent support of another group (for example, the Hanson cabinet in Sweden between 1932 and 1936 with the support of the peasants) or with alternative majorities (the Ekman liberal cabinets in Sweden during the inter-war period). In Norway, between 1908 and 1940 (except for the years 1910–1912 and 1913–1920) all the governments were homogeneous minority governments. In Denmark, since 1901, all the homogeneous governments have been minority governments, and this was the situation of the Krag cabinet before the elections of January 1968. This is possible either because the opposition is divided, or because it prefers not to oppose the government.

In some circumstances, even the Scandinavian countries have been obliged to form coalition governments (Sweden, 1936–1945 and 1952–1957; Denmark, 1950–1953, 1957–1964). In Norway since 1965, the Borden cabinet is a center or conservative coalition of four "bourgeois" parties. The same is true in Denmark of the Baunsgard government, which was formed after the elections of January 1968; it is a coalition of three parties of the right center.

However, by and large, the resemblances between these regimes and the British political system are numerous.

Second, in several other countries, such as the Netherlands, Belgium and more especially Italy, there is another kind of parliamentary government which seems comparable, however unpleasant this comparison may be, to the French system during the Third and Fourth Republics. The multiplicity of parties is a reflection of the deep divisions existing in the nation, more or less connected with ideological intransigency. A general attitude of individualism may result in the reluctance to accept the authority of a strong executive. The cabinet is expected to accept the will of the lower chamber (or both chambers) and not only on major points. Above all, because of the absence of a parliamentary majority, these countries are condemned to coalition governments—politically weak because they are based on fragile and limited compromises, unstable because, even supposing that the majority were numerically sufficient, it would always be of a very poor quality. These coalitions are permanently in danger of being broken up under numerous influences (lack of solidarity, homogeneity, clear opposition, leadership), each one being a factor of instability.

Until recent years, the Netherlands and Belgium enjoyed an acceptable stability and ministerial crises did not last too long. However, at present, particularly in Belgium where the traditional parties are deeply divided on the Flemish and Walloon problem, the difficulty of governing is almost as important as it has been in Italy since the retirement of de Gasperi. The allied parties do not consider themselves as really deprived of their previous autonomy. The President of the Council can never be a strong leader, but has to act as a conciliator and to take constantly into account the views of numerous important politicians outside or even within his own group.

In Italy, until 1953, the parliamentary system worked normally, with a number of rather unimportant changes of government, but, even during the de Gasperi era, the tendency to parliamentary supremacy was evident. Since 1953, the Christian-Democrats (internally divided into four tendencies) have never won a majority in the lower chamber. (They had 262 seats out of 590 in 1953; 273 out of 596 in 1958; 260 out of 630 in 1963; 266 out of 630 in May 1968.) The chamber elected in April 1963 comprised members of 11 parties, out of which six had an important representation. As a result, the Christian-Democrats, who had always been allied with other parties within coalition governments, were again compelled to some kind of "opening." The "opening to the right" (Pella in 1953, Zoli in 1957, Tambroni in 1960) was far from a success.

The "opening to the left," which had been advocated by President Gronchi and realized in 1962 with the Fanfani government, seemed to be the best solution, but the negotiations with the two socialist parties were so difficult that a temporary "monocolore" Christian-Democrat minority government had to be formed and it was replaced by the first Moro cabinet only in December 1963. It was overthrown on June 24, 1964, and replaced by a rather similar government. A third Moro cabinet was appointed on January 1, 1965 by President Saragat after his election. After a new crisis in January–February 1966, a fourth Moro cabinet was formed on March 17, 1966. In 1967, because of the proximity of the general elections, the Christian-Democrats, the two Socialist parties (which had been re-united in October 1966) and the Republicans continued to govern together, but associates on one issue were bitter opponents on others. The head of the coalition had to spend a great deal of time trying to persuade deputies and senators to support him, to negotiate abstentions, and to convince the leaders of his majority's groups and even his political "friends." The general elections of May 19, 1968, on the whole, confirmed the center-left majority, but the internal differences within the "united" socialist party (which is divided into five tendencies) made it impossible to form a new coalition government immediately. Again, a Leone Christian-Democrat minority government was formed on June 24, 1968. It remained in power, thanks to the abstention of the socialists and republicans, until the next congress of the socialist party in October 1968. New negotiations then had to take place.

In the Netherlands, with ten parties (11 in the elections of February 1967) and five having an appreciable representation, the political situation is also complicated, particularly because of the existence of religious parties. The difficulty of reaching an agreement results in long ministerial crises. In 1966 the fall of the Cals coalition cabinet (Catholics, labor and anti-revolutionary party) led to the formation of a transitional Zijlstra cabinet and, after the 1967 elections, 47 days were necessary to form the de Jong coalition government (Catholics, liberals and protestants).

In Belgium, the working of coalition governments has been made more and more difficult in the course of time. Recently, the Théo Lefèvre Christian-Social and socialist coalition cabinet fell on May 23, 1965, and a coalition of the same parties was formed (on July 27, only) by Mr. Harmel. On February 10, 1966, the socialist ministers resigned and the Harmel coalition was replaced (after 40 days) by the Van den Boeynants government, in which the Christian-Social party was associated with the liberals. But deep divisions on the linguistic problem compelled Mr. Van den Boeynants to resign on February 7, 1968, which resulted in a dissolution. At the general elections of March 31, 1968, the three major parties lost seats, and because of the extreme difficulty of the negotiations, it was only 78 days later that a new government could be formed. The 29 members of the Eyskens government (15 Catholics, 13 socialists, one without affiliation) had to be selected in such a way that there was an equal number of French-speaking and Flemish-speaking ministers in both parties.

The long duration of the crises which have been summarized reveals the weakness of the multi-party parliamentary system in Europe.

Third, curiously enough, Finland and France, which differ so deeply, seem to be comparable as regards their constitutions and political systems. In both countries, the cabinet must enjoy the confidence of Parliament (one chamber in Finland, the lower chamber in France), but in both countries cabinet government has to be combined with presidential preponderance and both Presidents are elected by the people (for six years by an electoral college elected by the votes of the citizens in Finland, for seven years directly by the citizens in France since 1962). Other resemblances might be difficult to find, but the attempts to reconcile some features of cabinet government with a kind of presidential rule are striking.

The democratic principle has now been established almost everywhere in Western Europe, without influencing appreciably the features of the authoritarian regimes of Portugal and Spain, where the organic Law of the State, ratified by a referendum on December 14, 1966 and several laws of June and July, 1967 have only recently initiated a possible evolution. However, the democrats believe that democracy is contagious and that in Greece, too, the military regime established by the *coup* of April 1967 only represents a temporary interlude.

The consolidation of democracy did not result in the same development and survival of liberty.

II. The Vicissitudes of Liberalism

All democracies have been founded upon the basis of liberty and organized in order to find a satisfactory balance between the liberty of the individual to live his life as he will, and the authority of the state to protect and enhance the welfare of all people. The importance of the individual, linked with the principle of the equality of all men, is the first and fundamental tenet of democratic theory in Europe, as it is everywhere.

Democracy and liberty disappeared together during the fascist and nazi interludes. Consequently, when they had to shape their new institutions in 1947 and 1949, both the Italian and German nations were careful to re-establish democracy and liberty at the same time. Austria took the same precaution and returned to its pre-war constitution. Likewise, the constitution of the French Fourth Republic was largely drafted in reaction against the abuses of power of the Vichy regime.

In other countries, where the principles of democratic government were unquestioned, economic and international crises have led to the use of emergency powers and to the lessening of liberty. In time of supreme crises, every nation changes its form of government somewhat. Usually, however, the enactments of parliaments have been the source of the increased powers of the executive and wholesale legislative delegations have been repealed after the crises.

Thus, however widely the institutions of European democracies differ, they all have a common tradition of liberty, but the ways in which the blessings of liberty may be secured vary greatly—because liberty means different things in different countries, because liberty is not absolute, but only relative, because there are different conceptions of political order and public interest, and because of the close affinity of economics and politics.

1. The liberal background.

The reconciliation of liberty and authority was the common purpose of the framers of all constitutions in Western Europe. Their inspiration is to be found in the British liberal tradition, from Magna Carta onwards, in the philosophers of the 18th century, in the French Declaration of Rights of 1789, in the American Bill of Rights of 1791 or in their political tradition.

Three main features sum up the theory of democracy in Western Europe:

A. Political freedom or the right to participate in government. The important points concern elections and the operation of the government.

The right to vote is obviously essential, and it has been indicated how universal suffrage was introduced in all countries. Likewise, the electoral system is important. In the course of time, electoral reforms have been adopted in the different countries in order to attain an equitable form of parliamentary representation.

The injustice of the British system of election by a simple majority has generally brought about the introduction of other rules elsewhere in Europe. Almost all countries have preferred proportional representation (P.R.), which works rather satisfactorily. However, it is probably responsible for giving rise to new groups and splinter parties, which leads to weak coalitions and short-lived governments in some countries.

This is the reason why in 1953, 1956 and 1964, electoral reforms in Germany have tempered the effects of P.R. by combining it in a very astute manner with the election of half the deputies by a simple majority, which favors major parties, while another rule tends to the elimination of minor parties. (Proportional representation works only for the parties that have polled five percent of the votes or obtained three seats by direct election.) The substitution of a majority system for the present rules is under consideration with a view to the elections of 1973, while the enforcement of such a reform at the next elections in 1969 has been denounced as an unacceptable maneuver by the liberal F.D.P. which would actually be seriously threatened or even eliminated.

In France, P.R. was briefly preferred to the majority system during the Third Republic and under the Fourth Republic. The Fifth Republic has returned to the special system called *"scrutin d'arrondissement,"* which was a characteristic of the Third Republic: that is, a candidate is elected on the first ballot if he receives an absolute majority of the votes cast; if no candidate fulfills the condition, a second ballot is held a week later, at which a relative majority secures election. The system encourages alliances between neighboring parties. Until recently, though, it failed to discourage small parties.

The essential characteristics of elections in Western Europe, as in other liberal democracies, are three in number.

First, the suffrage is exercised in entirely free elections. Of course, some electoral rules have been shaped by the majority in order to reduce the strength of the minority parties (French electoral law of 1951, Italian law of 1953), but any candidate or party normally has a chance to win or retain the support of the electorate.

Second, the elections themselves imply delegation to the elected representatives of a broad power to decide freely: in the intervals between elections, parliament is supposed to give expression to the will of the people. Yet, at intervals fixed by the electoral law, the government or, in fact, the majority parties, go before the people on the basis of their record and are either returned to office for another limited period or turned out in favor of the opposition. When the power of dissolution exists (as in all countries except Norway and, of course, Switzerland) and is really exercised or able to produce deterrent effects (as in Northern Europe and the French Fifth Republic) or when laws or decisions can be submitted to a referendum (particularly in Switzerland and France), the number of occasions on which the people can make their voice heard may be increased and the strength of parliament may be reduced.

Third, free elections mean choices between theoretically significant alternatives. The role of political parties has everywhere been considered as fundamental. The right to create new parties and to carry on political action is simply a form of the freedom of association. In some recent constitutions (France, Italy, Germany for example), their role has been recognized. In countries like Germany or Sweden, political parties have been granted subsidies on public funds. Quite exceptional is the possibility of forbidding or dissolving a party. In Germany, however, political parties are illegal under the constitution if, "as judged by their programs or the conduct of their adherents, they aim at impairing or destroying the basic system of a free and democratic organization of the state, or endanger the existence of the federal German Republic." This provision has been used twice, but, as yet, the government has not deemed it advisable to have recourse to it in the case of the alleged neo-nazi N.P.D.

As for the operation of the government, all our democracies put their faith in majority judgments and action, but they also organize responsible government, because the authority of the executive can be based only on popular support. In parliamentary regimes, the cabinet is responsible to parliament or to the lower house; in fact, it is also (or ought to be) responsible to the electorate. In France, the cabinet is responsible to the lower house and also to the president of the Republic, who, although legally not responsible, did not hesitate, himself, on several occasions of referendum or dissolution, to put directly the question of confidence before the nation.

B. Another feature of liberalism is the general recognition of civil liberties, considered as fundamental guarantees against arbitrary government. Either defined in more or less precise terms in the constitution or in a declaration of rights, or simply organized by statutes, or resulting from the principle of the supremacy of the law, civil liberties impose restraints on the power of the executive in every country in Western Europe. To be sure, liberty is a changing concept and many rights, once widely recognized, were gradually curbed by law. But the belief remains that the individual is the end and purpose of the state, and that social institutions exist to serve him.

C. Finally, liberalism also implies the equality of all men, for democratic freedom necessarily means freedom for all people, which leads to the abolition of inequalities. Moreover, any progress toward equality gives a feeling of liberation to all people who previously suffered important discriminations.

Historically, in Europe, the claim for liberty coincided with the establishment of limited government and usually appeared before the time when equality was widely claimed. At the same time, a relative equality has always been considered as a necessary component for democracy.

In a first stage, equality was simply the enjoyment of equal status under law and of equality of opportunity. Such a limited conception was in accordance with the basic principles of liberal democracy, individualism and free enterprise, which were dominant until World War I.

Later, particularly with the progress of socialism, most European countries were bound to develop progressive policies which could really improve the working-class conditions and support human welfare. Today, the field of welfare demonstrates particularly in the Scandinavian countries, but also in the others, the remarkable changes that have been brought about by the claim for social equality.

Despite these common features, however, the different European democracies are, in fact, very unequally liberal.

2. The different ways of doing the same things (or different things).

Political developments in Western Europe have demonstrated that democracy is capable of being put into practice, both in governmental and economic terms, in many different ways. The content of liberalism may also vary greatly.

For example, it has been pointed out that the word "liberty," especially in France or Italy, includes or has included the notion of escape from tyranny or abuses of power by government, while the word "freedom" may correspond to a more positive concept, supposed to evoke a normal expression of life itself. There is also a great political difference between liberty, considered as a protection of existing rights, and the claim for "a new liberty," that would mean a kind of liberation from our chains and lead to important social transformations. Government has long been considered as being limited to political democracy, but in all countries since World War I, the striking fact is the breadth of government activities. In many countries since World War II, the trend toward economic and social democracy has led to nationalizations and the creation of numerous public enterprises, as well as to government direction or at least regulation and control of the economy.

The discussion that follows will be limited to three basic matters connected with constitutional developments: (A) the structure of parliament (B) the limitation of power, and (C) the scope of local government.

A. Liberal democracy has generally been considered in the past as implying bicameralism. At the time when parliamentary government was introduced in European countries, bicameralism was synonymous with moderation: balance of power between two legislative bodies that were to differ from one another in such respects as their recruitment, qualifications for membership, and length of service. As emphasized in the famous conversation between George Washington and Thomas Jefferson, a second chamber should be a rather conservative body and function as a "check" upon a more democratic and radical lower chamber.

This expectation has long been realized, but even in those countries where the original pattern of bicameralism has apparently been maintained, the system has evolved so that, in modern constitutions, the decline of second chambers is visible (except, of course, in the federal states, where the functions of upper houses are peculiar).

Generally speaking, in the Netherlands and Belgium, the traditional bicameralism which was established by the old constitutions is still in operation. Both chambers have roughly the same powers (although in the Netherlands the upper chamber is not enabled to initiate or amend legislation) and the cabinet is responsible to both. Nevertheless, in actual fact, the political importance of the lower chamber has tended to increase.

The Italian constitution of 1947 is the only modern constitution that has established a true bicameralism; with different compositions and electoral systems, the Senate and Chamber of Deputies are constitutionally equal, and to remain in power, a cabinet must have the confidence of both chambers. Actually, however, the political complexion of senate and chamber has always been similar (the elections taking place at the same time), which considerably reduces the importance of bicameralism.

In Sweden and Norway, the structure of parliament is peculiar. In Sweden, there are two chambers with substantially equal powers, but the importance of the joint sessions of the two houses has grown. In Norway, the *Storting* is theoretically unicameral, but it selects one-fourth of the members who will constitute the *Lagting* and three-fourths who will compose the *Odelsting;* the two sections are, on the whole, equal in powers (even as regards the control of the cabinet), but the *Storting* in plenary assembly is vested with important powers.

In France, since 1946, the Council of the Republic and the Senate have received strictly limited powers: the cabinet is not responsible to the second chamber, and, in the legislative procedure, the National Assembly can always override the votes of the second house.

Bicameralism has changed greatly because, almost everywhere, the composition of the previously "conservative" upper chamber tended, in the course of time, to reflect the social structure of the country almost exactly like the lower house. Bicameralism, originally political in nature, has become only technical.

This is the reason why some countries (Finland, Denmark since 1953) have openly repudiated bicameralism and the French Senate will very probably be replaced in the future by a simple advisory body.

B. The limitation of political power, which is the most important safeguard of individual liberty, has been organized in all Western European countries, but in different ways, related to different traditions or aspirations.

First, the tendency to the supremacy of parliament, extremely apparent in France before the Fifth Republic, is still characteristic in modern Italy. In Northern Europe, a better balance of powers between the legislative and the executive has been realized, sometimes comparable (in Sweden and Norway) to the British one. A striking fact is that the American system of judicial review of legislation did not arouse the admiration of European nations. The ordinary courts either have been refused the power of judicial review, or were not powerful enough to establish "government by judiciary."

In the Irish Republic, the supreme court may control the constitutionality of a bill, but the bill can be referred to the court by the president of the Republic only. In France, the Constitutional Council must rule on the constitutionality of the organic laws and the regulations of the assemblies, but as for ordinary laws, they may only be submitted to the council and only by the president of the Republic, the premier, or the president of one or the other assembly which, in fact, has occurred only when parliament attempted to exceed the "domain of the law" to which the constitution restricts its competence.

Special constitutional courts have been created in Austria (by the constitution of 1920–1929) and, after World War II, in Italy and Germany.

In Italy, the constitutional court (which, by the way, could not be set up before 1955) can decide on the constitutionality of laws and decrees (and judge conflicts between the central government and regions and between the regions themselves). The court may take jurisdiction of the case when the issue of constitutionality is raised by the president of a court during the course of a judicial proceeding, or when it is raised by either party. This court has already ruled on a considerable number of important cases.

The German *Bundesverfassungsgericht* of Karlsruhe, which is separated from the non-political Supreme Court, may decide on the relations between the federal government and the *Länder,* on conflicts concerning the operation of the federal government and on the compatibility of federal law and Land law with the constitution. In other instances, it solves specific legal or political controversies (such as the case of antidemocratic parties, already mentioned). In this way, judicial review of the constitutionality of laws has been constitutionally introduced, and the court has exercised its power frequently.

In other countries, there is no control of the constitutionality of laws, which, it is true, is less important and alarming in unitary countries than it could be in federal states. Abuses of power by the legislature have been exceptional and public opinion is the best check against any attempt to violate the constitution.

Second, the problems of the limitation of executive power are different, and the political limitation of the executive depends on the features of the regime, already considered.

The principle of legality implies the protection of the people against executive or administrative action contrary either to the constitution, or to statutes. In continental Europe, this protection belongs either to the judicial courts, or, in the countries that have been inspired by the French model (such as Sweden, Finland, Italy, Germany and, since 1946, Belgium) to "administrative courts," which are in fact independent of the government. The differences between the various systems and techniques are too important or complex, and the problems involved in these problems are too numerous to be dealt with in this paper, but it may be said that the two systems which, a long time ago, were found to be in complete opposition, have evolved, so that the solutions accepted in these two systems are much closer today than they originally appeared to be.

A few words must be said on the special institution of the ombudsman. This has been introduced in the Scandinavian countries (in Sweden since 1809, Finland since 1919, Denmark since 1955, Norway since 1962) and transplanted to Germany in 1957 (*Wehrbeauftragte des Bundestages*) without great success. The ombudsman system works very well, especially in Denmark and Norway.

Generally speaking, the ombudsman is a parliamentary commissioner. Any person who is displeased with any administrative action or inaction may complain to the ombudsman who can also act on his own motion. He decides to dismiss futile complaints and to investigate the others. The ombudsman may criticize the administration or make recommendation for change, but has no power to change administrative action. His authority is due to his prestige, and to the publicity given to his action. This institution seems to protect against unfairness and to increase administrative efficiency. It has raised considerable interest in many countries, particularly in Great Britain, where the action of the parliamentary commissioner has been cautiously limited.

C. Beyond the controversies on centralization and decentralization, it appears clear (1) that democracy's essential aim is self-government, and (2) that an important restraint on the power of the executive may lie in a substantially autonomous system of local government, which helps to prevent the development of a huge, bureaucratic, uncontrolled, and perhaps arrogant central administration. Local government also contributes to political education and helps develop a widespread participation in the administrative process by the citizens, upon whom democracy should place the ultimate responsibility for the welfare of a pluralist society and for the security of the state.

All European democracies became pervaded with these ideas, but the objectives corresponding to such terms as states' rights, home rule, local self-government, and decentralization have been unequally and often imperfectly attained.

Of course, the most significant system of decentralized government appears in federal states. The *Länder,* provinces and cantons in Germany, Austria and Switzerland, are reasonably independent entities and usefully serve as intermediaries between the national government and the local units. In Germany, for example, the different political orientations of the *Länder* tend to increase the sensitivity of the central government to minority views and the *Länder* themselves are not simple regional units; they are states, with important functions and powers, with elected parliaments and responsible cabinet governments, and their autonomy is particularly significant where a long tradition of self-government exists (as in Hamburg and Bavaria).

But most European countries have been organized in unitary states, and the desire to protect a sometimes recent national unity against any kind of disintegration, as well as a tradition of uniformity or of equality, or the necessity of efficiency or rationality, or the persistence of strong central administrative structures inherited from authoritative regimes, have seriously limited the scope of decentralization.

As the term "decentralization" implies, local authorities, more often than not, have only such powers as have been conceded to them by the central government. Almost everywhere, the present organs of local government or administration have a long history and a certain tradition of autonomy, together with a tendency to decentralization, which has resulted in the devolution of powers to elected authorities at the regional and local levels. Local autonomy is enjoyed in some degree by every local authority, with an important diversity of initiative, functions, and scope of activities. In countries such as Belgium and the Netherlands, the provinces and communes have a large measure of autonomous government; in the Netherlands, the members of the provincial states elect the higher chamber of parliament, in Belgium, 48 senators are elected by the provincial councils. In Switzerland, communal powers are extensive. In Germany, the principle of communal autonomy has been established in the Bonn basic law and in the constitutions of the *Länder.*

However, in many countries, local authorities are subject to a very firm control by the executive. For example, aside from the elected councils, executive agents, who are officials, have been placed by the national government in local communities, not only for the purpose of attending to

national affairs, but also to control local action continuously and sometimes pervasively. The French system of the *"tutelle administrative"* (administrative guardianship) involves control of decisions (some of which
require the approval of the prefect) and also control of execution. Such a
system at least gives officials of the central government indirect influence
over the activities of local authorities. Thus, in Finland, Norway, Sweden,
and Denmark (as in France and Italy, in the departments and provinces)
the central government is represented in the counties by a governor or
prefect who is nominated, and may be dismissed, by the executive.

Local initiative is also restrained, of course, by lack of financial resources.
Liberal measures of decentralization were checked at a relatively early
stage by the rise of *étatism*. Because many problems formerly capable of
varying local solutions have become national issues, and because local
authorities are in need of financial assistance, the central government has
assumed additional functions. There has also been a general and substantial
increase in central control over local services (particularly the police
services), leading to closer co-ordination and possibly to uniformity. This
is of course a widespread modern phenomenon, but it is more visible in the
smaller European countries.

From this point of view, the problem of the regions in Italy is very sug-
gestive. Traditional local government is based on the commune and
province, largely comparable to the French commune and department. In
the province, the prefect exercises large powers over local affairs, controlling the commune and province administrative action approximately in
the same way as the French prefect does.

In order to develop local government without establishing federalism,
the Italian constitution of 1947 set up a new level of self-government
between the province and the capital: the region. Each one was to have
its own constitution and governmental structure, with an elected regional
legislative assembly and a responsible regional executive committee. The
constitution anticipated that the regions would have their own sources of
revenue and important powers were conferred upon the regional authorities.
(It also provided for administrative control of the region by a commissioner
of the government.) The creation of the regions seemed to announce an
entirely new form of local government and a considerable reduction of the
large influence of executive officials in the field of local action.

Unfortunately, 20 years after the constitution came into force, the reform
has not yet been completed. The five "autonomous regions with special
statute" (art. 116) have been organized with some variants in Sicily,
Sardinia, Aosta, Trentino-Alto Adige and Friuli-Venezia Giulia between
1946–1948 and 1963. These regions had to be organized thus because of
acute problems of underdevelopment or ethnic minorities. Yet the realization of the general constitutional scheme has been repeatedly postponed.

This is partly because of the changing attitudes of the political parties, partly because of the financial problems of the central government, and also because of the difficulty in reaching an agreement on the rules concerning the elections to regional parliaments, and the relations between the center and the regions—and in endowing the regional authorities with substantial resources without paralyzing the activities of the central government. In 1966, Prime Minister Moro pledged himself to secure the passage of whatever bills were needed to carry out the regionalist reform before the general elections of May, 1968. However, only the electoral law could be adopted, and it is only in late 1969 that the first elections to the regional councils are expected to take place.

In France, the necessity of transforming the economic regions—which have been created primarily to serve national governmental policy of development and planning, with a regional prefect and advisory bodies—has been recognized; regional reform is under consideration, in connection with the policy of "participation" and the revamping of the erstwhile weak Senate into a national economic council. A real reversal of France's traditional centralism would imply the emergence of elected regional councils with broad economic and financial responsibilities, but it would not be surprising to learn that the councils would be substantially controlled by a kind of commissioner of the government.

Thus, in Western Europe, the necessity has been admitted of bringing administration into line with democratic ideas, but at the local government level, democracy is very often tempered by a form of bureaucratic centralization. This is due to the wish to preserve national unity, and it is also linked with contemporary movements which tend to strengthen the executive.

III. Strengthening the Executive

The struggle against absolute monarchy or government has been carried on for years in Europe, and parliamentary government and democracy have generally been established with a considerable reluctance to accept the authority of a strong executive. Democrats often fear the power of government. A weak executive was accepted partly as the price which had to be paid for freedom. In Northern Europe and particularly in the Scandinavian countries, cabinet government developed more or less in the British way, but in other regimes, the legislature became the dominant organ—all the more since the divisions existing in the nation and the multiplicity of parties resulted (as has been mentioned above) in the absence of stable majorities and the formation of coalitions.

However, democracy is by no means synonymous with a weak executive. On the contrary, liberty is dependent upon authority for its existence, and there has been a rather general tendency to strengthen the executive in almost all countries where it had previously been deprived of the necessary authority and powers.

The growth of executive power is a general phenomenon. Its causes are well known. Efficient government in the modern state requires strong national leadership, an impulsive force, a co-ordinating authority that cannot possibly come from a numerous assembly. The growing importance of foreign affairs, the frequency of internal and international crises imply executive action, because initiative, energy and rapid decisions are indispensable. Mass communications have also given immense new assets to the chief executive, who seeks to mold public opinion and gain national support. The development of bureaucracy, which is necessary in modern government, also clearly contributes, on the whole, to increase the influence of the executive.

However, the democratization of the various political systems itself strikingly contributed to transform the executive into a powerful institution. The fear of tyranny had led to a distrust of executive power, but its limitation had been organized by the conservative forces of the old political class. With the expansion of the electorate and the vital role of political parties, government by the people was established, in which the citizens demand the power to decide by themselves and to choose their leader.

Of course, the growth of the executive is not equally visible in all European countries. The movement was limited, for example, in Germany and Italy after the war by the fear of dictatorship, in Switzerland by the traditional supremacy of the federal assembly, and in several parliamentary regimes by the multi-party system. Nevertheless, several attempts have been made to strengthen the executive, or, in any case, several changes have occurred, which can be seen in four ways.

A. In France, obviously, because of the presidential character of the regime, General de Gaulle has had "the supreme responsibility," the responsible cabinet has largely been his government, and no opposition or disagreement can appear between the President and the government. This results in a striking unity of the executive branch, which is a source of strength.

In most countries, executive decisions are made collectively, just as the responsibility for the decisions is collective.

The executive appears stronger when the collective character of decisions is lessened in relation to the dominant influence of the prime minister. The tendency to accept him as a real leader has developed clearly in all countries, except, of course, Switzerland and those countries where coalition governments and fluctuating majorities find it necessary to discuss nearly every problem in order to compromise. In other countries, the prime minister has emerged as the head of the government. He is, at the least, the leader of the dominant party; he can largely control the composition of the cabinet and is in a position to resolve any differences between ministers. His actual power naturally varies according to his personality, but he is always in fact the dominant figure of the executive and may be accepted as a national leader. This is of course related to the development of radio and television, and to the phenomenon of incarnation of power and management of public opinion. By means of television, his personality is brought into every home, not only as a voice, but also as a picture. If he is able to gain popularity and national support, this will increase his influence and his increased influence will help him to increase his popularity. This may happen even in countries where ministerial crises are relatively frequent because during a given period of time, the party leaders who are available for appointment as president of the council or prime minister are not very numerous and may well be considered as national personalities. The preponderance and authority of a prime minister are naturally more visible when governmental instability has been reduced.

B. Ensuring governmental stability is another means to strengthen the executive branch in parliamentary regimes.

In the northern countries, the party system and the general conditions of political life have, on the whole, confined ministerial instability within reasonable limits. Between 1905 and 1955, Sweden had 26 cabinets and only 16 Prime Ministers; in Norway, the figures were respectively 23 and 15, in Denmark 25 and 15, in the Netherlands 20 and 10, but in Belgium it was 46 and 21. In countries where the parliamentary regime works in the British way, where the tendency to the supremacy of the legislature did not develop, where a major party has been able to gain the majority (as in Sweden and Germany between 1953 and 1961), or where stable coalitions may work (as in Sweden and Norway, or Denmark and the Netherlands, or until recent years, Germany), or when minority governments may stay in power without being really opposed (as in Scandinavian countries), the dangers of instability are not important.

In other political situations (such as that in France before 1958, Italy more especially since 1953, Denmark and Belgium in recent years), the evil of instability may grow—and there have been attempts to promote stability through different remedies.

In a divided country, it is tempting to try to reduce the number of parties, but the merging of several existing groups into a united party is always very difficult and does not protect against the persistence of internal struggles within the newly united party. It is also tempting to proceed through electoral reforms, but the introduction of the British simple majority system in the countries where proportional representation has been accepted is politically very difficult (as appears today in Germany), and would probably not be enough to do away with a multi-party system.

Sometimes electoral reforms may favor the elimination of minor parties, as in Germany, but in Italy, the "premium to the majority system" of 1953 was a failure, and in Germany, the success was partly due to a previous tendency to political simplification.

There are essentially two methods for trying to stablize the executive.

One is the use—or the threat to use—the power of dissolution. To a certain extent, it is a disciplinary weapon against the opposition, for it may prevent the deputies from overthrowing ministries as recklessly as they please, without fear of electoral penalties. In Western Europe, the power of dissolution exists in all parliamentary constitutions except that of Norway. Its importance has often been overestimated. In countries like Sweden or modern Italy, governments have generally used this power only for choosing the best moment for general elections. In Belgium, the Netherlands, and Denmark, the power of dissolution has been used more frequently (in Denmark it is used almost automatically in the case of a ministerial crisis), but the results have often been disappointing (as they were during the Weimar Republic or in France during the Fourth Republic —when the constitutional conditions for a dissolution were fulfilled only once, in November 1955), mainly because of the electoral rules. With a majority system of voting, sudden general elections may lead to an important change in the composition of the house, even with a relatively small shift in public opinion. On the contrary, with P.R., small changes in public opinion have usually no consequences—or no important consequences— and the consultation of the electorate will very likely not give clear results (as happened in Belgium at the last elections).

The second method consists in laying down precise constitutional rules, in order to prevent ministerial crisis by "rationalizing" the parliamentary system. The techniques are numerous, including special rules for initiating a motion of censure, waiting period of some days before the vote on this motion, and special majority required for its adoption. Two techniques are particularly famous. One is the so-called "constructive motion of non-confidence" provided for by the Bonn constitution (art. 67): if the *Bundestag* wishes to overthrow the Chancellor, it must have agreed by an absolute majority on the person of his successor. The other is the machinery set up by the framers of the French constitution of 1958 (art. 49) in which the conditions under which the lower house may engage the responsibility of the government are so strict that in ten years only one motion of censure was adopted (October 1962). This resulted in the immediate dissolution of the assembly, and the elections gave the gaullists an important majority. It would, however, not be accurate to say that governmental stability in France is principally due to these constitutional rules.

C. The strengthening of the executive implies a certain amount of independence.

Parliamentary government means collaboration between the two branches, but does not in the least imply the subordination of the executive to parliament. The cabinet may be made relatively independent of the house by the "rationalization" of parliamentarianism—which appeared after World War I in most new European constitutions and was almost a complete failure. Nevertheless, some recent constitutions have returned to the various techniques of the so-called relationalization. Such provisions are particularly numerous in the Bonn basic law, and in the French constitution of 1958. They are, for example, related in France (1) to the agenda (2) to the fact that in the legislative process parliament must debate on the governmental text (3) to the possible limitation or rejection of amendments (4) to the vote or enforcement of finance bills, (5) to the committee system, and similar factors. Thanks to these rules, the cabinet may be empowered to govern without having to fight constantly against the opposition.

More significant are the rules tending to transfer to the electorate the power that determines the existence of the cabinet or of the chief executive. In Great Britain, the government is in fact largely chosen by the people and responsible to the electorate. In other countries, a somewhat similar situation may exist, as in Sweden and Norway, and also in the Irish Republic and Austria. In multi-party regimes, however, the power to form or to kill a coalition government is necessarily abandoned to the leaders of parliamentary groups, who calculate the chances of possible alliances or decide to break up a coalition, often without particular consideration of public opinion. Examples are France under the Third and Fourth Republics; Italy; to a lesser degree, Belgium; Germany, in 1965, where the electorate clearly plebiscited the "small coalition," which resulted, a year later, in the formation of the quite different "great coalition." The process appears to be undemocratic (or democratic in a very indirect manner).

In Finland and France, the president of the Republic is elected by universal suffrage (indirectly, in Finland). This rule is extremely important since, in both countries, but especially in France, the president has been vested with important powers and is in a position entirely different from that of a parliamentary chief of state. These differences were particularly apparent from the first days of General de Gaulle's presidency—and the constitutional revision of 1962, in deciding that the president would be elected by popular suffrage, legally changed the balance of power.

D. Finally, in almost all countries, the powers of the executive have been substantially increased. Even in Switzerland, the growth of centralization and the lessening of the subordination of the Federal Council to the Assembly are evident. In the conduct of foreign relations, the control of parliament is everywhere extremely limited, except through financial means. The tendency toward a directed economy has also contributed to confer new powers upon the executive branch.

Special rules for times of emergency or crisis have appeared, either in the constitutions—such as the famous Article 16 of the French constitution of 1958 and the new emergency rules which in 1968 have been adopted in Germany, after years of discussions—or in statutes.

Above all, in most countries, the power of the executive has been further increased in the field of legislation. In fact, because the cabinet is responsible for carrying out a definite program, it initiates, in all European countries, a very high percentage of all acts of parliament.

In France, the constitution of 1958 (Art. 34–37) has provided for a new division of the legislative function as a whole between the legislative and executive branch, so that the field of parliamentary legislation is now strictly circumscribed; parliament is authorized to deal only with those specific matters which are listed in Article 34, while all other matters may be dealt with by the executive.

Moreover, in all other countries, the domain of executive rule has been extended in the course of time.

The technique of delegated legislation, by which the government is given special powers to make legislative changes, has been provided for by several constitutions (Italy, art. 77; France, art. 38). In other cases, it is possible for the government to have its bills passed without a vote of parliament (Bonn basic law, art. 81, concerning the "state of legislative necessity"; France, art. 49, par. 3). In France (art. 11), the president may submit some bills for approval to the people by referendum, especially any bill dealing with the organization of governmental authorities, and, in this way, he may do without parliament.

In countries where the constitutions were framed a long time ago, constitutional practice has developed in similar directions. In the Swiss political system, for example, the two World Wars have considerably enhanced the powers of the Federal Council, which have become, at least temporarily, the dominant branch of the government. Between 1939 and 1950, the power to legislate by decree in very important matters has been delegated by the Assembly to the Federal Council.

The growth of the executive is, of course, much more apparent in the French Fifth Republic, but the same tendency also appears in other democracies, either because parliament had never claimed the right to dominate the executive (as in Northern Europe) or because parliaments have been obliged to accept restrictions upon their powers.

Conclusions

The political problems of Western Europe are obviously not peculiar to European countries. All democracies have to search for a satisfactory balance between liberty and authority, to reconcile the democratic ideology and the everyday working of governmental institutions, to preserve their great traditions and values and, at the same time, to change in a changing world.

Europe is a small continent, and Western Europe consists of a small number of small democratic countries between which many *rapprochements* have taken place. Some have years or centuries of common history. Most have the same ideal of free representative government. All are inclined to admit, with Winston Churchill, that "democracy is the worst form of government, except all those other forms that have been tried from time to time." All these nations try to promote the general welfare in a mixed economy of private enterprise and governmental action, or public enterprise. They are linked to each other by economic and political solidarity. The citizens of these countries are getting to know each other better and better.

Nevertheless, each one has its political traditions and all desire to preserve their autonomy and are more or less reluctant to surrender an important portion of their sovereignty. The European Community has been established by only six countries. It has made progress, but without reaching a high degree of political integration. The "outer seven" are still outside. When major controversies arise, the old theory of sovereignty makes it difficult to work out the essential compromises.

Another conclusion is that, when in these countries the structure of government had apparently ceased to be a major question, this was only a false appearance. Things have changed. The constitutional future of Germany will have to be fixed definitely, sooner or later. Italy will have to choose between a true regionalist reform and a simply decentralized state. Will the French institutions remain unchanged after General de Gaulle? Nobody knows. Belgium will have to find a solution to the very difficult problem of the two linguistic communities.

Finally, there is also, as in other parts of the world, the basic problem of the defense of democracy. Liberal democracy has been established in order to protect liberty against tyranny or possible oppression of the majority. Today, with some individuals or groups using violence here and there and claiming for themselves the right to coerce, to challenge, to paralyze public activities and to resist governmental authority, the question is how the majority will be able to rule democratically and to enforce the laws without using extreme repression. Revolutionary movements have often led to dictatorship. The future of democracy depends far more upon the people themselves than upon any institutions for, after all, freedom and civil liberties can prevail only where the people want them to survive.

Notes

1. In Spain, the nineteenth century was particularly perturbed. A limited monarchy was established repeatedly in 1812, 1820, 1869, and in 1874 after the second Restoration, but the regime did not really succeed. In Portugal, the constitution of 1826 also established a constitutional monarchy which lasted until 1910 but, in that country too, the king was the personal chief of the executive and the ministers were responsible to him.
2. That system, as early as 1848 and still more after 1874, admitted both popular initiative and referendum, either at the federal level or in the cantons. It is the opposite of any kind of Cabinet government. The Swiss have made the executive the formal servant of the legislature. Not only are the seven members of the Federal Council elected by the Federal Assembly, but the Assembly also resorts to postulates or motions to direct the executive's course in the conduct of administration as well as to oblige the Council to draft legislation in accordance with the will of the Assembly. There is no political responsibility of the Federal Council to the Assembly. The latter can only refuse to re-elect the councilors or some of them, but, in fact, they are re-elected. In the case of a possible divergence between the attitude of the Council and the Assembly's will, the councilors are bound to change their policy.
3. In Italy and Germany, after World War II, the authors of the new constitutions largely took into account the experience both of dictatorship and of the poor functioning of their previous parliamentary regimes.
4. The examples of France, where definite establishment of universal suffrage was effected in 1848, and Germany, where universal suffrage was introduced in 1871, are conclusive in this field.

   In democratic Switzerland, on the contrary, women are not entitled to vote in federal elections and women's suffrage has been introduced only in four cantons, since 1959.

11

Due Process Problems Today in the United States

Erwin N. Griswold

My role in this program is, I must confess, a somewhat awkward one. As a holder of public office, and as a lawyer appearing before the Supreme Court, I cannot appropriately discuss any pending case or specific problem. Nor can I, I feel, discuss any case which has been recently decided, and in which the United States, or one of its officers or agencies, was a party. When it is observed that nearly two-thirds of all the cases considered by the Court on their merits are United States government cases, the extent of this limitation becomes apparent.

Nor am I content to speak in simply general terms, and add my fulsome praise to the Fourteenth Amendment and the decisions which the Supreme Court has rendered in its construction and application over the past 100 years. There can be no doubt that it was a great event in American constitutional history which we are celebrating. Nor can there be doubt as to the great and important role which the Court has played in putting meaning and vitality into the Amendment, and particularly, into the general terms of its due process clause. I am grateful for the Fourteenth Amendment, and I have profound respect for the Court. Others, however, will deal with those topics with more authority than I can, even in the special context of "Constitutionalism in a Changing World."

In this situation, I am planning to focus my observations on a rather specific development in the relatively recent history of the Fourteenth Amendment. In doing this, I find myself encountering another dilemma. For, though I wish to measure my words, some of my observations may not indicate complete enthusiasm for every action that the Court has taken, especially in recent years. Almost from the beginning of its history, the United States Supreme Court has been the target of much extravagant

Erwin N. Griswold is Solicitor General of the United States.

and irresponsible criticism. One who ventures critical observations about the Court runs the risk that his remarks will be picked up by others and used in ways which were never intended. But to refrain from comment, or to limit one's self to flowery and empty praise, is no service to the Court, and is not a sincere way to give it the praise which is its due. I am a professional man, with a substantial academic background. I offer the remarks which follow as a genuine tribute to the Supreme Court and its justices, who carry the responsibility, pursuant to their oaths, to administer justice according to the Constitution of the United States, including the Fourteenth Amendment which became effective some time in June or July of 1868.

The most striking and far-reaching development with respect to the Fourteenth Amendment, I believe, is the extent to which it has been used by the Court to bring into effect against the States most of the terms of the first eight amendments to the Constitution, the Bill of Rights, in all their details, including the gloss which has been put on them by the decisions of 177 years. You may have noticed that that rather long sentence was rather carefully constructed; I did not say anything about "incorporation," or "selective incorporation," or "absorption." I do not propose here to discuss the whole problem. A good deal has been written about it, including much by various justices of the court in a considerable number of opinions. Some five years ago, Professor Louis Henkin wrote that "Students of the Court have been strangely silent about this interpretation of the Constitution," [1] and there is a good deal of truth in that observation today. Generally speaking, I think, the professional world is not aware how far the development has gone. Academic commentators have not fully foreseen the implications, or have perhaps been caught up in the "wave of the future" atmosphere that seems to surround this changing area of constitutionalism in our legal world.

Although the count could differ, and is not very important anyway, my own reading shows that there were forty-one decisions made by the Court on the merits over the past two Terms, in which Supreme Court law was applied in cases coming from state courts under the far-reaching umbrella of the Fourteenth Amendment. The formulation differs somewhat, but the statement is usually made in a wholly matter-of-fact way, which ignores the process that is involved. Thus, in *Powell* v. *Texas*,[2] the opinion by Justice Marshall refers to "the Eighth Amendment as applied to the States through the Fourteenth Amendment," while Justice Fortas, dissenting, refers to "the Eighth Amendment, made applicable to the States through the Fourteenth Amendment." [3] In *Mancusi* v. *DeForte*,[4] the Court refers to the respondent's "Fourth and Fourteenth Amendment rights," and thereafter refers to the Fourth Amendment exclusively. In *Board of Education* v. *Allen*,[5] the question was formulated as whether the state law was "in conflict with the First and Fourteenth Amendments." In *Sibron* v. *New York*,[6] the Court said that the case presented "questions under the Fourth and Fourteenth Amendments"; while in the related case of *Terry* v. *Ohio*,[7] the Court referred to "the Fourth Amendment, made applicable to the States by the Fourteenth," and thereafter referred to the Fourth Amendment exclusively. These examples could, of course, be multiplied. They are simply the ones which can be taken from the most recent volume of the United States Reports.

To be sure, this development has its roots in the period of 30 to 40 years ago. Prior to that, it had been text-book law that the first eight Amendments were not applicable to the states. In the leading case of *Twining* v. *New Jersey*,[8] for example, it was held that the Fourteenth Amendment did not make the self-incrimination provision of the Fifth Amendment applicable to the states. That was what I learned in law school, and I suppose that it is hard for me to adjust to change in my later years.

In *Gitlow* v. *New York*,[9] the majority of the Court assumed that "freedom of speech and of the press—which are protected by the First Amendment from abridgement by Congress—are among the fundamental personal rights and 'liberties' protected by the due process clause of the Fourteenth Amendment from impairment by the States." And, in a guarded way, this was asserted by Justice Holmes in his dissenting opinion in that case. Similar approaches were taken in several subsequent cases involving free speech, press, and assembly.[10] By 1940, this was phrased in terms of "The First Amendment, and the Fourteenth through its absorption of the First."[11] And similar references were made in a number of subsequent speech, press, and religion cases.[12] Yet in *Palko* v. *Connecticut*,[13] the Court speaking through Mr. Justice Cardozo, who had achieved great distinction as a State court judge, and as a legal philosopher, specifically disavowed the incorporation rule, and said:

> If the Fourteenth Amendment has absorbed them, the process of absorption has had its source in the belief that neither liberty nor justice would exist if they were sacrificed . . . This is true, for illustration, of freedom of thought and speech.

The current development, which has been moving relentlessly ahead for several years now, finds its foundation in *Adamson* v. *California*,[14] though the Court there again held that the self-incrimination provision of the Fifth Amendment did not bind the states. In reaching this result, the Supreme Court reaffirmed the established view in these words: "The due process clause of the Fourteenth Amendment . . . does not draw all the rights of the federal Bill of Rights under its protection." In that case, however, Justice Black filed a dissenting opinion, in which he said:[15]

My study of the historical events that culminated in the Fourteenth Amendment, and the expressions of those who sponsored and favored, as well as those who opposed its submission and passage, persuades me that one of the chief objects that the provisions of the Amendment's first section, separately and as a whole, were intended to accomplish was to make the Bill of Rights applicable to the states.

When this opinion was rendered more than 21 years ago, I thought it was interesting, rather surprising, and unpersuasive. I still feel that way. Of course one only has the view that comes to him from the light that he can focus on his own mind, and one must be constantly aware that his own light is unduly dim; but, for what it is worth, in my light there is no justification for this view. It seems to me obvious that textually it is wrong. It makes the due process clause of the Fifth Amendment meaningless, because it is wholly unnecessary, if all it does is to provide that the process due a man is that specified by the balance of the first eight amendments. And it reads large amounts of detail into the due process clause of the Fourteenth Amendment which surely are not there. As far as the historical basis for the conclusion is concerned—assuming that we could get beyond the words used in the Fourteenth Amendment, which are inept and inadequate to reach this result even if the historical basis for the conclusion were strong and clear—my own view is that it has been thoroughly demonstrated that this conclusion is not supported by the historical materials.[16]

Yet the view grows and grows, and now has, for all practical purposes, captured the present Supreme Court. This, to me, is nothing less than a tour de force. I trust it will not be misunderstood if I say that I can think of nothing in the history of our constitutional law which has gone so far since John Marshall and the Supreme Court decided *Marbury* v. *Madison* [17] in 1803. History has concluded that John Marshall was right. I do not think that the same conclusion necessarily follows on the development with which I am dealing. This view, I know, is not shared by most of those who have the votes. But this problem is one that will be with us for a long time, and it will have to be considered again and again, in the long view. Perhaps, in due time, it will be recognized that the Fourteenth Amendment cannot rightly be regarded as "incorporating" the first eight amendments, no matter how many times it has been said or decided that it does. This is a matter that cannot be determined for all time by *ipse dixit*. We can only hope that too much harm will not be done in the process of working these problems out.

What is the harm that may be done? Why am I concerned? Is it not a little odd that I should not see the great constructive nature of the contribution here, and join in the applause? Are not the first eight amendments good, and is it not a good idea to apply them to the states?

Yes, the first eight amendments are good, and it might well be a good idea to apply some of them to the states. But such a change as this, by no means interstitial, and not based on any clearly worded text, should not come about by judicial decision, no matter how desirable it may be thought to be. This, it seems to me, is a clear case of "tyranny of labels," and it is discouraging to me to see how quickly and easily the formula has been beguiling. It is an example, I think, of what Judge Cardozo called "The tendency of a principle to expand itself to the limit of its logic." [18] There is another quotation from Cardozo which seems to me to be relevant and appropriate. In *The Growth of the Law*,[19] he said: "The search is for the just word, the happy phrase, that will give expression to the thought, but somehow the thought itself is transfigured by the phrase when found." Here the effort was to develop content in the due process clause of the Fourteenth Amendment by looking for illustrations in the various and varying provisions of the first eight amendments. That proved a workable process, even though the answers were by no means automatic, but it also proved seductive. When some light was found in some of the first eight amendments, it suddenly develops that they not only give light, but they reach out to command and control. Thus has the thought of the due process clause of the Fourteenth Amendment been transfigured by the alluring specificity of the essentially unrelated language of the eight amendments which constitute our national Bill of Rights. More than half a century ago, Justice Holmes cautioned us against "pressing the broad words of the Fourteenth Amendment to a drily logical extreme." [20] It is hard for me to escape the conclusion that that is what has been done in these cases which bring to bear the very wording of the first eight amendments (or, so far, of most of them) as limitations on the powers of the states.

Though an initial reference is sometimes, or generally, made to the Fourteenth Amendment, the Court immediately turns to one of the first eight amendments and proceeds to apply its specific terms, and the decisions which have arisen under those terms. By this process, in recent years, the self-incrimination provision of the Fifth Amendment has been made applicable to the States,[21] despite relatively recent and powerful decisions to the contrary.[22] Also, just in the 1967 Term, the trial by jury provision of the Sixth Amendment was made applicable to the States.[23] It is disarmingly easy to slip over from the general language of the due process clause of the Fourteenth Amendment to the specific language of the first eight amendments when one says that the first eight have been "incorporated" or "absorbed." But this is just the sort of delusive process that lawyers are supposed to be skilled in guarding against.

Before long, in this process, we will have indictment by grand juries imposed on the states, though it has long been established that there is no such requirement, and there is nothing to indicate that procedure by information, adopted by more than half the states, is unfair, or abused, or is anything but the substantial reform which it was thought to be when it was advocated and painstakingly put into effect. Nor is there anything, to me, very persuasive in the view that trial by jury, even in criminal cases, is the only fair method of trial, or that it bears any relation to the "due process of law" which is the only relevant requirement of the Fourteenth Amendment. It is true that jury trial has great historical roots, and that it has a great emotional fascination for many American lawyers. But that does not make it an element of due process of law. The fact that many civilized nations in the world do not use juries in criminal cases is not wholly irrelevant. Indeed there are parts of this country today where most criminal trials are conducted without juries, and the standard of justice in those places seems to be as high as, if not higher than that in other parts of the country.

In the decisions during 1968, we just escaped a ruling that verdicts of less than a unanimous jury can no longer be accepted in the states.[24] It is odd that this should come to the United States, in the laboratories of the States, just at the time when in England, the source of the common law, the requirement of unanimity has been discontinued.[25] As a matter of fact, I rather like juries in criminal cases, and I like the rule of unanimity for verdicts in criminal cases. However, this is wholly irrelevant. Constitutional rules are not soundly based on the likes or dislikes of a majority of the Court, or on a desire to bring about changes which it is thought would be improvements.

On this basis, we will soon have a requirement of jury trials in all civil cases where the amount involved is over twenty dollars, as required in the Federal courts by the Seventh Amendment. How is this to be escaped if the Fourteenth Amendment "incorporates" the first eight amendments? Is there any reason within any conceivable notion of due process why such a result should be brought about? We may find, too, that the Second Amendment, dealing with "The right of the people to keep and bear Arms" is binding on the States. Is there any possible basis for finding such a result to be required by the general terms of the due process clause of the Fourteenth Amendment?

In his opinion in the *Adamson* [26] case, and in his recent Carpentier Lectures at Columbia University [27] Justice Black supports his view by saying that the first eight amendments give specific rules, while the due process clause is very general, so that judges, as he says, must fall back on "natural law," [28] and become "Platonic guardians" [29]—which I join with him and Judge Learned Hand in abhorring.

In his Carpentier Lectures in 1968, Justice Black put it this way: [30]

> But to pass upon the constitutionality of statutes by looking to the particular standards enumerated in the Bill of Rights and other parts

of the Constitution is one thing; to invalidate statutes because of application of natural law deemed to be above and undefined by the Constitution is another. In the one instance, courts proceeding within clearly marked constitutional boundaries seek to execute policies written into the Constitution; in the other, they roam at will in the limitless areas of their own beliefs as to reasonableness and actually select policies, a responsibility which the Constitution entrusts to the legislative representatives of the people.

This approach puzzles me. It seems to me that it greatly oversimplifies the situation. It uses a textual difficulty, in the generality of the due process clause—which after all is what is written in the Constitution of the United States—to support a specious slipping over into the supposed specificity of the first eight amendments. Of course it is not what the Constitution *says*. All that the Constitution says with respect to the states is that they shall not "deprive any person of life, liberty, or property, without due process of law."

Besides, there is the Fifth Amendment, and its due process clause. How is it to be interpreted, and given content? Is this to be regarded as invalid, under some sort of super-constitutional principle, because under it courts "roam at will in the limitless area of their own beliefs as to reasonableness and actually select policies"? Of course not. Judges must function as judges in construing and applying the due process clause of the Fifth Amendment. Is there any reason why they should not, or cannot, perform the same function, in construing and applying the same words, used to the same effect in the Fourteenth Amendment?

What the Court has done, it seems to me, is to read into the general terms of the due process clause of the Fourteenth Amendment not only words but ideas which are not there. It has read most of the first eight amendments as defining due process, without accepting the fact that in that process it has done wholesale what Justice Black has so effectively argued against on the retail level. There may be light in the observation of Carl Becker, the Cornell historian, who reminded us a generation ago that: [31]

> If we know . . . that the wish is father to the thought, that the heart has reasons that reason knows not of, it was, after all, reason that revealed this secret to us, and the secret, once revealed, enables reason to avoid illusions that would otherwise vitiate its conclusions.

It is true that the due process clauses are in very general terms, and that much of judging and judicial self-examination, and, indeed, humility, are involved in their interpretation and application. After all, though, that is what judges are for. Obviously enough, "due process" is an elusive concept; it cannot be pinned down by any template, even that of the first eight amendments. But it has deep common law and constitutional roots. It is the sort of concept with which judges in this country have been trained and accustomed to deal. Besides it is what the United States Constitution *says*. One does not have to be a literalist to think that the words actually used are relevant, even in a constitution, and this is especially true when the words are a concretion, with 750 years behind them. If the judges will focus on that, I have no doubt that they will work out adequate— and less rigid—solutions to the problems which come up (as the Court said, long ago) "by the gradual process of judicial inclusion and exclusion." [32] It will not be an easy task, but judging never is.

I am content to accept the collegiate conclusion on such questions, when the minds of the justices are focussed on the Fourteenth Amendment itself, and not turned away by the notion that there is something better or easier in the first eight amendments. Besides, such turning away offends my sense of judicial proprieties. Beyond question, it is the due process clause of the Fourteenth Amendment which is constitutionally and legally applicable in these cases involving the extent of state power. There is little to be said, it seems to me, in favor of putting that problem aside on the ground that it is difficult and something else is to be found in the first eight amendments. In many cases, of course, particularly in the area of criminal procedure, such as fundamental fairness,[33] right to counsel,[34] and to a speedy trial,[35] the due process requirement may lead to the same result. It should not, however, be automatic; and the decision should be one of due process, and not of something else.

Within months we were spared, by a single vote, the requirement that public drunkenness cannot be dealt with through the criminal law.[36] This was nearly done by carrying forward the process of reading the Eighth Amendment into the Fourteenth, already started in *Robinson* v. *California*,[37] reading conclusions into the Eighth Amendment that cannot be found in its words, and surely not in its history, and concluding on this basis that handling the problem of drunkenness through the criminal process is constitutionally invalid as a "cruel and unusual punishment." Indeed, as I read the opinions, the first part of the process was done; that is, the question was considered to be an Eighth Amendment question, and the division came on the application of the Eighth Amendment. But should not the focus have been on due process? Should we be frozen, in our handling of this ancient and intractable problem by a judge-made constitutional rule, never dreamed of during more than 150 years of our constitutional history, which would force one particular method of handling the problem on the states, a method which the judges do not understand (because no one does), and for which the medical profession is wholly unprepared?

In bringing these remarks to a close, I would like to make three general observations which seem to me to be relevant to the consideration of the problem of constitutionalism in our changing world.

1. For too long, this country has thought of the courts as the place to turn to for the resolution of problems. As Tocqueville observed 130 years ago: "Scarcely any political question arises in the United States which is not resolved sooner or later into a judicial question." [38] By extending the sweep in detail of the Fourteenth Amendment, we bring more and more state problems into the federal courts, and subject them to a uniform federal rule. Moreover, as Justice Black has pointed out,[39] it is surely odd, in the light of their well-known history, to look to the first eight amendments for limitations on *State* power, and this is not helped by looking at it through the Fourteenth Amendment with blinders on the eyes.

2. By the same process, we leave the states less and less free to conduct experimentation. Here again I can quote Justice Black on my side, for in his opinion in *Powell* v. *Texas*,[40] in the spring of 1968, he said that "experience in making local laws by local people themselves is by far the safest guide for a nation like ours to follow." Nevertheless, "incorporation" centralizes more and more of our law in Washington, and makes one law throughout a nation whose strength is thought to rest, in considerable measure, on its diversity and its federal nature. We are a nation, we should have due process throughout the nation, as the Constitution provides. But it is important to observe, I think, and to keep constantly in mind, that it is the fundamental and procedural fairness that is the essence of due process, and not the specifics of the first eight amendments.

3. Finally, it should be recognized that, to some extent, the states have been slow to meet their responsibilities in these areas, and the Supreme Court has, on some occasions, been impelled to act in order to fill what could be regarded as a legal vacuum. That was the situation in *Powell* v. *Alabama*,[41] *Brown* v. *Mississippi*,[42] and *Gideon* v. *Wainwright*,[43] and, to some extent, in *Mapp* v. *Ohio*.[44] If the states, through their legislatures and their courts, would meet their responsibilities more effectively, and would set higher standards, particularly in the field of the criminal law, we would have less intervention by the federal judiciary, and less need to debate about "incorporation."

Many of the results reached by the Court have been salutary, though I do not think they all have been. Whether they are consistent with or required by the constitutional provisions which the Court is expounding is another question. In this process, the Court has adopted a formulation and approach which I think is unwarranted and unsound. These important and difficult questions should be constantly subjected to reexamination. This, I believe, is of the essence in our Constitutionalism in a changing world.

Notes

1. Henkin, *"Selective Incorporation" in the Fourteenth Amendment*, 73 Yale L. J. 74 (1963). See also *The Supreme Court, 1963 Term*, 78 Harv. L. Rev. 179, 223–227 (1964); Frankfurter, *Memorandum on "Incorporation" of the Bill of Rights into the Due Process Clause of the Fourteenth Amendment*, 78 Harv. L. Rev. 746 (1965); *The Supreme Court, 1964 Term*, 79 Harv. L. Rev. 105–113 (1965). Compare Friendly, *The Bill of Rights as a Code of Criminal Procedure*, 53 California L. Rev. 929 (1965).
2. 392 U.S. 514, 531 (1968).
3. 392 U.S. at 558–559.
4. 392 U.S. 364, 366 (1968).
5. 392 U.S. 236, 238 (1968).
6. 392 U.S. 40, 43 (1968).
7. 392 U.S. 1, 8 (1968).
8. 211 U.S. 78 (1908). See also, *Hurtado* v. *California*, 110 U.S. 516, 520, 534–535 (1884), holding that the provision of the Fifth Amendment for indictment by a grand jury is not made applicable to the states by the due process clause of the Fourteenth Amendment.
9. 268 U.S. 652, 666, 672 (1925).
10. *Whitney* v. *California*, 274 U.S. 357, 372, 373 (1927); *De Jonge* v. *Oregon*, 299 U.S. 353, 364 (1937); *Lovell* v. *City of Griffin*, 303 U.S. 444, 450 (1938).
11. *Minersville School District* v. *Gobitis*, 310 U.S. 586, 593 (1940).
12. *Murdock* v. *Pennsylvania*, 319 U.S. 105, 108 (1943); *Douglas* v. *City of Jeannette*, 319 U.S. 157, 162 (1943); *Board of Education* v. *Barnette*, 319 U.S. 624, 639 (1943); *Everson* v. *Board of Education*, 330 U.S. 1, 8 (1947); *McCollum* v. *Board of Education*, 333 U.S. 203, 210 (1948).
13. 302 U.S. 319, 323, 326 (1937).
14. 332 U.S. 46, 53 (1947).
15. 332 U.S. at 71.
16. Fairman, *Does the Fourteenth Amendment Incorporate the Bill of Rights?*, 2 Stan. L. Rev. 5 (1949); Morison, *Does the Fourteenth Amendment Incorporate the Bill of Rights?*, 2 Stan. L. Rev. 140 (1949).
17. 1 Cranch 137 (1803).
18. Cardozo, *The Nature of the Judicial Process* 51 (1921).
19. Cardozo, *The Growth of the Law* 89 (1924).
20. *Noble State Bank* v. *Haskell*, 219 U.S. 104, 110 (1911).
21. *Malloy* v. *Hogan*, 378 U.S. 1 (1964).
22. *Twining* v. *New Jersey*, 211 U.S. 78 (1908); *Adamson* v. *California*, 332 U.S. 46 (1947).
23. *Duncan* v. *Louisiana*, 391 U.S. 145 (1968); *Bloom* v. *Illinois*, 391 U.S. 195 (1968).
24. *DeStefano* v. *Woods*, 392 U.S. 631 (1968), where it was held that *Duncan* v. *Louisiana* was not to be applied retroactively in such a case.
25. The Criminal Justice Act, 1967, c. 80, sec. 13.
26. 332 U.S. at 68–92.
27. "Due Process of Law," March 21, 1968.

28. 332 U.S. at 75, 91; Carpentier Lecture, March 21, 1968, p. 12.
29. L. Hand, *The Bill of Rights* 73 (1958), quoted in Justice Black's opinion in *Powell* v. *Texas,* 392 U.S. 514, 548 (1968).
30. Carpentier Lecture, March 21, 1968, pp. 11–12.
31. Becker, *Some Generalities that Still Glitter,* 39 Yale Rev. 649, 665 (1940).
32. *Davidson* v. *New Orleans,* 96 U.S. 97, 104 (1878).
33. *Brown* v. *Mississippi,* 297 U.S. 278 (1936); *Powell* v. *Alabama,* 287 U.S. 45 (1932).
34. *Gideon* v. *Wainwright,* 372 U.S. 335 (1963).
35. *Klopfer* v. *North Carolina,* 386 U.S. 213 (1967).
36. *Powell* v. *Texas,* 392 U.S. 514 (1968).
37. 370 U.S. 660 (1962). See also *Budd* v. *California,* 385 U.S. 909 (1966).
38. Tocqueville, *Democracy in America,* Pt. 1, ch. 16.
39. Carpentier Lecture, March 21, 1968, p. 8.
40. 392 U.S. 514, 548 (1968).
41. 287 U.S. 45 (1932).
42. 297 U.S. 278 (1936).
43. 372 U.S. 335 (1963).
44. 367 U.S. 643 (1961).

12

Constitutionalism in Canada: Legislative Power and a Bill of Rights

Bora Laskin

Canada was barely one year old when the Fourteenth Amendment became effective, and was not quite born when that amendment was first proposed to the United States Congress in 1866. Contemporary records indicate that far from considering any constitutional limitations upon the power to enact laws, the framers of the Canadian Constitution thought in terms of a federalism whose principle would be reflected in the composition of the organs of government, especially the Senate.[1] The central core of federalism, as now understood in Canada (namely, the division of legislative power), did not carry the significance at the time of Confederation that it later had.

The emphasis was on the proposed central legislature, and there was considerable feeling that a legislative union was being achieved in fact, if not in text; the powers to be exercised by the provincial or local legislatures would, it was thought, not be significantly different from the powers theretofore exercised by municipalities. What appeared to be a novelty to be reckoned with was the introduction of an intermediate level of government, between the imperial government in London on the one hand and the colonial governments of the various British possessions in North America on the other.[2]

The United States' brand of federalism, as then understood, was not worthy of emulation when it had bogged down in civil war. Even that aspect of federalism reflected in the United States' conception of equal Senate representation from the component states was rejected; Canada opted

Bora Laskin is a Justice of the Court of Appeal of Ontario.

for Senate representation on a basis of regions rather than of provinces.[3] Another aspect of federalism developed through convention, rather than law, in the composition of the national cabinet or executive. In the immediate post-Confederation period, not only provincial and regional influences but religious and linguistic considerations played their part in the selection of members of the national ministry; and this pattern was continued.[4]

In one major respect, Canadian constitutionalism aped that of the United States, namely, in judicial review of exercises of legislative power by the national Parliament and by the local or provincial legislatures.[5] There was no provision for such review in the written constitution; not even a general supremacy or paramountcy clause, such as is found in Article VI, clause 2 of the Constitution of the United States. However, judicial review was inevitable with respect to a constitution which was also, and perhaps predominantly in the early years of Canadian federalism, considered to be merely a statute of the Parliament of the United Kingdom; it was inevitable under a statute that conferred limited powers upon subordinate legislatures, whose enactments were subject not only to reservation and disallowance by imperial authority, but were also subject to be overborne by superior imperial legislation applicable to Canada. Judicial review was inevitable, too, under a system of judicature whose ultimate reach was to the Judicial Committee of the Imperial Privy Council, through which finality of decision could be had whenever it wished to hear an appeal even if Canadian legislation, federal or provincial, sought to bar it. This situation was not remedied in criminal cases until 1933,[6] nor in all other cases until 1949,[7] following conventional and statutory changes in the constitutional relations of Great Britain and the Dominions.[8]

There were, however, major differences between the judicial review obtained under the Canadian constitution and its operation in the United States. First, there was the fact that questions could be referred to the courts for a constitutional opinion, or for an opinion on the validity of proposed or actual legislation, without the need of having a "case or controversy."[9] Second, the range of inquiry into issues of constitutional validity was, in general, limited by the ordinary rules of statutory construction.[10] Third, judicial review in Canada was not, except obliquely, ever concerned with preservation of the doctrine of separation of powers.[11] Fourth, since the Canadian constitution had no bill of rights, Canadian courts did not develop the near-legislative function that is involved in the exposition and application of an entrenched bill of rights. Had such a responsibility fallen to them, its discharge could have been expected to influence their attitude to their function in interpreting the grants of legislative power; it would perhaps have made them more hospitable to extrinsic evidence, which is so much a part of adjudication on a constitutional bill of rights.

If the Canadian founding fathers thought about a bill of rights at all, it was by an almost instinctual assumption that the new federation would inherit British traditions. The closest they came to an expression of this assumption was by the inclusion in the preamble to the Confederation Act of a statement of the desire to federate "under a constitution similar in principle to that of the United Kingdom." Eighty years passed before there was any serious public debate in Canada about a bill of rights.[12] In part, the debate was inspired by the American Bill of Rights and the work of the United States Supreme Court in elaborating its meaning. In part, the debate was promoted by the work of the United Nations in formulating the Universal Declaration of Human Rights. The debate also had· a pragmatic basis in concern about such statutes as the Quebec Padlock Act, enacted in 1939 and finally struck down in 1957,[13] and the federal War Measures Act, a stand-by enactment that involved a wholesale delegation of power to the national cabinet upon a proclamation of the emergency of war or apprehended war, invasion or insurrection.[14] Experiences of executive action during World War II under this statute served to advance discussion of a constitutional bill of rights.

The Province of Saskatchewan enacted a statutory bill of rights in 1947, declaratory of the traditional political liberties, of certain legal liberties, and such egalitarian rights as the right to buy or rent property, to engage in professions or occupations, and the right to education without discrimination on the grounds of race, religion, ethnic or national origin. Penal sanctions and the injunctive process were the means of redress.[15]

The formal initiative for a constitutional, an entrenched, bill of rights had to come from the national government because it alone had the ear of the British government to enact the necessary constitutional amendment. Not all readers of this paper may be aware that the Canadian constitution, in origin a British statute of 1867, contained no provision for its amendment. Efforts to fashion a domestic amending procedure have failed over the years; and in the result, amendment depends on formal British action —taken, however, only at the behest of the national authorities. It remains, of course, a matter of internal politics whether an amendment can be safely sought without the consent of the provincial governments.[16]

The possibility of an entrenched bill of rights raised deep concern about what would happen to the balance struck over the years, by judicial decision and conventional practice, between national and state power. Promulgation of such a bill of rights, even if agreement on its language and range was reached, would of course flout the principle of parliamentary supremacy in a way which the mere distribution of legislative power does not. It is one thing to divide all law-making authority (and Canada clings to a doctrine of exhaustiveness of the distribution) between two levels of government; it would be a completely different thing to deny to both levels law-making authority in certain fields.

As matters stood under the Canadian constitution, it was not too clear whether civil liberty issues fell exclusively within federal or within provincial jurisdiction, or partly within the jurisdiction of each.[17] Indeed, one could not be certain of general agreement on what was comprehended within the term "civil liberties" or a "bill of rights." None of the traditional political liberties, nor of what may be called legal liberties (those matters associated with procedural fairness) was particularized in the catalogue of legislative powers assigned to the national and provincial legislatures. The only two guarantees in the written constitution concerned not individual rights but rather, collective rights; that is, the use of the English or French language in the national legislature or that of Quebec, and in the process and pleading in any federal or Quebec court;[18] and second, certain guarantees as to the continuation of separate schools, based on religious rather than linguistic considerations.[19] Nonetheless, on the theory that the Canadian constitution had distributed all law-making power, it was logical to conclude that freedom of speech, for example, or freedom of religion represented constitutional values—or "matters," to use the formula of the constitution—upon which legislative power could be exerted. To frame the situation in different words, the constitutional issue in civil liberties litigation in Canada was no different than it was in other types of litigation calling in question the validity of legislation. It was this: Was the particular suppression or enlargement or regulation within the competence of the enacting legislature?

There were sporadic debates in Canada for a decade starting in 1947 on the desirability of an entrenched bill of rights, and a number of inquiries were conducted in this connection. The British tradition of reliance on the common law, or at the most on a statutory declaration, had strong roots in the country; it was a statutory bill of rights that the national government brought forward in 1958 and that, after public and parliamentary debate, was enacted into law in 1960.[20] In my opinion, much confusion was generated about existing constitutional competence in the matter of civil liberties by journalistic references to "civil rights," a phrase well-known and well-worn in the United States. In context, the application of the phrase "civil rights" to the situation in the United States would not be misleading; but it was an unfortunate term to use in a Canadian context because the catalogue of exclusive provincial powers includes "property and civil rights in the province" as a class of subject.[21] The phrase is an historic one, going back (at least) to the Quebec Act of 1774.[22] In its setting there, it had reference, in my view, to the relations of citizens or inhabitants *inter se;* and did not embrace those aspects of public law, involving the relations of citizen and state, with which it is associated in American constitutional law.

My position on this question is by no means an unchallenged one; there is, for example, judicial opinion that freedom of religion is a civil right in the provinces, within the constitutional competence of a province to regulate or control or enlarge, but I should point out that there is equally impressive opinion to the contrary.[23] One of the purposes of the Quebec Act was to restore to the largely French-speaking inhabitants of Canada the right to resort to the French civil law for the resolution of their private controversies. It would be rather far-fetched to have the phrase "property and civil rights" import the application of the French law to issues of public law when British governmental institutions had been introduced into the country, with all that this connoted in the relations of the Crown and its new subjects.

When, after the American Revolution, loyalists swarmed into British North America and helped to populate not only Nova Scotia (from which New Brunswick was hived off in 1784) but also upper Canada, a new province under the latter name was established in 1792. The first enactment of its legislature was to introduce English law as the rule of decision "in all matters of controversy relative to property and civil rights"; and the statute went on to abolish the force of the "laws of Canada," that is the French civil law, in all matters of controversy relative to property and civil rights.[24] I regard this as providing support for my assessment of the limited and private law meaning of "civil rights," as it appeared in the list of provincial law-making powers under the Canadian constitution.

I should observe, and this may appear astonishing, that in the 85-odd years that the Judicial Committee of the Privy Council was Canada's court of last resort, and hence arbiter of the distribution of legislative power, it did not have to deal with a single civil liberties issue, at least so far as the traditional political liberties are concerned. Although the Supreme Court of Canada has experienced such litigation since becoming the final court, it cannot be said that it has drawn any clear line on the scope of authority of the national and provincial governments in this field.

All the cases have concerned the validity of restrictive provincial legislation, which it was sought either to strike down as invading federal legislative power or to restrict by a construction that would exclude a challenged activity from its reach. I shall take three examples to point up the character of our Supreme Court's work in bill of rights litigation. *Saumur* v. *City of Quebec,* decided in 1953, concerned the validity of a municipal by-law forbidding the distribution of books or pamphlets in the streets of the city without the written permission of the chief of police.[25] I shall not dwell on the approach that the Supreme Court of the United States has taken to such an enactment. In Canada there could be no First or Fourteenth Amendment considerations, but simply the question whether this by-law, on the assumption that it was authorized by provincial legislation, could be attributed to a head of provincial legislative power. The nine-Judge court which heard the case at its ultimate appeal level was deeply divided on the question of the validity of this by-law, and its application to the Jehovah's Witnesses who challenged it. Did it not relate merely to the regulation of the use of city streets? Was it not merely an ordinary police regulation? Even if it concerned freedom of expression or freedom of religion, were these not matters of civil rights in the province under the provincial catalogue of powers?

I do not propose to make any extensive analysis of the reasons of the court. It is enough to say that although four members of the Supreme Court were of the opinion, for somewhat different reasons, that the by-law was valid, and four were of the opinion that it went beyond provincial competence (and invaded federal legislative power, construed to embrace protection of religious freedom), the Jehovah's Witnesses succeeded in the result—because the ninth judge held that the by-law would be repugnant to an existing provincial statute protecting freedom of worship, if it were construed to preclude dissemination of religious tracts; hence it should be construed not to embrace such activity. On the strict constitutional issue, this judge had no doubt that freedom of religion and freedom of speech were civil rights in the province, and hence subject to provincial regulatory authority.

My second example concerns an amendment to a provincial labor relations statute prohibiting a trade union, as beneficiary of a revocable check-off of union dues under the act or under a collective agreement or of dues paid as a condition of membership in the trade union, from spending any of such money on or on behalf of any political party or candidate for political office. The net result of the amendment was to leave a trade union free to make collections for political purposes if it did so outside of the certification and other machinery of the act, and outside of the framework of collective bargaining or collective agreements. A bare majority of the seven-judge Supreme Court that sat on the case upheld the validity of this legislation, in its impact on both provincial and federal political activity and elections. The reason was that they viewed it as falling within provincial competence to regulate labor relations in enterprises within provincial regulatory power; and this competence could embrace the use of dues, whether compulsorily or voluntarily paid, with respect to union resort to the advantages of the act or under collective agreements.[26] The minority took the view that in extending the ban on political use of check-off money or membership dues beyond any connection with privileges conferred upon trade unions by the legislation, the legislature had shed any nexus with labor relations, and was simply interfering with political activity by unions and employees—and that this interference, at least in relation to federal politics, was beyond provincial competence.

To some extent, the views of the majority reflected the philosophy of the *Saumur* case; there seemed to be an unwillingness to assess the relative weight of the values that the legislation embraced. The fact that the province had a labor relations peg on which to hang the amendment appeared to satisfy the court that it was unnecessary to refine the thrust of the legislation, especially in the absence of protecting federal legislation so far as federal political activity was concerned.

Some two years later, in 1965, came another case, my third illustration, in which the majority's approach in the political check-off case was rejected, again in a bare majority decision. *McKay* v. *The Queen* concerned a municipal by-law which forbade the display on residential property of any signs or notices save those within a permitted class.[27] Election signs were not in this class, and the simple question was whether the by-law was enforceable against the display of signs promoting the candidacy of persons seeking election to the federal House of Commons.

The majority of the nine-judge court viewed the matter as one where provincial or provincially authorized legislation, for example, municipal by-laws, should not be construed to extend to objects beyond provincial competence. Since a province had no authority to regulate federal elections or campaigning therefor, it was proper to exclude such activity from the scope of the by-law. Not to do so would denigrate the federal constitutional value involved, and make it subservient to municipal zoning regulations. Yet this is what the dissenting four judges did; for them, there was only an incidental effect on federal electioneering activity, and they saw no need to restrict the general language of the by-law.

What my three illustrations point up is that, lacking any specification of civil liberty jurisdiction in the division of legislative powers and, notwithstanding the principle that all legislative power has been distributed to the one or to the other level of government, there is a reluctance to strike down provincial legislation merely because of its alleged interference with unexercised federal power, where such federal power depends on a refined assessment of constitutional values. The strong tradition of legislative supremacy, even though diluted under a federal system, appears to carry with it a tolerance for the legislative judgment when it has an undeniable constitutional foothold in some familiar legislative object; so that there is a wariness against too refined a scrutiny of the scope of the provincial enactment, which would necessarily involve both a value judgment *per se* and an attribution of power to the central authority.

It is well to point out that Chief Justice Cartwright supported the provincial position in the *Saumur* case, although he opposed it both in the political check-off case where he was one of the minority, and in the

McKay zoning by-law case where he articulated the views of the majority. In the *Saumur* case he made the following pronouncement: [28]

> In my view, freedom of the press is not a separate subject matter committed exclusively either to Parliament or the Legislatures [of the Provinces]. In some respects, Parliament, and in others the Legislatures may validly deal with it. In some aspects it falls within the field of criminal law, but in others it has been dealt with by provincial legislation the validity of which is not open to question, as for example the Libel and Slander Act [of Ontario]. . . . If the subject matter of a provincial enactment falls within the class of subjects enumerated in section 92 of the British North America Act such enactment does not, in my opinion, cease to be *intra vires* of the legislature by reason of the fact that it has the effect of cutting down the freedom of the press.

I do believe that the chief justice has moved away from this position, but it is still a force to be reckoned with in Canadian constitutional litigation respecting such values as are found in the American First and Fourteenth Amendments.

If there is any merit in my appraisal, it must strike the student of judicial review in Canada as rather odd that this willingness to respect the provincial legislative judgment evaporates when the courts are confronted with applications to review exercises of power by administrative tribunals under legislation that contains privative clauses. Indeed, there has been an intimation in the case law that total preclusion of judicial review by legislative direction may be unconstitutional, even though no issue of legislative power between the national and provincial legislatures is involved.[29]

This, of course, is a manifestation of a judicial bill of rights in Canada of which other illustrations are common both to Great Britain and to Canada. It takes its content from judicial courage or innovation and legislative abstention, and I say no more about it here.

On the Canadian constitutional side, however, one further observation may be made. If civil liberty matters are beyond provincial competence, at least so far as suppression is concerned, is there any social advantage or comfort to know that suppressive authority resides in the national Parliament, on the theory that what is outside of provincial competence must necessarily be within federal power? It would, in my view, be a distinct gain to have such a position clearly enunciated; and if that was the position it would certainly help the government of Canada to carry its proposal, recently renewed, to entrench a bill of rights in the constitution.

One judge of the Supreme Court of Canada, Justice Abbott, expressed the view in 1957 that the right of free expression and debate on public issues was not only beyond provincial control, but was beyond abrogation (to use his word) by the national Parliament itself.[30] This blunt introduction of a constitutional limitation on both levels of government, without express supporting words in the Canadian Constitution, was grounded on implications from other parts of the constitution: first, the requirement that the parliament meet at least once a year; second, the provision for national elections at least every five years; and, third (more fragile but reflecting a norm), the statement in the preamble to the constitution that it was to be similar in principle to that of the United Kingdom. What all this envisages, according to the proponents of the limitation (and they include eminent scholarly opinion), is a representative, democratic working of parliamentary institutions, involving freedom of political discussion, assembly and organization or association. To date, although Justice Abbott reiterated his proposition in a later case, his is the only judicial voice that has uttered it.[31]

Reference was made earlier to the enactment in 1960 of a statutory bill of rights, by the Parliament of Canada. A considerable literature has grown up around it, much beyond its deserts as an effective measure.[32] It is an admonitory statute that prescribes a rule of construction for federal statutes; in brief, it is addressed by the Parliament to itself and to the courts which are directed to *construe and apply* existing and future federal enactments so as not to abridge or infringe any of the declared rights or freedoms, unless any such enactment expressly recites that it shall operate notwithstanding the Canadian Bill of Rights. The traditional political and legal liberties are set out in the statute, which has also borrowed from the language of the Fifth and Fourteenth Amendments. Section 1 (a) and (b) of the Act is in these terms:

> It is hereby recognized and declared that in Canada there have existed and shall continue to exist without discrimination by reason of race, national origin, colour, religion or sex, the following human rights and fundamental freedoms, namely
>
> (a) the right of the individual to life, liberty, security of the person and enjoyment of property, and the right not to be deprived thereof except by due process of law;
>
> (b) the right of the individual to equality before the law and the protection of the law.

The remainder of section 1 lists freedom of religion, freedom of speech, freedom of assembly and association, and freedom of the press.

Some of the procedural safeguards which in the United States have their source in the Fifth and Fourteenth Amendments are specifically set out in section 2 of the Canadian Bill of Rights. Experience to date indicates that due process in the Canadian statute will have no substantive implications, although a distinguished retired Judge of the Supreme Court of Canada, Ivan Rand, suggested in an article on the matter that it imported a standard of reasonableness; in his words, "the setting up for all law infringing rights, privileges and liberties, a standard of rational acceptability in the regulation of human conduct and relations." [33] On the procedural side, due process (apart from principles of natural justice) does not seem to have meant more than application of the relevant statute according to its terms. The debate, familiar to students of American constitutional law, and perhaps also to constitutional historians in Great Britain as well as in the United States, whether due process of law means anything more than "according to law" in a literal sense, does not seem to have agitated the Canadian judiciary. Apart from consistent concern for natural justice—the right to a fair hearing—dealt with, however, in another part of the Bill of Rights, due process has raised no large issues.

The Canadian Bill of Rights is limited in its operation to federal legislation, but despite some doubt, it appears that it also reaches common law principles which operate in the areas of federal jurisdiction.[34] It does not, however, purport to bind provincial legislatures, even in the realm of the political liberties in respect to which it is arguable that federal jurisdiction is paramount if not exclusive.

Within its limitation to purely federal legislation and common law operating as such, it will be ineffective to modify legislation that is enacted in contrary terms, if all it does is express a rule of construction. At the risk of undue repetition, let me reiterate that the Canadian Bill of Rights enjoins the courts to *construe and apply* all federal legislation, past and future, to conform to the fundamental rights that it expresses. If this is merely a rule of construction, it is easy enough to say that it must yield to a contrary expression; and on such a view, the statutory declaration of rights would be fragile indeed. Yet such an appreciation of the enactment would not give adequate weight to the word "apply"—for the admonition to the courts is to construe and apply, and there is force in the suggestion that it is an offending statute that must bow to the Canadian Bill of Rights, and not *vice versa*.[35]

Future legislation incompatible with the Canadian Bill of Rights raises difficult questions about the nature of parliamentary supremacy, and whether one parliament can bind a successor to follow a particular mode or form of enactment. An easier test of the position of our courts, and especially of the Supreme Court of Canada, on the force of the Canadian Bill of Rights is to see how its declared freedoms operate upon pre-existing federal legislation which might be thought to be in conflict.

A test occurred in a 1963 decision, *Robertson and Rosetanni* v. *The Queen* which arose out of a prosecution of a bowling alley operator for carrying on business on Sunday, in breach of the Lord's Day Act.[36] This

Sunday observance statute, enacted by the national parliament in 1906, was posited on Christian tenets and had its constitutional justification in the federal criminal law power, a power considered ample enough to support prohibitory legislation to ensure respect for religious convictions. Parliament could not have enacted the Lord's Day Act as a general Sunday observance measure to secure a secular object of repose or recreation, the basis of a fairly recent case decided in the Supreme Court of the United States.[37]

Since the Lord's Day Act had a sectarian purpose, could it stand in the face of the injunction in the Canadian Bill of Rights that federal legislation, whether pre-existing or in the future, must be construed and applied so as not to abridge, *inter alia,* freedom of religion? The Supreme Court, sitting in its quorum of five, decided, with one dissent, that there was no incompatibility in the two measures, because only if the Lord's Day Act imposed religious observances on unwilling persons or restrained anyone in his exercise of his own religious profession, would there be a derogation from freedom of religion. The Lord's Day Act did not compel unwilling persons to become Christians or observe any religious rites; it had merely a secular business consequence upon those who did not believe in Sunday observance.

To put the matter in American constitutional terms, it would appear that the Canadian Bill of Rights in declaring for freedom of religion does so only to protect the free exercise thereof; it does not preclude federal legislation respecting an establishment of religion.[38] This is not a desirable result, especially in view of earlier expression by the Supreme Court of Canada that "all religions are on an equal footing." [39]

Teeth were found in the Canadian Bill of Rights in a recent judgment of an intermediate appellate court, which held that a provision in the federal Indian Act, making it an offense to be intoxicated off a reserve, was discriminatory legislation and violated the prescription of equality before the law in the Canadian Bill of Rights.[40] There was moreover, discrimination against Indians collectively, "by reason of race," within the terms of the Canadian Bill of Rights. The court rejected an earlier construction of the "equality before the law" provision by another intermediate appellate court, which read it as meaning equality before the courts.[41] In the case under discussion, there was an approximation to the United States equal protection doctrine. It remains to be seen whether the Canadian Supreme Court will take the same view; an appeal is on its calendar for hearing at its current session.[42]

If the Canadian Bill of Rights does not develop any teeth (and, in any event, its frailty as mere legislation which can be repealed or outflanked is obvious), then the protections which are embedded in the Fourteenth Amendment against state encroachment can come in the Canadian provinces only by affirmative legislation (either provincial or federal according to the matter involved), or according to an evolutionary common law. This is true, for example, of the right to counsel, although here the courts themselves have been known to act; it is true of the rule in *Miranda* v. *Arizona;* [43] it is true of search and seizure situations and the consequent rejection of illegally obtained evidence. And it must be remembered that just as legislation can be benign, it can also be harsh; and common law rules are also at the mercy of legislative winds of change.

A debate is again in the offing in Canada on an entrenched bill of rights. Prime Minister Trudeau raised the question early in 1968 when he was still minister of justice.[44] He restated his desire to entrench protection for individual and linguistic rights, after he formed a government following the national election of June 25th, 1968. It would be merely guessing to purport to predict the outcome.

Notes

1. Waite, *The Life and Times of Confederation* (1962), esp. Chap. 8.
2. *Ibid.*
3. See the British North America Act, 1867, 30 & 31 Vic., c. 3 (U.K.), s. 22, as amended in 1915 and in 1949; hereinafter referred to as the B.N.A. Act.
4. Rogers, *Federal Influences on the Canadian Cabinet,* 11 Can. Bar Rev. 103 (1933).
5. For a general assessment, see Strayer, *Judicial Review of Legislation in Canada* (1968).
6. 1933 (Can.), c. 53, s. 17. The validity of this provision was sustained in *British Coal Corp.* v. *The King,* [1935] A.C. 500.
7. 1949 (Can. 2nd sess.), c. 37, s. 3; now s. 54 of the Supreme Court Act, R.S.C. 1952, c. 259. Power to enact this measure was affirmed in *Atty.-Gen. of Ont.* v. *Atty.-Gen. of Canada,* [1947] A.C. 127.
8. The story can be found in various places; e.g., *Abolition of Appeals to the Privy Council: A Symposium,* 25 Can. Bar Rev. 557 (1947); Livingston, *Abolition of Appeals from Canadian Courts to the Privy Council,* 64 Harv. L. Rev. 104 (1950).
9. The legislation, federal and provincial, providing for such references is noted in Laskin, *Canadian Constitutional Law* 146–149 (3rd ed. 1966).
10. *Id.,* at 152 et seq.
11. See Willis, *Administrative Law and the British North America Act,* 53 Harv. L. Rev. 251, 252 (1939).
12. See How, *The Case for a Canadian Bill of Rights,* 26 Can. Bar Rev. 759 (1948); *Note,* 26 Can. Bar Rev. 706 (1948).
13. *Switzman* v. *Elbling and Atty.-Gen. of Que.,* [1957] S.C.R. 285.
14. Now found in R.S.C. 1952, c. 288, as amended by 1960 (Can.), c. 44, s. 6.
15. 1947 (Sask.), c. 35; see now Saskatchewan Bill of Rights Act, R.S.S. 1965, c. 378.
16. For a review of efforts to secure an amending procedure, see Favreau, *The Amendment of the Constitution of Canada* (1965).
17. See, for example, Schmeiser, *Civil Liberties in Canada* 13 (1964).
18. B.N.A. Act, s. 133.
19. *Ibid.,* s. 93; and see *Ottawa Separate School Trustees* v. *Mackell,* [1917] A.C. 62.
20. 1960 (Can.), c. 44.
21. B.N.A. Act, s. 92 (13).
22. 1774 (U.K.), c. 83.
23. The contrary opinions are revealed in *Saumur* v. *Quebec and Atty.-Gen. of Que.,* [1953] 2 S.C.R. 299.
24. 1792 (U.C.), c. 1; see now Property and Civil Rights Act, R.S.O. 1960, c. 310.
25. [1953] 2 S.C.R. 299.
26. *Oil, Chemical and Atomic Workers International Union, Local 16–601* v. *Imperial Oil Ltd.,* [1963] S.C.R. 584.
27. [1965] S.C.R. 798.

28. [1953] 2 S.C.R. 299, at p. 386.

29. The cases are mentioned in Laskin, *op. cit. supra* note 9, at 789.

30. In the *Switzman* case, *supra* note 13, at 328.

31. In the *Imperial Oil Ltd.* case, *supra* note 26, at 599.

32. The most comprehensive treatment is by Tarnopolsky, *The Canadian Bill of Rights* (1966).

33. Rand, *Except by Due Process of Law,* 2 O.H.L.J. 171, 187 (1961). [It is sad to record the death of this distinguished retired judge on January 20, 1969.]

34. Driedger, *The Canadian Bill of Rights in Lang* (ed.), *Contemporary Problems of Public Law in Canada,* 31, 44.

35. *Id.,* at 38, 40–41; and see also Laskin, *An Inquiry into the Diefenbaker Bill of Rights,* 37 Can. Bar Rev. 77, 132 (1959).

36. [1963] S.C.R. 651.

37. *McGowan* v. *Maryland,* 366 U.S. 420 (1961).

38. See *Note,* 42 Can. Bar Rev. 147 (1964).

39. *Chaput* v. *Romain,* [1955] S.C.R. 834, at p. 840.

40. *Regina* v. *Drybones* (1967), 64 D.L.R. 2d 260. This case is noted in 46 Can. Bar Rev. 141 (1968).

41. The rejected construction was voiced in *Regina* v. *Gonzales* (1962), 32 D.L.R. 2d 290.

42. The judgment of the Supreme Court of Canada came down on November 20, 1969, and by a six to three majority the Court concluded that there was a conflict between relevant terms of the federal Indian Act and the Canadian Bill of Rights, and that in such a case the provisions of the Indian Act must give way. The dissenting Judges, of whom Cartwright C.J.C. was one, decided in effect that the force of the Canadian Bill of Rights was exhausted once the effort to construe the Indian Act in the light of the provisions of the Canadian Bill of Rights showed a conflict; in such a case, the Indian Act had to be given its conflicting effect. Chief Justice Cartwright, who had dissented in the *Robertson and Rosetanni* case (see footnote 36), expressly admitted to a change of mind about the effect of the Canadian Bill of Rights.

43. 384 U.S. 436 (1966).

44. Trudeau, *A Canadian Charter of Human Rights* (1968).

13

Freedom and the Communist Constitutions

Harry Schwartz

In the mid-1950's, Milovan Djilas once wrote that the most subversive act one could perform in a Communist-ruled state was to insist upon the full and literal implementation of the laws in the statute books. The writer was reminded of that remark a few years ago when the papers reported that a Soviet poet had paraded for a time in Moscow's Red Square carrying a sign that said, "Defend the Soviet Constitution." Mr. Djilas's remark also prepared me for the sequel to that poet's demonstration: his arrest.

What Djilas had in mind, of course, was the yawning chasm that exists between the letter of the law and the reality in the Soviet Union and the states it dominates in Eastern Europe. The letter of the law in these countries normally provides constitutional "guarantees" for all civil rights. In the Soviet Constitution, for example, Article 123 declares "Equality of the rights of citizens of the U.S.S.R., irrespective of their nationality or race, in all spheres of economic, government, cultural, political and other social activity, is an indefeasible law." Article 124 speaks of ensuring "citizens freedom of conscience," adding that "freedom of religious worship and freedom of anti-religious propaganda is recognized for all citizens." Article 125 proclaims that "the citizens of the U.S.S.R. are guaranteed by law: (a) freedom of speech; (b) freedom of the press; (c) freedom of assembly, including the holding of mass meetings; (d) freedom of street processions and demonstrations. These civil rights are ensured by placing at the disposal of the working people and their organizations printing presses, stocks of paper, public buildings, the streets, communications facilities and other material requisites for exercising these rights." Article

Harry Schwartz is University Professor, State University College, New Paltz, N.Y. and a member of the Editorial Board of the *New York Times*.

128 asserts that "the inviolability of the homes of citizens and privacy are protected by law." [1]

The simple truth is that these and similar guarantees in the Soviet Constitution—and in the constitutions of the Soviet-dominated states—have been proved repeatedly to be worthless. This was true during the Stalin era; the present Soviet Constitution with its "guarantees" was actually adopted at a time of particularly rampant official lawlessness. This was true, though to a lesser extent, during the Khrushchev era. This is true now in the Brezhnev-Kosygin era when many of the practices of the Stalin era have been reinstated.

This discrepancy is well realized by thoughtful and intelligent people in the Communist world, and when they have the opportunity, the bolder spirits among them have commented on and deplored the situation. Thus, the noted Czechoslovak writer, Ludvik Vaculik, made these remarks in a speech before the Fourth Congress of the Czechoslovak Writers Union in June 1967, that is, at a time when Antonin Novotny still ruled in Prague:

> According to the letter [of the law], it might appear as if a code of rights and duties really existed in our country which (according to Article 19 of the Constitution) "ensures the free and general development and assertion of the personality of the citizen, and, at the same time, the consolidation and development of socialist society." I have found in my work in newspapers and radio that in actual fact the citizen rarely invokes his constitutional rights because anyone, even at the periphery of power, can attach conditions to the exercise of these rights, conditions which are not included in the Constitution and which, in common decency, cannot be written into it. Often of late I have read the Constitution and have arrived at the conclusion that it is badly compiled and perhaps because of this, has lost the respect of citizens and authorities alike. As far as style is concerned the Constitution is grandiloquent, but is very vague in many of its important provisions. . . . The prolix language and the fuzzy ideas of the Constitution render it impossible to enforce. In this manner the supreme legal norm becomes a program and an expression of good intentions, rather than a legal guarantee of the rights of the citizens. [2]

Mr. Vaculik was speaking as a citizen of a Communist dictatorship, as a person still in the power of that dictatorship. He chose his words with care, and could assume his listeners would understand his sometimes elliptical language. But it would be useful here to spell out what he had in mind when he spoke of the "conditions to the exercise of these rights, conditions which are not included in the Constitution and which, in common decency, cannot be written into it."

The essence of the matter is that freedom exists only to echo the party line, the official policy of the state and of the Communist Party that directs that state. Ideas contrary to the party line are simply barred from the press, the radio, television, films, books and the like by the censorship and other controls over those media. Free speech is harder to limit, but there have been many periods in Soviet history when men have gone to jail for an ill-advised remark or for telling a joke that could be interpreted as critical of the regime.

A few examples of how this system of repression works in practice—in complete contradiction to the constitutional guarantees—may make these ideas concrete.

In early 1966, the Soviet writers Andrei Sinyavsky and Yuli Daniel were placed on trial, and then convicted and imprisoned for having sent various of their writings abroad where they were published. In the course of the trial, both men were asked why they had not taken their writings instead to Soviet publishers. Their answers, which were not contradicted by the prosecution, speak eloquently of the real situation. Yuli Daniel's answer was, "I knew very well that Soviet editors would not publish anything on such controversial topics. My writings have a political tinge, and they would not have been printed on political grounds." Andrei Sinyavsky was even more terse, saying, "Because they could not be published here." [3]

Judging by the recent sales of his books, the most famous living Soviet writer, so far as the West is concerned, is Alexander Solzhenitsyn. But his latest two books which are now so popular in the West, *The First Circle* and *The Cancer Ward,* have been denied publication in the Soviet Union. Here is Mr. Solzhenitsyn's summary statement of his view of the writer's position in the Soviet Union today, given in his May 1967 letter to the Soviet Writers Union:

> Not having access to the podium at this Congress, I ask that the Congress discuss:
>
> 1. The no longer tolerable oppression, in the form of censorship, which our literature has endured for decades, and which the Union of Writers can no longer accept.
>
> Under the obfuscating label of Glavlit [the Soviet censorship organization], this censorship—which is not provided for in the Constitution and is therefore illegal, and which is nowhere publicly labeled as such—imposes a yoke on our literature and gives people unversed in literature arbitrary control over writers. A survival of the Middle Ages, the censorship has managed, Methuselah-like, to drag out its existence almost to the 21st century. Of fleeting significance, it attempts to appropriate to itself the role of unfleeting time—of separating good books from bad . . .

. . . Many members of the [Writers] Union, and even many of the delegates at this Congress, know how they themselves have bowed to the pressures of the censorship and made concessions in the structure and concept of their books—changing chapters, pages, paragraphs or sentences, giving them innocuous titles—just for the sake of seeing them finally in print, even if it meant distorting them irremediably.[4]

As for freedom of demonstration in the Soviet Union, the reality of this "constitutional guarantee" was vividly evidenced in late August 1968. Then, shortly after the Soviet and satellite invasion of Czechoslovakia, roughly a half dozen Soviet citizens sought to stage a protest demonstration. They had no sooner begun to unfurl their banners than they were set upon by secret police agents who had been following them, beaten up, and taken off to jail. Later most of the demonstrators were sentenced to prison terms.[5]

There was, of course, one Communist-ruled nation that tried, in 1968, to implement honestly the constitutional guarantees of civil liberties. The essence of the Czechoslovak "Spring" that lasted until August 20, 1968 was the existence of almost untrammeled free speech, free press, freedom of assembly and the like. Past injustices were freely admitted; many lies spread by the Czechoslovak rulers in the past were exposed publicly. Persons who had been unjustly imprisoned for their political views earlier were promised legal rehabilitation and compensation for their sufferings. Non-Communist political groups sprang up and held legal meetings. The censorship by secret police personnel was abolished. However, it was precisely these features of the Czechoslovak scene that proved intolerable to the Soviet Union and its satellites. Repeatedly, during the January-August period, the Kremlin and its allies demanded the reimposition of censorship in Czechoslovakia so as to end free speech, free press, free radio and free television, that is, they demanded that Czechoslovakia stop honoring its constitutional guarantees and go back to the previous illegal situation. The invasion of Czechoslovakia that followed was a tactic born of desperation, the only means seen available to stop the rot that freedom had brought to Communist power in Prague. What motivated the Soviet leaders, of course, was the fear that the liberties won and being used in Czechoslovakia might be demanded in the Soviet Union itself and elsewhere in Eastern Europe. After all, had not the rioting Polish students in early March 1968 shouted in the streets of Warsaw, "Long live Czechoslovakia"?[6]

Even this brief survey has made plain how bleak the situation is. The constitutional guarantees of civil liberties in the Communist nations are a form of hypocrisy, literally the tribute vice pays to virtue. Yet it is a mark of slight progress that in recent years, Soviet leaders have seemed to exercise their repressive rule with something suggesting a bad conscience.

Under Khrushchev, for example, the practice was begun of incarcerating heretics and dissidents in insane asylums—on the pretext that they were mad. An insane asylum is hardly a desirable place to be, but it has some virtues as against a formal prison or slave labor camp. Some dissidents— notably Pavel Litvinov and Mrs. Yuli Daniel—were allowed to remain at large months after their disgust with Soviet repression of civil liberties had been expressed publicly. At the Sinyavsky-Daniel trial of 1966 and at several other subsequent related trials, sympathizers of the accused were not afraid to congregate outside the courtroom building and express their sentiments, even though secret police agents were busily engaged in taking their pictures. Moreover, as of this writing Alexander Solzhenitsyn is still at liberty, although his books have appeared in the West without state approval.

The essence of the matter is that Soviet authorities find themselves in an embarrassing situation. On the one hand, they admit the gross illegalities of the Stalin regime and are pledged to complete observance of what is called "socialist legality." On the other hand, their insecurities and their lack of confidence in their people's loyalty are so great that they fear even the smallest infection by independent thought. Caught between these two tensions, Moscow has opted for the most part to put security, as the Soviet secret police understands the term, ahead of legality, including constitutional rights. However, many of those involved know what they are doing and have some degree of bad conscience about it—something that could not be said of Stalin. Yet all this is too tenuous a basis for suggesting that constitutional protection of civil liberties has any bright future in the Soviet world. Rather, for the immediate, foreseeable future, such protections seem very flimsy indeed.

Notes

1. For a full text of the Soviet and other Communist nations' constitutions, see Jan F. Triska, *Constitutions of the Communist Party-States* (1968).
2. Quoted from Research Departments of Radio Free Europe, *Czechoslovak Press Survey*, No. 1946, September 4, 1967, pp. 5–6.
3. *On Trial*, translated, edited and with an introduction by Max Hayward 56 and 122 (1966).
4. The full text of Slozhenitsyn's letter is in *Problems of Communism*, September-October 1968, pp. 37–39.
5. Cf. the relevant issues of *The New York Times*, August-October, 1968.
6. On the Czechoslovak developments in 1968, cf. Harry Schwartz, *Prague's 200 Days* (1969).

14

Due Process in Developing Nations

Thomas M. Franck

The theme of this paper concerns the application of due process to the jurisprudence of developing countries—the due process concepts that come to us via the Fifth and Fourteenth Amendments but that have their roots in the norms, particularly the procedural norms, of the English common law. This examination will be confined to those developing countries which were formerly under British rule, and which have therefore been exposed to English and American, Australian and Canadian jurisprudence. Undoubtedly, however, a similar study could be made of the Franco-phonic states by lawyers versed in the civil law's equivalent traditions.

In the 1956 case of *Nyali* v. *Attorney General* [1] (a dispute that had a Kenyan *situs*), Lord Denning made this memorable statement which establishes our theme: "Just as an English oak, so with the English common law; you cannot transplant it to the African continent and expect it to retain the tough character which it has in England. It will flourish indeed but it needs careful tending. So with the common law. It has many principles of manifest justice and good sense which can be applied with advantage to peoples of every race and color all the world over; but it has also many refinements, subtleties and technicalities which are not suited to other folk. These off-shoots must be cut away. In these far off lands the people must have a law which they understand and which they will respect. The common law cannot fulfill this role except with considerable qualifications."

Today, transplant similes would no doubt speak of organs rather than trees, and of the rejection phenomenon in the body politic. Perhaps that is progress. The present writer prefers Lord Denning's older word-pictures. It is important for us to know not only that our sturdy oak endures, but also that it is not to a jurisprudential desert that it has been transplanted.

Thomas M. Franck is Professor of Law at New York University and Director of its Center for International Studies.

Particularly in the area of procedural human rights, much that the common law posits is also indigenous to tribal or customary law. This discovery makes anthropologists of us all; it is rather like finding that one has been speaking prose all one's life to learn that a firm grasp of common law concepts also gives one a practical, if selective, grounding in the basic jurisprudence of, say, the Barotse tribe. The point is delightfully developed by Professor Max Gluckman of Manchester University in his 1963 Storrs lectures at Yale.[2] In these he points out that the Lozis have such venerable legal maxims as: "hard cases make bad law" and "no man may be a judge in his own cause." When we speak of transplantation, then, we really speak of grafting Western common law onto a body of local law which is frequently already both compatible and receptive to it. Perhaps, then, we should have used the distasteful organic simile after all.

To some extent, customary law exceeds our own in its social concepts. Thus while our law emphasizes the *form* of a real property transaction, characterizing it rigidly as sale, lease or mortgage, the Wanyaturu of Tanzania emphasize circumstantial evidence of the socio-economic context in which the transaction occurs, and their courts have held that "land sold in time of famine may subsequently be redeemed"—thereby creating a sort of constructive mortgage.[3] We might ponder which property concept embodies the more developed sense of due process.

So, too, we must be careful to avoid the sin of institutional pride or cultural myopia. We have no business, for example, to think of courts *per se* as our western gift to Africa or Asia. President Jomo Kenyatta in his pioneering anthropological study, *Facing Mount Kenya,*[4] has given us a colorful account of practice at what might be called the Kikuyu "prebar" —the assembly of elders which, with elaborate and remarkably functional procedures, anticipated the Western system of adjudication. Some form of judicial system is to be found in most tribal states, as well as the princely states of India and Malaysia and elsewhere in Southeast Asia. It is, of course, also a highly developed indigenous institution in Arab countries and countries under Arab influence or rule.

The coming of the colonial era to British Africa, Asia and the Caribbean led to the transplantation of which Lord Denning spoke. Three winds of change wafted those little acorns of English—and, to a lesser degree of Scots—jurisprudence around the world: one the educational system, a second the judiciary, and a third the Colonial Office.

In the former British Empire, legal training, more than any other aspect of education, was centralized in Britain: whether at the great universities, the perhaps not-so-great but vastly serviceable and willing Inns of Court, or in the system of external degrees. The first law schools in all of formerly British Africa are barely a decade old, even though the oldest college was established nearly 200 years ago. Consequently, there continues to be much of a sense of very real fraternity among men now in early middle-age who are, or are becoming, the judges, attorneys-general and ministers of the new nations. It is not surprising that, for example, Nigerian and Caribbean lawyers are staffing so many judicial posts in the less developed East and Central African nations, for the training these men received qualifies them professionally and culturally for a world-wide legal mission.

Closely interrelated to common legal education is the commonality of the law itself, both legislative and judicial. United Kingdom statutes did not ordinarily apply to the colonies, but special British statutes did, and applied equally to them all. Likewise, the statutes enacted in one of the colonies usually were made to conform to the formulation used in others. A most remarkable example of this is the Indian Penal Code of 1860, which is to be found, in one form or another, in the northern region of Nigeria, the Sudan, and the Northern region of Somalia. In East Africa the Indian Code was replaced in the 1930's by a new but related model based on the Queensland Code of 1899. The same source has supplied the rest of Nigeria, other than the North, Kenya, Uganda, Tanganyika, Zanzibar, Northern Rhodesia, Nyasaland and Gambia. The Ghana Code is based on the St. Lucia Code of 1889. Similarly, the colonial courts applied English common law except where it was excluded by statute or where, as in the exceptional cases of Ceylon and Southern Rhodesia, a modified civil law system, the Roman-Dutch, prevailed. For each colony, the highest court of appeal was the Judicial Committee of the Privy Council, and cases from other high courts, including not only the House of Lords but also the highest courts in other colonies, were frequently cited.

With independence, both the statutory and judge-made colonial law was invariably kept in effect by the new states. This was so even after violent revolution, as in Nigeria.

The last of the three sources of commonality is the Colonial Office. This may at first seem odd, since the service was not noted for its obsessive preoccupation with jurisprudence, and perhaps least with the jurisprudence of due process. Nevertheless, the same colonial office which fathered preventive detention, rustication, deportation, and the imperial-put-down, also launched most of the new ships of state on the rough seas of independence, in elaborate constitutional vessels constructed with a great many planks of due process and human rights.

One may be permitted a slightly raised eyebrow at the 329 pages of the Kenya Constitution of 1963. Typical is the way it develops the simple concept that no man shall be deprived of life without due process: [5]

> 15.(1) No person shall be deprived of his life intentionally save in execution of the sentence of a court in respect of a criminal offense under the law of Kenya of which he has been convicted.

(2) Without prejudice to any liability for a contravention of any other law with respect to the use of force in such cases as are hereinafter mentioned, a person shall not be regarded as having been deprived of his life in contravention of this section if he dies as the result of the use of force to such extent as is reasonably justifiable in the circumstances of the case:

(a) for the defense of any person from violence or for the defense of property;

(b) in order to effect a lawful arrest or to prevent the escape of a person lawfully detained;

(c) for the purpose of suppressing a riot, insurrection or mutiny; or

(d) in order to prevent the commission by that person of a criminal offense, or if he dies as the result of a lawful act of war.

Were the British being holier than themselves in turning over the keys to the kingdoms with such extraordinarily detailed instructions? Perhaps. Yet it also takes 360 words to describe the terms of freedom of religion in the Indian constitution,[6] and the Indians wrote that instrument themselves.

No. I rather think the remarkable length and detail of the new constitutions' due process and civil rights clauses, which contrast so strikingly both with Britain's unwritten and America's succinct approach to the same subjects, is due to a number of very good reasons.

A detailed enunciation was, this writer thinks, intended to help the courts. When a state achieves independence, its political branches of government are usually endowed with powerful popular support earned during the political struggle for independence. However, no similar popularity supports the judiciary. On the contrary, the judges tend to be holdovers from colonial times, when they and the courts had to enforce unpopular laws. Moreover, while at, or even before independence, leadership of the executive and legislative branches is assumed by indigenous leaders, the judiciary, through lack of trained local candidates, often remains for a time, even after independence, wholly or partly staffed by expatriates. Obviously, such a judiciary is in a comparatively weak position *vis-a-vis* the political branches of government. If, therefore, the judges are to succeed in adjudicating the relationship between the individual and the state, or between parts of a federation and the central government, it is well that their discretion be, and appear to be, limited. An extensively detailed constitution allows courts to shift some of the burden of criticism—if such there is to be—from themselves to the text of a contract to which the political leaders have themselves agreed.

Second, the social fabric of the new state is often extremely complex, rent between numerous tribes, races, regions and status groups. A detailed setting out of the rights of each can have a hortatory effect, even if it is difficult to enforce. Constitutions that are purely hortatory, like those of some socialist countries, are of little value. But in a developing state a constitution has three roles: to regulate, to reassure, and to educate. Detailed exposition is meant to serve the last two of these purposes.

Third, the post-World War II momentum towards enumerating "universal" democratic principles influenced the constitutional draftsmen. As a signatory to the European Convention for the Protection of Human Rights and Fundamental Freedoms of 1950,[7] Great Britain expressed its willingness to make its own law and the law of its dependencies conform to the convention's detailed civil law code-like provisions.

How have the norms of due process fared in the new nations since their independence? Ever since Pliny exclaimed, *"ex Africa semper aliquid novi,"* probably in despair, we have grown conditioned to bad news about these states; so much so, it is to be feared that we hear it even when it is not there.

It would be impossible for the writer, in this brief paper, to attempt to justify the proposition that in the new nations the arm of government which is best weathering the stormy years of independence, of rising expectations, of neo-colonialism, of modernization, is the judiciary, and that therefore the legacy of due process, of procedural due process in particular, is alive and well in the preponderance of the new Anglo-phonic states.

No more can be done here than to indicate a few examples.

In Ceylon, during the troubles following the assassination of Prime Minister Bandarnayke, a special panel of judges to hear treason cases was set up. The authorizing law provided that the panel would consist of any three judges of the Supreme Court selected by the Minister of Justice. In the case of *Queen* v. *Lujange,*[8] the first such panel decided that the enabling act violated the constitutional doctrine of separation of powers. No such concept is expressed in the Ceylon Constitution, and the panel reached its decision by a wide-ranging search through the constitutional doctrine and practice of the Commonwealth and the United States, including a scholarly analysis of Dean Pound's "historical criterion theory." They found that choosing the judges to hear a particular case was inherently a judicial function and could not be exercised by the Minister, even when acting under legislation. It is, in the present writer's opinion, remarkable that a panel of Supreme Court judges, chosen by the Minister to hear a case of the gravest national importance at a time of deep crisis, would hold itself unconstitutional because it had been chosen by executive rather than judicial fiat.

Let us look at another instance. In Tanzania, an ordinance granted a local board power to grant liquor licenses. The respectable Bukoba Gymkhana Club was turned down recently without a hearing, on the ground that club rules require applicants for membership to be nominated and seconded by other members. It was alleged that this practice was *de facto* discriminatory since almost all members are non-blacks. It may have been so—the writer suspects it was—but the High Court of this independent new nation properly concluded that the denial of the license *without a hearing* was a violation of natural justice.[9] It reversed the board.

Similar cases have recently come from Cyprus and Malaysia. It would not be too much to say that practice in the new states has helped to clean up the residue of unfettered executive discretion left by *Liversidge* v. *Anderson* [10] and *Duncan* v. *Cammell, Laird & Co.*[11]

In the same vein, it can be reported that tenure of judges, with the exception of the Ghana debacle at the time of Dr. Nkrumah, has generally survived the vicissitudes of political fortune that have rocked other branches of government. Thus, too, the practice regarding right to counsel, judicial impartiality, notice and specificity of charges, pre-trial bail, disclosure of evidence, confrontation of witnesses and privilege against self-incrimination does not today vary substantially between the developed and developing states of the English law tradition. This appears remarkable, but it is very little remarked upon in the West.

The major exception is preventive detention and it fares much better in getting attention. Preventive detention laws apply in some of these countries, even as they applied in some of them when they were colonies, and even as they have applied in emergencies in Britain and, more unusually, even in America's past.[12] However, in other new states there is no preventive detention, and where there is, as in the case of India, the law may have some safeguards in the form of binding substantive judicial review of all detention orders. Used very sparingly, as in India or Tanzania,[13] the operation of these laws may be less iniquitous than bad bail practices elsewhere, or laws establishing presumptions against, or shifting the burden of proof to, the defendant in a criminal action such as may be found in the United States in its Federal Firearms Act of 1960,[14] or the Official Secrets Act of Canada.[15] This certainly does not make preventive detention juridically desirable, but does place it in cultural perspective.

It must be remembered, too, that when nations resort to arbitrary arrest of persons suspected of committing or being about to commit crimes, they generally do so not from free-floating draconianism but because the rural society, the tribal networks, and the sparseness of the police makes it difficult for the state to protect itself by means as efficient as those available to, say, the city of New York—in which approximately one adult male in 90 is a policeman, and in which the state has the most sophisticated devices of crime detection at its disposal.

This introduces the next point, which is that the state of due process in the developing countries must be judged in the context of the socio-economic and cultural condition of each society. We must listen not only to the words but to the music. If we do that, we may find that the literal application of American or British concepts of due process in other states and circumstances may at times have the opposite of their intended effect.

In the case of *Olawoyin* v. *Attorney General*,[16] decided in the Northern Region of Nigeria in 1960, the court was asked to rule on the constitutionality of a law which made it a criminal offense to send children to schools run by political, as distinguished from state or religious agencies. The plaintiff had children of school age whom he wished to enroll in a political school, and he alleged that the prohibition violated the constitution. The chief justice refused to decide this issue, saying, after a survey of Indian and United States cases, that "courts of law exist to determine, and where necessary to protect, the rights of persons . . . In my opinion it would be contrary to principle to make the declaration asked for in vacuo" because the children had not in fact yet been enrolled in the illegal school.

But Nigeria had no "case or controversy" clause in its constitution. Was it wise for this court to insinuate it, to co-opt from the United States a procedural rule which requires a man to break the law in order to test it? Should people in the Northern Region of Nigeria be encouraged by the law to break the law? Or, on the other hand, should people unfamiliar with the concept of constitutional rights be discouraged from trying to enforce them by the prospect of arrest and jail if they lose, a kind of judicial game of truth-or-consequences? Would it not be better for the Nigerian courts to give opinions before, rather than after the crime? Incidentally, the *Olawoyin* case is also illustrative of the point that foreign courts trying to apply our legal concepts sometimes fail to keep up with the rapid evolution of those concepts at the hands of our own judges.[17]

Two other illustrations involving questions of the appropriateness of bilateral transfer of normative legal concepts from developed to developing countries come from India—the first country to achieve independence and constitutional democracy after World War II, and perhaps the developing country most attached to the form of western due process.

The Indian Constitution's Article 15 [18] says that "the State shall not discriminate against any citizen on grounds only of religion, race, caste, sex, place of birth or any of them." In a 1951 decision, *Madras* v. *Champakam*,[19] the Indian Supreme Court held that this provision prevented discrimination in favor of certain backward castes, tribes and classes of the community. As in the preceding case, the writer is not convinced that even the concepts being co-opted from the American constitution need bring us to this conclusion. Equal protection of the law really means, one would have thought, protection designed to foster equal opportunity: the right to vote, that equally to buy property, equally within one's capacity to receive as good an education as one's inherent potential allows. And where the socio-economic conditions of part of the population deny them this opportunity, it is at least arguable that the law should compensate for such socially-imposed inequality by creating extra opportunities to over-come it to the limits of one's capability.

In any event, the Indian government did amend Article 15 after the *Champakam* decision, to make exactly this point: "Nothing in this Article . . . shall prevent the State from making any special provision for the advancement of any socially and educationally backward classes of citizens or for the Scheduled Castes and Scheduled Tribes." [20]

A similar problem arose in connection with the too-literal transplantation of western concepts of property rights, and this generated the greatest parliamentary-judiciary controversy in Indian Constitutional history. As originally adopted, the constitutional safeguard for property rights, contained in Article 31 of the constitution, simply provided that there must be "compensation for the property taken. . . ." [21] It did not, however, go further to use either general terms like "due process" or specific ones like "adequate" or "full" or "just" compensation. Neither did the constitution say anything about compensation for property, which while not actually expropriated, was devalued by government regulation. Nevertheless, a flood of litigation followed the early attempts at land reform. Controversy first arose over state laws abolishing the great Zamindaris. State supreme courts held such laws unconstitutional as discriminatory in that compensation was less than market value, and that one class was thus being discriminated against.

The first amendment act of 1951 forbade judicial invalidation of land reform legislation solely on the ground that it would be unequal in application or because of its social purpose. Land reform could now again begin to move forward—but at once it was again stalled. During the period 1953 to 1954, the courts continued to stretch judicial review of questions of fair compensation to the remaining limits. In *Sagir Ahmed* v. *Uttar Pradesh*,[22] the Supreme Court found Article 31(2) applicable to intangible as well as tangible property, in this case a bus franchise. Then came *State of W. B.* v. *Bela Banerjee* [23] which precipitated the Fourth Constitutional Amendment. In that case, land was acquired for the resettlement of refugees from Pakistan. The act limited compensation to market value on December 31, 1946, in order to take the profit out of land speculation caused by the resettlement. This time it was the Supreme Court which held that Article 31(2) meant that compensation must be full and fair, which in turn meant the market value. As a result, Article 31 was again amended in 1955, this time to read "and no such law shall be called in question in any court on the ground that the compensation provided by that law is not adequate." [24]

One would have wished India to have been spared such a damaging rearguard war with inappropriate concepts of due process.

These changes in the Indian Constitution to make it better adapted to indigenous social needs seem to be well within, and not violative of, the spirit of due process which is meant to foster justice, not to perpetuate historic injustice. It is thus interesting to note a more recent case that puts this adaptive process again in doubt, at least prospectively. In *Golak Nath* v. *State of Punjab*,[25] by a 6–5 decision, the Indian Supreme Court held that the Indian Parliament has no power to abridge Part III of the constitution, the part dealing with fundamental rights, not even by constitutional amendment. The case reversed a number of prior decisions, but applied the United States doctrine of prospective overruling to save the validity of such prior amendments as we have been discussing.

Art. 13(2) of the constitution, provides "the state shall not make any law which takes away or abridges the rights conferred by this part (fundamental rights) and any law made in contravention of this clause shall, to the extent of the contravention, be void." The court said this precludes all amendments to Part III of the constitution, because even a constitutional amendment is "a law made in contravention" of Part III. This seems to strain legal credulity. It may be that the Indian Supreme Court, by this narrow majority, has at least temporarily again borrowed the worst of due process: its proclivity for stifling innovation. Moreover, the Indian court, again borrowing from the worst rather than the best of our due process, has chosen to take this intractable stand on an issue not of human, but of property rights.

Thus an overly punctilious concern with the *forms* of due process in developing countries may emphasize the first word—"due"—to the detriment of the second word—"process." However, there is also a bright, countervailing tendency. Some new states have made radical, experimental departures from form in order to strengthen substances.

The political process is at the heart of all legal norms, and a number of new nations in different economic and cultural circumstances from the United States have risked imaginative experimentation in their search for a serviceable system to preserve the essence of participatory democracy by discarding unworkable western forms. This is not, of course, to say, that all the developing countries which have overthrown their Westminster or Capitol Hill models have done so to make democracy work better. Some have, however, and of these, Tanzania is probably the most interesting model. By adopting the one-party system, the Tanzanians slaughtered a sacred cow of democracy and risked being placed in the same conceptual dock with the Marxian-proletarian dictatorships. In fact, however, the innovative Tanzanian one-party system has had the opposite effect, being the inspiration for liberalization in Yugoslavia and, more recently, in Czechoslovakia. In Tanzania an attempt has been made within the one-party context to retain a meaningful element of representative government in a society which, in order to mobilize for rapid modernization, has decided to impose severe restrictions on the right to participate in *organized* dissent. In brief, a diversity of candidates is permitted, but not of parties. One is moved to wry contrast with the system now prevailing in the United States, which seems to conduce to a diversity of parties but not of candidates.

In western democracies, the existence of an organized opposition is intended to ensure the proper functioning of government and the discreet use of power through a system of checks and balances. President Nyerere of Tanzania has said,[26] "we recognize that the system of 'checks and balances' is an admirable way of applying the brakes to social change. Our need is not for brakes—our lack of trained manpower and capital resources, and even our climate, act too effectively already. We need accelerators powerful enough to overcome the inertia bred of poverty, and the resistances which are inherent in all societies."

An account by Professor Ruth Morgenthau of the parliamentary elections in Tanzania in September 1965 concludes that [27]

> Based on universal suffrage, the elections were honestly run and offered the voters genuine choices between two rival candidates in more than a hundred single member constituencies. Although the top dozen leaders of the party and government remained almost the same, there was a dramatic turnover in the National Assembly as a whole—a change far more sweeping than the Parliamentary shifts usually encountered in multi-party systems. Barely a quarter of the incumbent members were re-elected as a result of decisions not imposed from above, but freely taken by the voters.

Just as opposite political processes may in opposite social circumstances conduce to the same results, so with judicial process. One must always look to the social context, not just to the rule.

In Kenya, where, as in Britain, the police are considered less inclined to resort to illegal searches and seizures than in this country, there is no widespread feeling that when on occasion such searches occur, the guilty party should win the game on a technical foul. But if the admissibility of evidence illegally obtained encourages the police to become a menace to the general public, it may be predicted that the rule will change.

In Tanzania, unlike other East African countries, all confessions made anywhere except before a judge or magistrate are excluded. An extraordinary instance of this rule's operation came to the writer's attention in a recent, terse report of a Tanzanian criminal appeal, the case of *Maina* v. *The Republic,*[28] in which a conviction for possessing a drug was being sought on evidence of a statement made by the accused to a police inspector that a certain cigar was his. The judge ruled that "If the appellant knew that the cigar contained (the drug) then such statement would be a confession and inadmissible. . . . On the other hand, if the appellant made such a statement not knowing the cigar contained (the drug) that would demonstrate his innocence." Why does Tanzania have such a rule? Because, of the East African countries, it has by far the greatest shortage of private practitioners, so that a man in custody could generally not expect to have counsel during his period of pre-trial arrest. In a country with better legal services, the same rule would be of doubtful social utility.

In short, there are elements of commonalty in the practice of the new and the old Anglo-phonic states, which encourages the conclusion that constitutional or common law concepts of due process are adaptive. If we pride ourselves on this, we must be prepared to see the transplanted concepts *actually* adaptive, to the point where in form, though not in substance, they may become nearly unrecognizable. But unless we *can* recognize them in such changed circumstance, we have not really understood our own norms, for we will have mistaken their letter for their spirit.

The days of western colonial empire are past, and new groupings are proving difficult to fashion out of the plethora of new nations. This is not a new event in history. Writing of the Christian West as it was after the collapse of the Roman Empire, Mattingly said: [29] "Christendom was torn by the gravest internal conflict, by religious schism, doctrinal dispute, and the endemic warfare of class against class, people against people, faction against faction, king against king. But Latin Christendom still knew itself to be one. This sense of common bond, political as well as religious, never found adequate expression in political institutions. The actual social structure of power, the difficulties of travel and communication, the confused pattern of local and regional differences prevented any such expression. The authority of the Holy Roman Empire . . . shrank every time an emperor invoked it. . . . But the collapse of the empire and the schism of the papacy underlined a sense of unity which had never really depended on any fountainhead of authority. . . . Its combination of Roman pride and Christian faith was more than a mere aspiration; it was almost a reality."

So, now, perhaps, with the spirit of our law.

Notes

1. [1956] 1 Q. B. 1.
2. Gluckman, *The Ideas in Barotse Jurisprudence* (1965).
3. *Kisina* v. *Mkiya,* 1963(1) Tanganyika Digest of Appeals No. 55 of 1962.
4. Kenyatta, *Facing Mount Kenya* (1938).
5. Constitution of Kenya, Ch. II, § 15(1) and (2), 1963.
6. Constitution of India, Part III, §§ 25–28, 1949 as amended to October 5, 1963.
7. Documents and Decisions of the European Commission of Human Rights, 1955–7, at p. 4 (1959).
8. (1963) 64 N.L.R. 313.
9. *In re Bukoba Gymkhana Club,* High Court of Tanganyika (1963) E.A. 478.
10. [1942] A.C. 206.
11. [1942] A.C. 624.
12. Cf. *Ex parte Merryman,* 17 Fed. Cas. 144 (C.C. Md. 1861); Public Laws of the U.S. of America, 3rd Session, 37th Congress, pp. 755–58, 12 Stat. 755, XII; 48 U.S.C. Sec. 532 (1940); Frank, *Martial Law in Hawaii,* 44 Columbia Law Rev. 639 (1944), *Duncan* v. *Kahanamoku,* 324 U.S. 304 (1946); and *R.* v. *Home Secretary* [1942] 1 K.B. 87 (C.A.).
13. India Preventive Detention Act 1950, Act No. 4 of 1950; Tanganyika, Preventive Detention Act, No. 60 of 1962 and Zanzibar, Preventive Detention Decree, Presidential Decree No. 3 of 1964.
14. Explosives Act, 18 U.S.C. 837, 74 Stat. 87 (1960).
15. Official Secrets Act of 1939.
16. (1960) N.R.N. L.R. 53, affm'd All N.L. Rev. 269.
17. Cf. Sedler, *Standing to Assert Constitutional Jus Tertii in the Supreme Court,* 71 Yale Law Journal 599 (1962) and Bickel, *Forward: The Passive Virtues, The Supreme Court,* 1960 Term, 75 Harv. Law Rev. 40 (1961).
18. Constitution of India, Part III, Art. 15, § 1, 1949 as amended to October 5, 1963.
19. (1951) S.C.R. 525.
20. Constitution of India, Part III, Art. 15, § 4, 1949 as amended to October 5, 1963.
21. Constitution of India, Part III, Art. 31, 1949.
22. (1955) 1 S.C.R. 707 (1952–4) 2 C.C. 248.
23. (1954) S.C.R. 558.
24. Constitution of India, Part III, Art. 31, 1949 as amended to October 5, 1963.
25. A.I.R. 1967 S.C. 1643.
26. Nyerere, "How Much Power for a Leader?" *Africa Report,* July, 1962.
27. Ruth S. Morgenthau, "African Elections: Tanzania's Contribution" 10 *Africa Report,* 12, 12 (No. 11, Dec. 1965).
28. Crim. App. No. 49 of 1964 (Tanganyika).
29. Mattingly, *Renaissance Diplomacy,* 1955, pp. 16–18.

15

The United Nations and Racial Discrimination

C. V. Narasimhan

It is, indeed, fortunate that the Centennial of the Fourteenth Amendment should coincide with the celebration by the United Nations of the International Year for Human Rights, commemorating the 20th anniversary of the Proclamation by the United Nations of the Universal Declaration of Human Rights.

The other day an ambassador in the United Nations came to discuss with me the scheduling of an appointment on October 4, 1968. I explained to him that I was completely tied up that afternoon because I had been invited to speak at the Law School of New York University, on the subject of "The United Nations and the Fourteenth Amendment." The ambassador nodded wisely and said, "Of course you should do it; after all, the United Nations has been mainly responsible for the Fourteenth Amendment!"

Even if the United Nations was not responsible for the Fourteenth Amendment, the Fourteenth Amendment has certainly influenced legal thinking and the constitutional provisions of many states during the last 100 years. It has also influenced the United Nations Charter itself. There is, for example, a close parallel between the provisions of the Fourteenth Amendment and the Preamble to the United Nations Charter which refers to the "equal rights of men and women and of nations large and small," and also Article 2 (1) of the Charter which asserts the principle "of the sovereign equality of all its members." More specifically, in Article 1 (3) of the charter, under the heading "Purposes and Principles," it is stated that one of the purposes of the United Nations is to "achieve international co-operation in solving international problems of an economic, social, cultural, or humanitarian character, and in promoting and encouraging respect

C. V. Narasimhan is an Under-Secretary General of the United Nations.

for human rights and for fundamental freedoms for all without distinction as to race, sex, language, or religion."

The preoccupation of the United Nations with the problem of discrimination, racial or otherwise, has found expression not only in the charter, but in the actual operation of the various organs. One of the committees of the General Assembly, the Third Committee, has dealt every year with problems of human rights and—increasingly in recent years—with problems relating to discrimination. Under Article 62 of the United Nations Charter, the Economic and Social Council may "make recommendations for the purpose of promoting respect for, and observance of, human rights and fundamental freedoms for all."

Among the subordinate organs may be mentioned, in addition to the Commission on Human Rights, the Sub-commission on Prevention of Discrimination and Protection of Minorities. The Sub-commission is composed of 18 persons selected by the Commission on Human Rights to serve, in their capacity as individuals and not as representatives of member states, for a normal term of three years. The Sub-commission meets annually for some three weeks and has been an active force in the work of the United Nations directed toward the elimination of discrimination.

The specialized agencies of the United Nations have also shown considerable interest in the problem of discrimination. For example the International Labor Organization has been concerned with the prevention of discrimination in employment and occupation. Similarly, both the Sub-commission and UNESCO have interested themselves in problems of discrimination in education. In 1960, for example, the General Conference of UNESCO adopted a Convention and Recommendation against Discrimination in Education.

While racial discrimination has by no means been confined to South Africa, the fight against discrimination in the United Nations has been mainly directed against the policy of apartheid and practice of racial discrimination in South Africa. The question of the racial policies of the Government of South Africa was raised in 1946, at the very first session of the General Assembly, by the Government of India in the form of a complaint relating to treatment of people of Indian origin in South Africa. Two years later, South Africa urged that, under Article 2 (7) of the Charter, the Assembly should decide that the racial policies of South Africa were a question which came essentially within the domestic jurisdiction of South Africa and outside the competence of the General Assembly. This proposal was rejected by the General Assembly. In 1950, at the fifth session of the Assembly, the *Ad Hoc* Political Committee, while considering the problem of apartheid, decided that it was competent to deal with this problem and recommended certain specific proposals for adoption by the Assembly. On December 2, 1950, the General Assembly adopted a resolution in which it expressed the view that "the policy of racial segregation (apartheid) is necessarily based on doctrines of racial discrimination."

Until then, the problem of apartheid had been dealt with mainly in the context of complaints by India and Pakistan in regard to the treatment of persons of Indian and Pakistani origin. It was at its next session, in 1951, that the General Assembly considered the question of the racial situation in South Africa in much broader terms by including an additional item entitled "The question of race conflict in South Africa resulting from the policies of apartheid of the Government of South Africa." South Africa again protested against the inclusion of this item in the agenda on the basis that, under Article 2 (7) of the Charter, the Assembly was incompetent to consider this item; this contention was again rejected.

In 1952, the General Assembly established a commission of three members to consider the racial situation in South Africa in the light of the purposes and principles of the Charter and the relevant resolutions of the United Nations. The Assembly invited the Government of South Africa to co-operate with this commission but that Government refused to recognize it. The commission submitted three reports which were dealt with by the Assembly in 1953, 1954, and 1955.

Since that time, the question of apartheid has been considered by the Assembly practically every year and also on various occasions, starting in 1960, by the Security Council. Thus the Security Council called upon the Government of South Africa, in 1960, to abandon its policies of apartheid and racial discrimination. In January 1961, the then Secretary-General, Mr. Hammarskjöld, visited South Africa at the invitation of the Government, but no mutually acceptable solution of the question could be reached in his discussion with the Prime Minister of South Africa. In 1963, the Security Council requested the Secretary-General to appoint a group of recognized experts "to examine methods of resolving the present situation in South Africa." The group of experts appointed by the Secretary-General suggested that the Security Council should invite the South African Government to take part in discussions under UN auspices on the formation of a national convention, fully representative of all the people of South Africa. If no satisfactory reply was given by the South African Government, the group of experts recommended that the Security Council should apply economic sanctions. The question came up before the Security Council again in 1964 in the context of the Rivonia trial instituted against the leaders of the anti-apartheid movement.

In 1962, the Assembly established a Special Committee on the Policies of Apartheid of the Government of the Republic of South Africa. This committee has been engaged in reviewing the racial policies of South Africa and has submitted an annual report on the matter to the Assembly.

In addition to the action taken in the General Assembly and the Security

Council dealing with the specific problem of apartheid, the Assembly has also begun to pursue a more general line. On November 20, 1963, the Assembly proclaimed the United Nations Declaration on the Elimination of all Forms of Racial Discrimination. On December 21, 1965, two years later, the General Assembly adopted and presented for signature and ratification the International Convention for the Elimination of all Forms of Racial Discrimination. In many ways this is one of the most important and comprehensive instruments in the field of human rights, and ranks in importance with the two Covenants on Human Rights which the Assembly adopted in December 1966.

As of October 1968, 72 states had signed the convention and 23 governments had ratified it. The convention comes into force when 27 governments have ratified it. The United States of America has signed, but not yet ratified, the convention.

On the recommendation of the Assembly, the United Nations has also celebrated, and an increasing number of governments have begun to celebrate, March 21 of every year as International Day for the Elimination of Racial Discrimination.

The interest evinced by the United Nations in regard to the problem of discrimination is, of course, only a part of its total concern with the whole field of human rights. During recent years the preoccupation of the United Nations with human rights has increased enormously. As already pointed out, 1968 was the 20th anniversary of the Universal Declaration of Human Rights which was adopted on December 10, 1948, as a resolution by the General Assembly. As is well known, Mrs. Eleanor Roosevelt, of honored memory, was one of the main architects of this declaration. It is not for the present paper to deal with the contents of the declaration or the tremendous influence it has exerted throughout the world, both at the international level and at national levels. Not only have its provisions inspired a number of international conventions, both within and outside the United Nations; they have also significantly influenced national constitutions, municipal legislation, and, in some cases, even court decisions. In some instances, the very text of provisions of the declaration has been incorporated in international instruments or national laws. The declaration has become a yardstick for measuring the degree of respect for, and compliance with, internationally accepted standards of human rights.

After the proclamation of the Universal Declaration of Human Rights in 1948, the Commission on Human Rights was entrusted with the task of preparing draft international covenants. In 1954, it prepared the preliminary texts of two draft covenants, one dealing with political and civil rights and the other with economic, cultural and social rights. These were sent, through the Economic and Social Council, to the General Assembly and were considered, article by article, at each session of the Assembly from 1955 to 1966, primarily in the Third Committee of the Assembly. It may have appeared to some that the Third Committee was progressing at a snail's pace, but ultimately the two covenants and the Optional Protocol to the Covenant on Civil and Political Rights were adopted by the General Assembly on December 16, 1966. The Covenant on Economic, Social and Cultural Rights was adopted by 100 votes to none, the Covenant on Civil and Political Rights by 106 votes to none, and the Optional Protocol to the Covenant on Civil and Political Rights by 66 votes to two, with 38 abstentions. Apart from differences in language, the importance of the two covenants derives, of course, from the fact that they contain provisions for implementation. As of October 1968, 31 states had signed the covenants but not even one government had ratified either covenant. The United States was not among the signatories.

The year 1968, as stated, was celebrated by the United Nations as International Year for Human Rights. One of the major events of the year was the holding of the International Conference on Human Rights in Teheran. On May 13, this conference adopted a proclamation, from which the following are significant excerpts:

> The primary aim of the United Nations in the sphere of human rights is the achievement by each individual of the maximum freedom and dignity. For the realization of this objective, the laws of every country should grant each individual, irrespective of race, language, religion or political belief, freedom of expression, of information, of conscience and of religion, as well as the right to participate in the political, economic, cultural and social life of his country;
>
> States should reaffirm their determination effectively to enforce the principles enshrined in the Charter of the United Nations and in other international instruments that concern human rights and fundamental freedoms;
>
> Gross denial of human rights under the repugnant policy of apartheid is a matter of the gravest concern to the international community. This policy of apartheid, condemned as a crime against humanity, continues seriously to disturb international peace and security. It is therefore imperative for the international community to use every possible means to eradicate this evil. The struggle against apartheid is recognized as legitimate;
>
> The peoples of the world must be made fully aware of the evils of racial discrimination and must join in combating them. The implementation of this principle of non-discrimination, embodied in the Charter of the United Nations, the Universal Declaration of Human Rights, and other international instruments in the field of human rights, constitutes a most urgent task of mankind, at the international

as well as at the national level. All ideologies based on racial superiority and intolerance must be condemned and resisted.

One of the interesting aspects of the Fourteenth Amendment is the question of the right of the federal government to intervene to enforce its basic guaranty that, "No State shall make or enforce any law which shall abridge the privileges or immunities of citizens of the United States; nor shall any State deprive any person of life, liberty, or property, without due process of law; nor deny to any person within its jurisdiction the equal protection of the laws." Section five of the amendment contains an express enforcement provision: "The Congress shall have power to enforce, by appropriate legislation, the provisions of this article."

From what has been said above, it will be seen that there is a close parallel between the position of the federal government trying to prevent the practice of racial discrimination in regard to citizens of a state of the United States, and the position of the United Nations in its efforts to prevent a member state of the United Nations from practicing discrimination on any of its citizens. However, it is obvious that, by and large, the United Nations has not succeeded in this effort, despite the assertion by both the General Assembly and the Security Council that they are competent to deal with the problem of racial discrimination within the territory of a member state, such as the Republic of South Africa, notwithstanding the provisions of Article 2 (7) of the United Nations Charter.

This failure stems mainly from two circumstances. In the first place, the General Assembly is not a world legislature and has no means of enforcing its resolutions, which are mainly recommendatory in character. Secondly, the organ which can take mandatory action, namely, the Security Council, has so far shown itself unwilling to go to the extent of imposing economic sanctions against South Africa although, in the comparable case of Rhodesia, mandatory economic sanctions on a selective basis were imposed by the Security Council.

Another parallel between the rights of individuals and the rights of States is also of interest. At the beginning of this paper, it was stated that in the Preamble to the Charter there is a reference to the equal rights "of nations large and small." Reference was also made to the provisions of Article 2 (1) of the Charter, which states the principle of "the sovereign equality" of all members of the United Nations. It is, of course, well known that this equality is a theoretical concept. In fact, this principle applies to member states of the United Nations only in respect of their membership in the General Assembly. Other principal organs, such as the Economic and Social Council and the Trusteeship Council, have only a select membership. The members of the Economic and Social Council are elected by the General Assembly, while the membership of the Trusteeship Council consists mainly of the administering powers and an equal number of non-administering powers elected by the General Assembly. In the Security Council, the lack of application of the principle of sovereign equality of all member states is even more obvious. There are five permanent members, who are also vested with the veto, while there are only ten elected members to represent the remaining 120 member states.

If the achievements of the United Nations in the elimination of racial discrimination have fallen far short of the goals of the Charter, its record in respect of another Charter objective, namely "to develop friendly relations among nations based on respect for the principle of equal rights and self-determination of peoples" [Art. 1 (2)] has been somewhat more satisfactory. As is well known, the number of founding members of the United Nations at the time of its establishment in June 1945 was only 51. In 1968, there were 125 members. Of these, no less than 56 members were states which joined the United Nations subsequent to the founding of the organization, after having emerged from colonial tutelage to the state of independence and sovereignty. In addition, three territories, Western Samoa, Nauru and the Cook Islands, had also attained independence but had not elected to seek membership in the world body. This is certainly one of the more encouraging chapters in the story of the United Nations since its establishment. At the same time, this has given rise to problems.

The main problem is that the dynamic progress of the process of decolonization has brought into the United Nations an influx of new members of a magnitude that was not envisaged by the founding fathers. This phenomenon has also given rise to the problem of the "microstates." There are many, both individuals and governments, who fear that this large influx of new members, many of them small in area, property and resources, may, over a period of time, weaken the organization. It has been suggested that special steps should be taken to bring about some parity between the right to vote in the General Assembly and the reality of political and economic power wielded by the major powers. Various suggestions have been made in this regard such as the establishment of a bicameral legislature, the institution of weighted voting in the General Assembly for certain issues including the budget, and the abolition of the veto in the Security Council. It is unlikely that any of these suggestions will ever be adopted, as the solutions proposed will adversely affect the interests of either the large number of small states, of whom a two-thirds majority must vote in favor of a Charter amendment, or of the five permanent members, all of whom must concur to validate a proposed amendment of the charter.

From what has been said, it will be clear that both in the United States and in the world at large, the fight for true equality and the struggle against discrimination are far from being won. But progress is being made, and in the long run the human spirit will prevail.

It is, of course, easier to make progress towards equality, and put an end to discrimination, at any rate in the strictly legal sense, within a country. It is more difficult at the international level. However, it is to be hoped that over a period of time, with the relentless pressure of international public opinion, good sense will prevail even in those areas of the world where, at the present time, there is blind adherence to the outmoded doctrine, and discredited practice, of racial discrimination.

16

Fourteenth Amendment: Retrospect and Prospect

Earl Warren

It is both fitting and necessary that an event of this sort should be held to take measure of this nation's first century of experience with the Fourteenth Amendment. This conference has demonstrated to me once again that a centennial observance can be both a stimulating and a sobering event.

To a scientist contemplating our ageless universe, a century can be as fleeting as a falling star streaking to a flaming death in the earth's atmosphere. But to ordinary mortals contemplating their own mortality, 100 years impart a permanence and stability to an institution or—in our case—a document. Particularly in today's rapidly changing world, endurance for 100 years is a marvelous achievement, and one worthy of celebration. However, endurance for 100 years provides not only proof of survival but also a needed perspective for an evaluation of progress made or opportunities lost, and it is in this latter respect that a centennial observance can be a sobering experience. For we find in such observances an opportunity to pause and to take stock—to determine if the promises and hopes of a century past have come to fruition—and to put the lessons of the past 100 years to work in plotting a course for the next century.

The Fourteenth Amendment is sorely in need of such a sobering evaluation. That amendment—along with the Thirteenth and Fifteenth Amendments—wrote into our basic charter of government a solemn commitment by the American people to the goal of equality before the law. By that commitment, the American people pledged through their government that no opportunity would be denied an individual because of his race or his color or his country of origin. Yet, as we stand here today, 100 years after that solemn commitment was undertaken, we would be less than honest with ourselves if we did not admit that only now do we as a nation stand

Earl Warren is former Chief Justice of the United States.

on the threshold of translating that promise of equality into realistic action.

I do not mean to imply that the past century has been without its achievements. Only the most cynical among us would contend that the Negro —the intended beneficiary of the solemn commitment of the Fourteenth Amendment—is no better off today than he was in those tragic days immediately following the Civil War. But the steps we have taken in the last 100 years toward fulfilling the promise of equality have been halting and uncertain. We have learned in recent years—and at a cost which this nation cannot long bear—that promises and piecemeal progress are no substitute for true equality. We have seen that the rising aspirations of Negro Americans and their just desire for meaningful participation in American life will no longer be stilled by the promise of a better tomorrow. We have seen further that we can no longer counsel patience when men are denied the employment they seek, when their children are denied a quality education, and when their families are denied adequate housing and the food necessary to sustain life simply because their skins are black. And we have received dire warnings that, unless we quickly put our national house in order, the fires fanned by racism will ultimately consume the entire structure. No thoughtful American can long ignore the tragic implications of the warning issued by the Presidential Commission which studied the causes of recent riots in our major cities. "This is our conclusion," the commission wrote. "Our Nation is moving toward two societies, one black, one white—separate and unequal." [1]

That warning, and the events that prompted it, form an appropriate —if somewhat urgent—backdrop to this Centennial Conference. They remind us that, in taking measure of a century of experience with the Fourteenth Amendment, we deal not with some musty historical document or with an abstract legal doctrine. Rather we deal with problems and issues which are more pressing today than they were when the amendment was drafted and ratified.

I make no pretense of having easy solutions to the many problems which plague our nation today and which touch upon the principles of democracy embodied in the Fourteenth Amendment. Merely to catalogue those problems and the correlative principles in the amendment would be too ambitious an undertaking on this occasion. I propose a more limited inquiry. I shall examine what I view as the core commitment of the Fourteenth Amendment—the pledge to the newly freed slaves that henceforth they would enjoy equality with their former masters—and what I perceive as the reasons that the commitment has so long remained a promise unfulfilled. In particular, I shall focus on the respective roles played by Congress and the Supreme Court in enforcing the Fourteenth Amendment during the past century.

Such an examination will necessarily dwell upon the failings of the past, and the tone of my remarks may occasionally sound negative and harsh in their criticisms. By the emphasis I have chosen, I do not mean to denigrate the achievements of the past century. Indeed, without those achievements, I could not say with confidence that I believe we stand at the threshold of making the Fourteenth Amendment's promise of equality a reality. But the past century has also been marked by a number of failings and misdirections, and unless we fully understand the nature of those failings, we may find that our next century of experience with the Fourteenth Amendment will be one of delusion rather than progress.

I

The roots of American democracy are firmly embedded in the doctrine of equality. When Thomas Jefferson took his pen in hand to write the Declaration of Independence, he listed as the first of the "self-evident" truths "that all men are created equal." Those were strong words for that age, but they were hardly novel or original. As Professor Robert Harris has observed, the Declaration of Independence succinctly and eloquently summarized the major elements of Western democratic thought which gave birth to the American Revolution.[2] Equality was a consistent theme in the works of those men who made the major contributions to Western political theory up to the time of the Revolution. The writings of John Locke were particularly influential among the men who led the American Revolution, and the concept of the equality of men was an important part of Locke's theories of the social compact and natural law. It was to be expected that Lockean concepts of equality should find expression in the words of the men who fought to establish this nation.

The progress of the nation toward its stated goal of equality is, however, a story filled with ironies. Thus, the author of the ringing words of the Declaration of Independence was a slaveholder, and some of his writings suggest that he viewed the Negro as anything but the white man's equal.[3] And, while the document which heralded the birth of the nation spoke of the equality of all men, the constitution which welded the former colonies into a single government relegated the Negroes imported from Africa as slaves to a second-class status. Yet, ultimately, it was the slavery compromise of 1787 which made possible and necessary the commitment to equality now embodied in the three Civil War amendments. For, while the slavery compromise forced an abandonment of the concept of equality, it was a compromise held together by the mortar of convenience and expediency.

As sectional differences developed and grew in the new nation, the compromise began to crumble, and the institution of slavery came to symbolize the bitter divisions in the country. As new compromises were attempted to preserve that most inhumane of human institutions, the fight against slavery assumed the posture of a moral crusade in the North and parts of the West. The Abolitionists, as had Thomas Jefferson before them, drew upon the theories of John Locke in formulating their legal and moral arguments against slavery.[4] But moral pleas fell on deaf ears, and appeals to the fundamental creed of equality contained in the Declaration of Independence were of no avail. Sectional cleavages widened; the South clung stubbornly to the institution of slavery; and the nation was plunged into a tragic civil war when the efforts to preserve the Union by peaceful means failed.

The work of reconstructing the divided and battlescarred nation after the Civil War took many forms. Most relevant for our purposes were the successful efforts to write into our charter of government a constitutional basis for the nation's commitment to the concept of equality. Within five years after the guns of the Civil War had been silenced, Congress had proposed and the country had ratified three amendments which purported to give the newly freed slaves civil and political equality with all other Americans. The Thirteenth Amendment told the Negro that slavery could have no place in this nation and that he could no longer be treated as chattel, to be bought and sold at the caprice of his white master. The Fourteenth Amendment conferred national citizenship on the Negro and told him that he could expect due process and equal protection before the law. The Fifteenth Amendment gave the Negro the most potent weapon in the democratic arsenal—the vote—and promised him that he could participate fully in the American political process. The three amendments had a common feature—they designated the Congress as the governmental body that would take action to ensure that the new commitment to equality would be fulfilled.

For someone who lived in the period immediately following the Civil War and who viewed the nation as morally bound to make good on its long delayed promise of equality, there was good reason to be optimistic about the future. The Civil War had demonstrated that there could be no compromise with the concept of the equality of all men if the nation were to remain faithful to its basic creed. The war, despite its many tragic consequences, had at least been the vehicle for ridding the nation of the institution of slavery. The constitution contained specific provisions reducing the abstract adherence to concepts of equality to tangible and solemn commitments. And Congress, which was proving quite responsive to the aspirations of the newly freed slaves, had reserved for itself the task of translating those commitments into meaningful action. Yet, within 18 years after the Civil War had ended, all cause for optimism had evaporated, and the Negro was cast adrift without hope of meaningful national action in his search for the rights and the equality which had been promised him.

The reasons for this abrupt reversal in the national attitude toward the

Negro and the commitment to equality are complex, involving interwoven political, economic, and social factors which are difficult to unravel. However, I should like to isolate one course of events during the critical 18-year period immediately following the Civil War—the approach taken by Congress, through its enforcement powers, and by the Supreme Court, through its decisions, to the Fourteenth Amendment's Equal Protection Clause. That story is, in a sense, a familiar one. But, viewed from our present perspective, that story reveals quite starkly that the cause of Negro equality was needlessly deterred and inhibited during the immediate post-Civil War period.

II

Much has been written concerning the "original understanding" of the Fourteenth Amendment,[5] and there is no need to stir those murky waters again. This much can safely be said of the purposes of the Fourteenth Amendment: It was designed to make national citizenship paramount to state citizenship, to confer national citizenship upon the newly freed slaves, and to secure for the former slaves the equal enjoyment of certain civil rights. Whatever conclusions one draws from the debates preceding the adoption of the Fourteenth Amendment, there can be no doubt that the Negro was its intended beneficiary. However, several critical questions were left open. For example, what were the nature and the scope of the civil rights the Negro was to enjoy equally with whites? Against whom were those rights to be secured? And what body of government was to undertake this definitional task?

As we shall see, the Supreme Court reserved to itself the ultimate responsibility for answering those questions, and the answers the court provided were to inhibit significantly the development of Negro equality. But Congress became the initial arena for the task of translating the new commitment to Negro equality into meaningful action. This was a natural consequence of the plain wording of the Fourteenth Amendment. Section Five provides that "Congress shall have the power to enforce, by appropriate legislation, the provisions" of the amendment. This was a rather clear mandate to Congress to undertake the task of defining and securing the rights guaranteed the Negro by the amendment, and Congress quickly seized the initiative. By 1875, it had enacted five major pieces of civil rights legislation, guaranteeing Negroes a broad range of rights and pledging the use of federal power to back up the guarantee. The Negro was given the right to enter into contractual relationships, to enforce his legal rights in courts of law, and to acquire and convey property.[6] Two statutes made effective the Negro's rights to vote by prescribing federal criminal penalties for any interference with that right.[7] The Negro was given federal protection against private conspiracies to injure, threaten or oppress him,[8] and against anyone who, acting under color of law, sought to deprive him of the rights, privileges and immunities secured by the constitution.[9] Finally, the Negro was guaranteed by federal law the same right of access to places of public accommodation that whites enjoyed.[10] Some of those statutes were passed under the enforcement clauses of the other two Civil War amendments,[11] but *in toto* those statutes represented important steps along the path leading to the equality promised by the Fourteenth Amendment.

By 1875, the Supreme Court had not become significantly involved in the questions of Negro equality under the Fourteenth Amendment. Yet, by 1875, legislative action in support of Negro equality had run its course, and Congress was not to pass another civil rights statute until 1957. This legislative retrenchment reflected the national mood of the period. Reconstruction was in its terminal stages, and even some of the Negro's staunch supporters had become disenchanted by the excesses of the Reconstruction program in the South. It had also become obvious to many that political gain, rather than moral righteousness, was motivating many of the radical Republicans who were speaking for Negro rights in Congress.[12] In addition, problems other than Negro equality and Reconstruction began to occupy the attention of the nation and Congress. The nation was just beginning to enter a period of rapid industrial growth and expansion, only to be dealt a crippling blow by the severe depression of 1873. Disclosures of the corruption of the Grant administration had weakened the faith of the people in the governmental process. Finally, the bitterly contested election of 1876 had brought the nation to the brink of another civil war before a special commission appointed by Congress declared the Republican candidate for the Presidency, Rutherford B. Hayes, the victor over Samuel J. Tilden.[13]

The efforts to resolve the electoral deadlock which persisted through the early months of 1877 had a particularly decisive impact on the developing national program to secure equality for the Negro. Recent scholarship has uncovered convincing proof that the dispute was resolved partly at the expense of the Negro.[14] Southern Democrats, who in concert with their Northern colleagues might have blocked any congressional certification of Hayes' victory prior to inauguration day, acquiesced in the Electoral Commission's decision which awarded the presidency to the Republican candidate.[15] In exchange for their acquiescence, the Southern Democrats had received assurances that Hayes would support federal appropriations for making internal improvements in the Southern states and would withdraw the remaining federal troops from the South, thus bringing Reconstruction to a close. While economic gain backed by the Federal Treasury appeared to be the principal concern of Southern Democrats, the withdrawal of federal troops would mean returning to the Southern states full control over their internal affairs. And this, in turn, meant that the Southern Negro would be required to look to state governments, rather than to federal power, for the protection and enforcement of his rights.[16]

The interplay of these several factors, capped by the electoral compromise of 1877, placed a damper on the enthusiasm for affirmative legislative action in support of the Negro which had characterized the immediate post-Civil War period. But none of these factors, either standing alone or in combination, necessarily suggested that the Negro could no longer look to Congress for assistance in his struggle to attain equality. At worst, Congress in the late 1870's seemed only to reflect a national mood of retrenchment, and the Negro's setback could be expected to be as temporary as that national mood. In addition, significant legislative gains had already been made, and diligent enforcement of existing statutes could measureably advance the Negro toward achieving equality.

But the Supreme Court was yet to make its influence felt. It is true that there were straws in the winds of judicial decisions before Congress had definitely abandoned the cause of Negro equality. In the *Slaughterhouse Cases*,[17] the court virtually reduced the Privileges and Immunities Clause of the Fourteenth Amendment to a nullity. And, in two 1876 decisions, the court frustrated federal efforts to bring prosecutions for interferences with the Negro's right to vote. In *United States* v. *Reese*,[18] the court held unconstitutional §§ 3 and 4 of the Civil Rights Enforcement Act of 1870 [19] because the reach of those statutory provisions was not limited to discrimination based on race. And, in *United States* v. *Cruikshank*,[20] the court ruled that an indictment charging fraud and violence against Negroes in Louisiana state elections was defective. The court held that several of the rights allegedly infringed—including the right to peaceably assemble with others, the right to petition for redress of grievances, and the right to bear arms—were not rights secured by the Federal Constitution and, therefore, could not come within the protective umbrella of federal legislative power. Although the indictment alleged interference with the right to vote, the court ruled that the indictment was defective because it did not allege that the interference was racially motivated. Those decisions offered little solace to Negroes who would be required ultimately to look to the federal courts for the enforcement of their rights.

However, for supporters of Negro equality, the judicial outlook was not wholly gloomy prior to 1883. The *Cruikshank* decision had been the most damaging because it had reduced the number of civil rights which could receive federal protection, but the impact of the other decisions could be viewed as mixed. Although the Privileges and Immunities Clause had been stripped of potentially expansive meaning in the *Slaughterhouse Cases,* the Supreme Court had made clear in that same decision that the Equal Protection Clause was to be principally a bulwark for Negro rights.[21] Similarly, although the *Reese* decision struck down a portion of the 1870 Enforcement Act on overbreadth grounds, that case did not take from Congress the power to legislate against racially motivated interferences with the right to vote. In addition, other provisions of congressional enforcement legislation had survived lower court tests.[22] Finally, in 1879, the Supreme Court decided two cases which represented clear victories for the cause of Negro equality. In *Strauder* v. *West Virginia,*[23] the court invalidated as contrary to the Equal Protection Clause a state statute which limited jury duty to white persons.[24] And in *Ex parte Virginia,*[25] the court sustained the constitutionality of § 4 of the 1875 Civil Rights Act [26] which made it a federal crime to exclude any citizen from a state or federal jury because of his race or color.

The Supreme Court rendered its decisive judgment on the Fourteenth Amendment in 1883. In two decisions that year—*United States* v. *Harris* [27] and the *Civil Rights Cases* [28]—the court undertook the task of defining the scope of congressional enforcement power under the Fourteenth Amendment. In the *Harris* case, the court declared unconstitutional § 2 of the so-called Ku Klux Klan Act of 1871,[29] which made it a crime for two or more persons to conspire to or to go in disguise upon a highway or upon another's property for the purpose of depriving anyone of the equal protection of the laws. The *Civil Rights Cases* struck down the public accommodations provisions of the Civil Rights Act of 1875.[30]

The court found a common defect in the two statutes—namely, that Congress had sought to regulate directly the acts of private persons. In the view of the court, such legislative power was possessed only by the states in our constitutional scheme, and the Fourteenth Amendment had in no sense altered the division of power between the state and federal governments. The court construed the Fourteenth Amendment as giving Congress only the power to correct or nullify state laws or the acts of state officials or state agents which contravened the amendment's provisions. From those two 1883 decisions grew the state action doctrine, and that doctrine has remained to this day an integral part of the lexicon of Fourteenth Amendment adjudication.

In the view of Charles Warren, the 1883 decisions "practically put an end to attempts on the part of the Federal Government to settle the negro question by means of indictments in the Federal Courts." [31] I think that the eminent historian of the Supreme Court understated the full impact of the *Harris* decision and the *Civil Rights Cases*. Another commentator has more recently observed that, as a result of the state action doctrine, "the heart of the Fourteenth Amendment was doomed to death by judicial limitations." [32] The Fourteenth Amendment as a guardian of Negro rights did, indeed, lapse into a moribund state after the 1883 decisions. That consequence is all the more tragic because, in my view, the state action limitation on congressional enforcement power was both unnecessary and unjustified.

III

The state action doctrine declared in 1883 found its source in the Supreme Court's concept of federalism. Unfortunately, its concept of federalism was of pre-Civil War vintage. The limitations which the state action doctrine placed upon congressional power might well have been sound if the constitution in 1883 read as it did in 1860. However, three amendments had been added to the constitution after 1860, and the remarkable aspect of the *Harris* decision and the *Civil Rights Cases* is that they are devoid of any searching inquiry into whether the Fourteenth Amendment had altered to any degree the federal-state balance of power which had existed prior to the Civil War. This omission is important, in my view, in assessing the viability of the state action doctrine which emerged from those decisions.

Under the influence of Chief Justice Chase, the Supreme Court had been receptive to expansions of national power during the 1860's. However, with changes in the court's composition, a reaction to the trend toward nationalism had set in during the 1870's,[33] and the reaction found expression in traditional, pre-war concepts of federalism.

The decisions in *Harris* and the *Civil Rights Cases* represent a high-water mark of that reaction.[34] The court did recognize the obvious in those decisions—namely, that the limitations contained in § 1 of the Fourteenth Amendment acted upon state power. But the court failed to recognize any corresponding expansion of national power in § 5 of the amendment. In fact, the interrelationship between §§ 1 and 5 received scant attention in the two 1883 decisions, and the court seemed to view the Tenth Amendment as a limitation upon the power conferred on Congress by § 5.[35] The juxtaposition of the Tenth Amendment with the Fourteenth Amendment illustrates quite clearly the states' rights bias of the court which decided *United States* v. *Harris* and the *Civil Rights Cases*.

By my comments, I do not intend to belittle the importance of federalism in our constitutional scheme. I have long believed that strong and viable state governments are crucial to our democracy, and I would oppose any attempt to usurp state power through the process of judicial decision. However, the constitution is not a rigid and unbending document, and those who drafted it did not necessarily expect that the form of government they prescribed or the balance they struck between state and federal power would remain unchanged as long as the nation existed. Otherwise, the framers would not have included in the constitution the machinery for amending that document. I have always believed that, if fundamental changes are to be made in our constitutional scheme, these changes should be made through the amending process. That process was employed after the Civil War, and there is evidence that the three Civil War amendments were designed, in part at least, to alter the federal-state balance which had existed prior to 1860.[36] But the Supreme Court in 1883 rejected any such construction of the Fourteenth Amendment. In fact, one detects in the *Harris* decision and the *Civil Rights Cases* a sense of disbelief that any fundamental alteration in federal-state relationships could have been intended by the resort to the amending process.

I find the court's reluctance to recognize any expansion of congressional power in the Fourteenth Amendment particularly puzzling since the most convincing argument for such an expansion was far more familiar to jurists of the nineteenth century than it is today. That argument focuses on the meaning of the word "protection" in the Equal Protection Clause. Under John Locke's theory of the social compact, man surrendered to government his right of unrestrained freedom in his relations with others in society. In exchange for surrendering that right, man received from government the promise of protection in the enjoyment of those natural rights which all men possessed. This concept of legal protection that was owed to all men by government was an important premise in the legal arguments against slavery advanced by the Abolitionists prior to the Civil War.[37] It was a concept which also found repeated expression in the congressional debates which preceded the adoption of the Fourteenth Amendment.[38] And it was a concept which was not unfamiliar to Supreme Court justices of the nineteenth century.

When Justice Washington enumerated in *Corfield* v. *Coryell*[39] those privileges and immunities "which belong of right to the citizens of all free governments," his list began with the privilege of "[p]rotection by the Government."[40] In fact, Justice Bradley, who wrote the majority opinion in the *Civil Rights Cases,* quite clearly articulated the legal protection argument nine years earlier when he wrote the lower court opinion on circuit in *United States* v. *Cruikshank*.[41]

The legal protection concept would have provided a clear doctrinal basis for a finding in 1883 that Congress had the power under § 5 of the Fourteenth Amendment to prohibit and punish private discrimination against Negroes. The reasoning would have taken this form: The word "protection," as used in the Fourteenth Amendment, was in a sense a term of art having definite content and meaning. Thus, when the amendment declared that "[n]o state shall . . . deny to any person within its jurisdiction the equal protection of the laws," it did more than simply require the states to refrain from affirmative action which discriminated against Negroes. The amendment went further and placed upon the states an obligation to provide to Negroes and whites alike that legal protection which government owes to all men. And, if the states were to withhold such protection from the Negroes, Congress was empowered to correct the deficiency by appropriate legislation, which could include statutes which reached private action.[42]

Whatever the merits of the legal protection argument, it found no support in the Supreme Court in 1883. Pre-Civil War notions of federalism held sway in the court, and the enforcement powers of Congress under the Fourteenth Amendment were severely curtailed. The practical impact of the 1883 decisions was to turn the enforcement scheme for the Fourteenth Amendment on its head and to deal a serious setback to progress toward the goal of achieving Negro equality.

As I have mentioned, the Fourteenth Amendment prescribed its own enforcement scheme, designating Congress as the federal branch that was to be responsible for implementing its provisions. I have also made reference to the 1879 decision in *Strauder* v. *West Virginia*,[43] in which the court ruled that the Fourteenth Amendment by its own force operated to invalidate state laws which discriminated against Negroes.[44] When the *Harris* decision and the *Civil Rights Cases* are read with *Strauder* in mind, one is forced to conclude that the court reduced § 5 to a useless appendage to the Fourteenth Amendment in 1883. *Strauder* makes § 1 of the amendment self-executing, and the *Harris* decision and the *Civil Rights Cases* decree that the congressional enforcement power under § 5 is to be no broader than and is to add nothing to the amendment's self-executing provisions. Congress was in effect told in 1883 that any enforcement legislation it might enact would be—in the words of Professor Corwin— "gratuitous meddling." [45] An amendment which seemed, on its face, to expand federal legislative power became a vehicle for the expansion of federal judicial power. This result has been aptly described as "a departure from and a distortion of the Constitution that has few parallels in American constitutional development . . . ." [46]

Events were to show that the Supreme Court, having assumed for itself in the 1880's the role of enforcing the Fourteenth Amendment's pledge of equality, was ill-equipped—both institutionally and philosophically—to carry out that role effectively. The institutional limitations on the court are obvious. Under our judicial system, federal courts cannot seize the initiative and devise innovative solutions to pressing social problems. The courts must wait until a justiciable controversy arises between two parties with adverse interests. And, even when such a controversy comes to a court, any number of factors—including procedural defects and an inadequate record —may prevent a decision which will have an impact beyond resolving the particular dispute between the parties before the court. In addition, a court is far more limited than a legislature in devising effective remedies, a shortcoming which is particularly apparent when broad social problems are at issue. A more important drawback to judicial enforcement of social policy is that a court cannot act until someone in society becomes dissatisfied with the *status quo* and takes the initiative by filing a lawsuit.

In terms of Fourteenth Amendment equal protection litigation, the initiator had to be the Negro in search of the rights he had been promised. But the Negro was in a poor position in the late nineteenth century to seize the initiative and blaze new trails in the law. For one thing, litigation costs money, and the Negro was still struggling to achieve economic—as well as civil and political—equality with the white man. For another, the burden of initiative placed on the Negro required a rare quality of courage. Particularly in the South, any Negro who tampered with the prevailing dogma of white supremacy could expect economic reprisals, harassment and even death for his efforts. There was no NAACP in those days to carry the financial burden of litigation and to act as an institutional lightning rod for the individual Negro, who found survival a far more immediate and real problem than vague promises of equality. It is not surprising, therefore, that a major line of Fourteenth Amendment decisions in the Supreme Court involving Negro rights in the late nineteenth and early twentieth centuries presented the issue of racial discrimination in jury selection.[47] In those cases, no initiative on the part of the Negro was necessary. He was brought coercively into the judicial process through criminal prosecution, and the equal protection question was presented to the Supreme Court when the Negro sought relief from his conviction.

Lack of economic resources and intimidation by whites were not the only barriers faced by Negroes who had to look to the Supreme Court for the protection of their rights. The course of Fourteenth Amendment adjudication in the late nineteenth century offered little encouragement to Negroes who expected the Supreme Court to champion their cause. Soon after the *Civil Rights Cases,* the Fourteenth Amendment underwent a strange metamorphosis in the court, becoming principally a guardian of corporate —rather than Negro—interests.[48] The late nineteenth century was the era of rampant laissez-fairism, and state legislatures were working to establish a measure of control over the demonstrable evils of industrialization. Corporate lawyers turned to the Due Process Clause of the Fourteenth Amendment in their search for a judicial shield against economic and social legislation.

Their arguments found a receptive audience in the Supreme Court, and the Due Process Clause came to take primacy over the Equal Protection Clause in Fourteenth Amendment adjudication. The story of the development of the substantive due process doctrine as a device to invalidate social and economic legislation is a familiar one,[49] and there is no need to review that story in any detail at this time. However, there is a certain tragic irony to that story which deserves comment. A principal purpose of the Civil War amendments was to transform the Negro from a piece of property into a human being in the eyes of the law. Yet, in the late nineteenth and early twentieth centuries, the Fourteenth Amendment was invoked more successfully in the Supreme Court to protect property rights than to safeguard human rights. That result can be explained in part by the failure of the court to comprehend the scope of the due process limitation on governmental action. It would seem to belabor the obvious to observe that the words "due process of law" impose, at most, a requirement of procedural regularity in the actions of government and its agents, and not a check on the substance of legislation enacted according to regular procedures. Yet, at the same time that the substantive due process doctrine was flowering, the court exhibited an extreme reluctance to apply the Due Process Clause of the Fourteenth Amendment to correct alleged procedural irregularities in state criminal trials.[50] The court not only brushed aside suggestions that the Due Process Clause made the specific guarantees of the Bill of Rights applicable to the states,[51] but until the early 1930's it also refused to apply the Fourteenth Amendment's more general command of procedural regularity to upset a state criminal conviction. It was only when the toleration by state courts of inhuman treatment of criminal defendants became intolerable that the Supreme Court finally interceded.[52] It is perhaps fitting that the court's intercession came in cases in which Southern Negroes had been subjected to the most extreme forms of Southern injustice.

The Equal Protection Clause was not completely overlooked during the period when the Due Process Clause became the focus of judicial attention. Yet, even the Equal Protection Clause came to be invoked more frequently on behalf of property rights than Negro rights.[53] The Supreme Court's major equal protection pronouncement on Negro rights after the *Civil Rights Cases* was *Plessy* v. *Ferguson*,[54] a decision that was hardly calculated to inspire confidence in the Negro that the court would be the champion of his rights. In only two areas of concern prior to World War II did the court consistently seem receptive to Negro claims of discriminatory treatment. The first area, which I have already mentioned, was discrimination in jury selection. The second area involved allegations of discrimination in voting contrary to the Fifteenth Amendment.[55] However, aside from those two lines of decisions and a handful of other cases,[56] Negroes made little significant progress in their struggle for equality through the judicial process prior to the late 1930's.[57]

IV

The remarkable feature of the Supreme Court's Fourteenth Amendment decisions in the late nineteenth and early twentieth cnturies is that they failed to grasp the importance of the nation's commitment to equality and the increasingly desperate plight of the Negro. Perhaps this failing is particularly apparent to us at this period in history when racial problems seem to dominate our national life. In addition, hindsight often imparts a certain arrogance to historical judgment, and occasionally we are tempted to deal harshly with the men who were responsible for what we view as errors of the past. I like to think that, if I had been a member of the Supreme Court in 1883, I would have voted with the first Justice Harlan in the *Civil Rights Cases.* But my confidence in that judgment is somewhat tempered by my awareness that men, after all, are fallible and that their thoughts and deeds are too often shaped by the times in which they live. We can detect in the history books no great public opposition to the course of Fourteenth Amendment adjudication which denied the Negro any meaningful progress toward equality in the late nineteenth and early twentieth centuries. At worst, the Supreme Court justices of that period simply reflected the prevailing national attitude toward the Negro and his plight. If those justices are to be faulted, it must be because they failed to comprehend the significance of the Fourteenth Amendment's promise of equality and the potentially explosive impact of repressing too long the Negro's quest for equality.

However, if we eliminate the human factor from the historical inquiry, we cannot escape the conclusion that the Supreme Court embarked on a course of judicial decision in 1883 which seriously undermined effective implementation of the nation's commitment to equality. In my view, the court's fundamental error was in denying Congress a meaningful role in Fourteenth Amendment enforcement. The Negro faced a variety of barriers —some obvious and some quite subtle—in his struggle to become a full and equal member of American society, and the federal courts were simply not equipped to undertake the broad range of programs necessary to tear down those barriers. Those courts could proceed only on a case-by-case basis in their efforts to relate abstract notions of equality with the real world of racial prejudice, discrimination and distrust. The judicial conclusion in *Plessy* v. *Ferguson* [58] that separation of the races satisfied the constitutional command of equality dramatically illustrated that abstract judicial concepts will not necessarily reflect the real world.

A legislature has far more institutional flexibility than a court in dealing with pressing social problems. A court must wait until an appropriate case is presented to it before it can take any action on a problem; a legislature can initiate corrective action as problems arise. A court's official knowledge of the Negro's problems is limited to the facts presented by the parties to a particular lawsuit; a legislature has broad powers of investigation to inquire into all facets of racial discrimination and prejudice. A court's mandate acts directly only upon the parties to a particular case; a legislature can prescribe rules which are binding on all persons in society.

These and other differences in the judicial and legislative processes help to explain why progress toward the goal of equality was so painfully slow after the Supreme Court effectively restricted the enforcement powers of Congress.

Some may think that I am placing undue faith in the legislative process as the answer to many of our racial problems. But we cannot escape the plain fact that the Fourteenth Amendment, by its own terms, designated Congress as the principal enforcer of the amendment. We can only speculate on whether Congress would have acted more vigorously in the late nineteenth and early twentieth centuries if the Supreme Court had not placed the state action limitation on congressional enforcement power in 1883. I have already noted that civil rights legislation had seemed to have run its course several years prior to the *Civil Rights Cases*. And I have had enough political experience to know that legislatures more than courts tend to reflect and follow the mood of the general public. However, there is some very recent evidence that the *Civil Rights Cases* had a prolonged inhibiting impact on the exercise of congressional power. Just four years ago, when both public opinion and the mood in Congress favored renewed legislative efforts on behalf of the Negro, Congress resorted to its commerce power in enacting the public accommodations title of the Civil Rights Act of 1964.[59] There was general agreement in Congress at that time that reliance on Fourteenth Amendment enforcement powers would place the public accommodations provisions of the statute on shaky constitutional grounds. It is a rather sad commentary on the development of Fourteenth Amendment doctrine that Congress felt compelled to equate Negro rights with the movement of goods to enact civil rights legislation.

Despite the errors of the past which I have discussed, events of the past decade suggest that the Negro now stands on the threshold of achieving the legal equality that was promised him 100 years ago. That such a possibility exists can be attributed in large part to the Negro's indomitable spirit and his persistent faith in our democratic process. Particularly after he was required to share equally the burden of arms in World War II, the Negro repeatedly resorted to the courts for assistance in his struggle to attain equality. Aided by the financial resources and the remarkable legal talent of organizations such as the NAACP, he won a series of court victories in the post-war period,[60] highlighted by the school desegregation decision of 1954.[61] The Negro's peaceful demonstrations against a segregated society in the South, and the violent reactions to those demonstrations awakened the nation's conscience to the realities of racial injustice. Demands for effective legislative action grew, and Congress responded by enacting five civil rights statutes in an eleven-year period.[62]

Perhaps the most significant development in recent years has been the changed attitude of the Supreme Court toward congressional enforcement powers. In three decisions during the 1965 Term—*United States* v. *Guest,*[63] *South Carolina* v. *Katzenbach,*[64] and *Katzenbach* v. *Morgan*[65]— the court took a major step toward removing the restrictions that the *Civil Rights Cases* had imposed on congressional enforcement power. In *Guest,* six justices made clear that they would no longer impose the state action limitation on congressional power under § 5 of the Fourteenth Amendment. The other two decisions indicated that the court would respect the congressional determination that particular legislative action was necessary to secure Negro equality. The *Morgan* decision was, in my view, particularly significant. There the court sustained the constitutionality of a provision of the Voting Rights Act of 1965[66] which extended the franchise to certain Puerto Rican citizens, despite the fact that they could not meet the state requirement of literacy in the English language. The court reached that conclusion even though the court itself had ruled seven years earlier that such literacy requirements do not necessarily violate the Fifteenth Amendment.[67] That decision, in effect, told Congress that it shared with the court the responsibility for construing and applying the provisions of the Civil War Amendments to assure that the nation's pledge of equality will be fulfilled.

Some may view with alarm the prospect that the court may be willing to share with another branch of government the responsibility for constitutional interpretation. I do not join in that alarm. The three branches of the Federal Government were, after all, created by the constitution, and the three branches share equally the responsibility for implementing the provisions of the constitution. For too many years the Supreme Court has had virtually the sole responsibility for giving content and meaning to the broad mandate of the Fourteenth Amendment. I welcome the new willingness of the legislative and executive branches to participate in that difficult task. In fact, I believe quite strongly that the Supreme Court's work will be made measurably easier if, in the future, Fourteenth Amendment adjudication becomes principally a matter of construing statutes enacted by Congress to secure Negro equality. Justice Stewart's historic opinion in *Jones* v. *Alfred H. Mayer Co.*[68] in 1968 illustrates the meaningful progress that can be made when Congress enacts and the court construes statutes defining the scope of Negro rights.

V

My emphasis has been on the importance of greater participation by Congress in the task of translating the Fourteenth Amendment's promise of equality into meaningful action. I do not mean by my emphasis to suggest that, because Congress has now assumed a more active role, the court should show less concern for the problems of Negro equality. Although the court's Fourteenth Amendment decisions in the late nineteenth and early twentieth centuries frustrated the Negro's just expectations, I think it is fair to conclude that the court's decisions during the 1950's provided the necessary impetus for concerted national action on behalf of Negro equality in the past decade. The seriousness of the nation's current racial problems will not permit any slackening of effort by any branch of the government. All governmental agencies—local, state and national—must employ their total resources in seeking solutions to the problems of racial hatred and distrust. Vigorous executive and legislative action on behalf of the Negro will be of no avail if the judiciary succumbs to the ambivalent attitude that characterized early Fourteenth Amendment decisions.

There is another important reason why the Supreme Court must remain in the forefront of Fourteenth Amendment enforcement in the future. I have suggested several reasons why the legislative process can provide imaginative new approaches to the problem of securing Negro equality. However, the role played by the Supreme Court in the 1950's in awakening the nation to the need for broad national action on behalf of Negro rights illustrates the unique contributions that the judicial process can make to the task of fulfilling the promise of the Fourteenth Amendment. The essential function of the Supreme Court in our democracy is to act as the final arbiter of minority rights, and the Fourteenth Amendment is a basic repository of those rights. By remaining a responsive forum of last resort for Negroes and other minority interests, the court can assure that the spirit of the Fourteenth Amendment will become a tangible reality of American life. Thus, although the court in *Katzenbach* v. *Morgan* invited Congress to share the constitutional responsibility for implementing the nation's commitment to the goal of equality, the court made quite clear that it would not hesitate to strike down any legislation which restricted or abrogated the equal protection guarantee.[69] Moreover, the court in recent years has incorporated the important procedural safeguards of the Bill of Rights into the Due Process Clause of the Fourteenth Amendment,[70] thus assuring that all criminal defendants will be entitled to equal justice whether they are tried in federal or state courts. Because the Supreme Court bears a special responsibility for making the judicial process conform to the societal values embodied in the Bill of Rights, the court must give careful scrutiny to any legislation which tends to dilute those values. Finally, the court can make important contributions to Fourteenth Amendment enforcement in areas which touch only indirectly upon Negro rights. Thus, I am confident that the court's recent reapportionment decisions[71] will have the long-range effect of creating more representative legislative bodies at all levels of government which will be responsive to the Negro's just demands.

Those who drafted and fought for the adoption of the Fourteenth Amendment 100 years ago did more than commit this nation to the concept of the equality of all men. They also expressed a basic faith in our constitutional system and in our ability to solve through democratic processes the most complex problems of human relationships. It is our responsibility to ensure that their faith was not unfounded. Our task is not an easy one. The possibility that our nation is moving toward "two societies, one black, one white—separate and unequal" suggests that our system of government may be facing a new challenge to survival as serious as that presented by the Civil War. Abraham Lincoln described that earlier challenge as whether a nation "conceived in Liberty, and dedicated to the proposition that all men are created equal . . . can long endure." The nation did survive the terrible agony of the Civil War, and I am confident that it will survive the present racial crisis and its special agonies if we remain faithful to the solemn commitment to equality embodied in the Fourteenth Amendment 100 years ago.

Notes

1. Report of the National Advisory Commission on Civil Disorders 1 (1968).
2. R. Harris, *The Quest for Equality* 2 (1960).
3. *Id.*, at 15.
4. J. Ten Broek, *The Antislavery Origins of the Fourteenth Amendment* 86, 101 (1951). Ironically, the pro-slavery forces in the South also took refuge in the theories of John Locke to support their positions. *Id.*, at 109–110.
5. See, e.g., H. Flack, *The Adoption of the Fourteenth Amendment* (1908); R. Harris, *supra,* note 2, at 24–56; J. Ten Broek, *supra,* note 4; Bickel, *The Original Understanding and the Segregation Decision,* 69 Harv. L. Rev. 1 (1955); Fairman, *Does the Fourteenth Amendment Incorporate the Bill of Rights? The Original Understanding,* 2 Stan. L. Rev. 5 (1949); Frank & Munro, *The Original Understanding of "Equal Protection of the Laws,"* 50 Colum. L. Rev. 131 (1950); Graham, *The Early Antislavery Background of the Fourteenth Amendment,* Wis. L. Rev. 479, 610 (1950).
6. Act of April 9, 1866, 14 Stat. 27. This statute was enacted prior to the adoption of the Fourteenth Amendment. However, it was re-enacted subsequent to that amendment's ratification. Act of May 31, 1870, 16 Stat. 140, 144. In fact, some of those who worked in Congress for approval of the Fourteenth Amendment believed that the 1866 Act stood on shaky constitutional grounds, and they urged adoption of the new amendment to impart *post facto* validity to the 1866 Act. See H. Flack, *supra,* note 5, at 78–81, 94–96; R. Harris, *supra,* note 2, at 32.
7. Act of May 31, 1870, 16 Stat. 140; Act of Feb. 28, 1871, 16 Stat. 433. These statutes were designed principally to secure the right to vote protected by the Fifteenth Amendment.
8. Act of May 31, 1870, 16 Stat. 140.
9. Act of April 20, 1871, 17 Stat. 13.
10. Act of March 1, 1875, 18 Stat. 335.
11. See notes 6–7, *supra.*
12. Partisan motive was particularly apparent in the provisions of Section Two of the Fourteenth Amendment. See H. Flack, *supra,* note 6, at 97–127.
13. The story of the electoral deadlock of 1876 and the successful efforts to break that deadlock is recounted in P. Haworth, *The Hayes-Tilden Disputed Presidential Election of 1876* (1906); 7 J. Rhodes, *History of the United States 1850–1877,* at 206–285 (1906).
14. See C. Woodward, *Reunion and Reaction* (rev. ed., 1956).
15. The scholars who have studied the disputed election of 1876 have come to conflicting conclusions on the question of which candidate *should* have won the Presidency. The election deadlock centered principally on 19 contested electoral votes from South Carolina, Florida and Louisiana. Tilden, who had accumulated 184 certain electoral votes from other states, needed only one of the contested votes to win the election. In each of the contested Southern states, conflicting sets of electoral votes had been forwarded to Congress by electors favorable to each candidate. In each instance, the Electoral Commission appointed by Congress accepted the votes of the Hayes electors and thereby gave the Republican candidate the

Presidency. The critical decision made by the Electoral Commission was to refuse to inquire into the regularity of the post-election canvass of the votes in the three states. The canvasses had been conducted by Republican appointees who invalidated large numbers of Democratic ballots, wiping out Tilden's popular vote majorities. One author has concluded that, although there were irregularities in the post-election canvasses, Hayes was entitled to the electoral votes of South Carolina, Florida, and Louisiana because the Tilden popular vote majorities in those states had been produced by fraud and voter intimidation. See P. Haworth, *supra,* note 13, at 329–343. However, more recent studies of the 1876 election have concluded that Tilden was at least entitled to the electoral votes of Florida and therefore the Presidency. See C. Woodward, *supra,* note 14, at 19–20.

16. Woodward, *supra,* note 14, at 265–266.
17. 16 Wall. 36 (1873).
18. 92 U.S. 214 (1876).
19. Act of May 31, 1870, 16 Stat. 140.
20. 92 U.S. 542 (1876).
21. 16 Wall. 36, 81 (1873).
22. See, e.g., *United States* v. *Hall,* 26 Fed. Cas. 79 (No. 15,282) (C.C.S.D. Ala. 1871); 2 C. Warren, *The Supreme Court in United States History* 600 n. 1 (rev. ed., 1928).
23. 100 U.S. 303 (1879).
24. Cf. *Neal* v. *Delaware,* 103 U.S. 370 (1881).
25. 100 U.S. 339 (1879).
26. Act of March 1, 1875, 18 Stat. 335, 336–337.
27. 106 U.S. 629 (1883).
28. 109 U.S. 3 (1883).
29. Act of April 20, 1871, 17 Stat. 13.
30. Act of March 1, 1875, 18 Stat. 335.
31. 2 C. Warren, *supra,* note 22, at 612.
32. Silard, *A Constitutional Forecast: Demise of the "State Action" Limit on the Equal Protection Guarantee,* 66 Colum. L. Rev. 855, 857 (1966).
33. See 2 Warren, *supra,* note 22, at 533–550; E. Corwin, *American Constitutional History* 70 (A. Mason & G. Garvey, eds., 1964).
34. 2 Warren, *supra,* note 22, at 608.
35. See *Civil Rights Cases,* 109 U.S. 3, 14–15 (1883).
36. I have already noted that some congressional supporters of the Fourteenth Amendment thought that the 1866 Civil Rights Act was beyond the power of Congress and that the new amendment would give to Congress the power it lacked in 1866. See note 6, *supra.* In the view of those congressmen, the Fourteenth Amendment was quite clearly designed to expand federal legislative power.
37. Ten Broek, *supra,* note 4, at 96–98.
38. See *id.,* at 192–222; H. Flack, *supra,* note 5, at 210–277.
39. 6 Fed. Cas. 546 (No. 3,230) (C.C.E.D.Pa. 1823).
40. 6 Fed. Cas., at 551.

41. 25 Fed. Cas. 707 (No. 14,897) (C.C.D.La. 1874).
42. The legal protection argument is developed at greater length and in somewhat differing forms in R. Harris, *supra,* note 2, at 42–56, and L. Frantz, *Congressional Power to Enforce the Fourteenth Amendment Against Private Acts,* 73 Yale L.J. 1353 (1964).
43. 100 U.S. 303 (1879).
44. Cf. *Neal* v. *Delaware,* 103 U.S. 370 (1881).
45. Corwin, *supra,* note 33, at 81.
46. Harris, *supra,* note 2, at 56.
47. See, e.g., *Martin* v. *Texas,* 200 U.S. 316 (1906); *Carter* v. *Texas,* 177 U.S. 442 (1899); *Smith* v. *Mississippi,* 162 U.S. 592 (1895); *Bush* v. *Kentucky,* 107 U.S. 110 (1882).
48. The process began in 1886 when the court ruled for the first time that the Fourteenth Amendment was intended to protect corporations as well as natural persons. *Santa Clara County* v. *Southern Pacific R.R.,* 118 U.S. 394 (1886).
49. Professor Corwin, as befitted his genius, was particularly incisive in his contemporary analyses of the defects in the substantive due process doctrine. See Corwin, *supra,* note 33, at 67–125.
50. See Schafer, *Federalism and State Criminal Procedure,* 70 Harv. L. Rev. 1, 1–5 (1956).
51. See, e.g., *Hurtado* v. *California,* 110 U.S. 516 (1884); *Twining* v. *New Jersey,* 211 U.S. 78 (1908).
52. See, e.g., *Powell* v. *Alabama,* 287 U.S. 45 (1932); *Brown* v. *Mississippi,* 297 U.S. 278 (1936).
53. Professor Harris studied 554 decisions in which the Supreme Court ruled on equal protection claims. He found that 426 of those decisions, or 76.9 percent of the total, involved legislation affecting economic interests. R. Harris, *supra,* note 2, at 59. The frequency with which equal protection claims were presented to the court led Justice Holmes to remark on the occasion that such claims were "the usual last resort of constitutional arguments." *Buck* v. *Bell,* 274 U.S. 200, 208 (1927).
54. 163 U.S. 537 (1896).
55. See, e.g., *Guinn* v. *United States,* 238 U.S. 347 (1915); *Myers* v. *Anderson,* 238 U.S. 368 (1915); *Nixon* v. *Herndon,* 273 U.S. 536 (1927); *Nixon* v. *Condon,* 286 U.S. 73 (1932); *Lane* v. *Wilson,* 307 U.S. 268 (1939). Not all of the pre-World War II voting rights cases were favorable to the Negro litigant. See *Grovey* v. *Townsend,* 295 U.S. 45 (1935), overruled by *Smith* v. *Allwright,* 321 U.S. 649 (1944).
56. See *Buchanan* v. *Warley,* 245 U.S. 60 (1917) (racial zoning); *Harmon* v. *Tyler,* 273 U.S. 668 (1927) (same); Missouri *ex rel. Gaines* v. *Canada,* 305 U.S. 337 (1938) (segregated schools). But see *Corrigan* v. *Buckley,* 271 U.S. 323 (1926) (restrictive covenant).
57. For a survey of the decisions by the Supreme Court and other courts involving Negro rights through the early 1940's, see B. Nelson, *The Fourteenth Amendment and the Negro Since 1920* (1946).

58. 163 U.S. 537 (1896).
59. 78 Stat. 241.
60. E.g., *Shelley* v. *Kraemer,* 334 U.S. 1 (1948); *Sweatt* v. *Painter,* 339 U.S. 629 (1950); *McLaurin* v. *Oklahoma State Regents,* 339 U.S. 637 (1950); *Barrows* v. *Jackson,* 346 U.S. 249 (1953).
61. *Brown* v. *Board of Education,* 347 U.S. 483 (1954); *Bolling* v. *Sharpe,* 347 U.S. 497 (1954).
62. Civil Rights Act of 1957, 71 Stat. 634; Civil Rights Act of 1960, 74 Stat. 86; Civil Rights Act of 1964, 78 Stat. 241; Voting Rights Act of 1965, 79 Stat. 437; Civil Rights Act of 1968.
63. 383 U.S. 745 (1966).
64. 383 U.S. 301 (1966).
65. 384 U.S. 641 (1966).
66. 79 Stat. 437, 439.
67. *Lassiter* v. *Northampton County Board of Elections,* 360 U.S. 45 (1959).
68. 392 U.S. 409 (1968).
69. 384 U.S., at 651, n. 10.
70. See *In re Oliver,* 333 U.S. 257 (1948) (right to a public trial); *Mapp* v. *Ohio,* 367 U.S. 643 (1961) (Fourth Amendment exclusionary rule); *Gideon* v. *Wainwright,* 372 U.S. 335 (1963) (right to counsel); *Malloy* v. *Hogan,* 378 U.S. 1 (1964) (privilege against self-incrimination); *Pointer* v. *Texas,* 380 U.S. 400 (1965) (right of confrontation); *Klopfer* v. *North Carolina,* 386 U.S. 213 (1967) (right to a speedy trial); *Washington* v. *Texas,* 388 U.S. 14 (1967) (right of compulsory process); *Duncan* v. *Louisiana,* 391 U.S. 145 (1968) (Sixth Amendment right to jury trial); *Washington* v. *Texas,* 388 U.S. 14 (1967) (right of compulsory process); *Duncan* v. *Louisiana,* 391 U.S. 145 (1968) (Sixth Amendment right to jury trial).
71. E.g., *Baker* v. *Carr,* 369 U.S. 186 (1962); *Gray* v. *Sanders,* 372 U.S. 368 (1963); *Wesberry* v. *Sanders,* 376 U.S. 1 (1964); *Reynolds* v. *Sims,* 377 U.S. 533 (1964); *Avery* v. *Midland County, Texas,* 390 U.S. 474 (1968).